A Time *of* Departing

*H*ow Ancient Mystical Practices are
Uniting Christians with the World's Religions

Ray Yungen

2nd Edition

Lighthouse Trails Publishing
Eureka, Montana U.S.A.

Published in Eureka, Montana by
Lighthouse Trails Publishing, LLC
www.lighthousetrails.com

Library of Congress Cataloging-in-Publication Data

Yungen, Ray.
  A time of departing : how ancient mystical practices are uniting Christians with the world's religions / Ray Yungen.— 2nd ed.
    p. cm.
  Includes bibliographical references and index.
  ISBN-13: 978-0-9721512-7-6 (softbound : alk. paper)
  ISBN-10: 0-9721512-7-3 (softbound : alk. paper)
  1. Christianity and other religions—New Age movement. 2. New Age movement—Relations—Christianity. I. Title.
BR128.N48Y86 2006
239'.93—dc22
                                        2005029534

Note: Most Lighthouse Trails books are available at special quantity discounts. Contact information for publisher in back of book.

Printed in the United States of America

To Mother and Dad
who did so much for me

Acknowledgments

Thank you to all the wonderful brothers and sisters in our Lord who stood beside me, aided me and encouraged me in the making of this book. You know who you are, and I am forever indebted. May God bless you all for your steadfastness and courage in your defense of the faith that is so precious to believers around the world.

Contents

Now the Spirit speaketh expressly, that in the latter times some shall depart from the faith, giving heed to seducing spirits, and doctrines of devils. (1 Timothy 4:1)

One

The Invisible Denomination

"Christian" yoga, spiritual disciplines, spiritual formation, the silence, sacred space, and contemplative prayer—do any of these sound familiar? If you haven't heard of them yet, chances are it's just a matter of time before these terms start showing up in your own church. And very possibly you will not realize the implications such concepts can have.

A New Age spirituality has infiltrated much of the Christian church, and an attempt to reorient evangelicalism is taking place outside the radar of most believers. Prominent Christian leaders are now making unprecedented statements, urging followers to practice meditative techniques. Big-name pastors are attending conferences where yoga workshops and labyrinths (maze-like structures) are part of the program. The term *New Age* itself is rarely explained from most pulpits and only then as a far-out belief system practiced by gurus and Hollywood celebrities.

While many Christian leaders have given the impression that nothing is amiss, a New Age, mystical spirituality has become intricately woven into the fiber of countless churches, youth organizations, and Christian educational institutions.

Listen to these quotes, and you will see exactly what I mean:

Zen Buddhism should be taught in every 5th grade class in America.[1]—**M. Scott Peck**, author of *The Road Less Traveled*

I do yoga, tai chi which is a Chinese martial art and three kinds of meditation-vipasana, transcendental and mantra (sound) meditation.[2]—**Jack Canfield**, author of *Chicken Soup for the Soul*

I began practicing meditation, specifically breath prayer, once again. I integrated the use of Tai Chi and yoga.[3] —**John M. Talbot**, Catholic monk and musician

I look for inspirational messages from a variety of sources besides Jesus. Our folks get to hear words of wisdom from great prophets and spiritual leaders like Buddha, Mohammed . . . Yogananda and the Dalai Lama.[4]—**Ken Blanchard**, author of *The One-Minute Manager*

I must add, though, that I don't believe making disciples must equal making adherents to the Christian religion. It may be advisable in many (not all!) circumstances to help people become followers of Jesus and remain within their Buddhist, Hindu, or Jewish contexts."[5]—**Brian McLaren**, a leader of the Emerging Church movement

We need to become aware of the Cosmic Christ, which means recognizing that every being has within it the light of Christ."[6]—**Matthew Fox**, author of *The Coming of the Cosmic Christ*

Has a mystical spirituality indeed infiltrated the church? And if it has, what's the big deal? What's so bad about it anyway? And what proof is there? This book is my attempt to answer these questions in a reasonable, well-documented, and compelling fashion.

In order to grasp how this mystical spirituality has entered the church, we must first understand the underlying layers of the New

Age to see how it has seeped into the fabric of our society. Every facet has been affected—business, medicine, education, politics, and finally, the church. By the time you have finished this book, I believe you will be convinced that the church is in harm's way.

The Scope of the New Age

In the decade of the 1980s, the term *New Age movement* inspired a sense of dread in many conservative Christians. This fear stemmed from the conviction that something evil and sinister surrounded this movement and that ominous clouds were looming on the spiritual horizon. In the 1990s, this backlash largely subsided, and most Christians forgot about what had seemed so threatening a few years earlier.

But this movement has *not* gone away. In fact, it is very much with us and in ways that may surprise many Christians. By the time the new millennium arrived, the New Age had ever so quietly permeated Western culture so that today many Christians are acclimated to New Age and Eastern spirituality. *A Time of Departing* unveils this new spiritual paradigm and reveals the many different manifestations it has taken.

For those who believe we may be on the threshold of the "latter times," then I Timothy 4:1 should be of keen interest, because if we are indeed in those times, shouldn't there be some evidence of this falling away somewhere? Furthermore, what sort of Christian would be so vulnerable as to accept "deceiving spirits?" You might be surprised at the answer.

> Now the Spirit speaketh expressly, that in the latter times some shall depart from the faith, giving heed to seducing spirits, and doctrines of devils. (1 Timothy 4:1)

My hope and prayer is that *A Time of Departing* will help the followers of Jesus (His church) to recognize the subtle teachings of deceiving spirits—spirits that are *reinventing* Christianity by introducing

Eastern mystical practices. It will be shown that these practices may cause unsuspecting participants to abandon the Christian faith in favor of interspirituality (a merging together of all faiths). This new spirituality, even now, is manifesting itself within some of our most widely recognized evangelical churches.

This book is not just another attempt to explain the New Age. It is, rather, an alert to the church as to how and through whom this belief system is creeping into our pulpits, Sunday school classrooms, prayer groups, and Bible studies. It is a critical time to heed the warning of the apostle John:

> Beloved, believe not every spirit, but try the spirits whether they are of God, because many false prophets are gone out into the world. (1 John 4:1)

Let us first examine the magnitude and influence the New Age has in current society.

New Age pundit David Spangler wrote that in 1965, concerning the movement he had embraced: "There weren't many places where such a vision was being taken seriously or even considered."[7] In 1992, two and a half decades later, secular journalist Michael D. Antonio, speaking of the same movement, noted quite a remarkable change:

> [S]ociologists at the University of California at Santa Barbara estimate that as many as 12 million Americans could be considered active participants and another 30 million are avidly interested . . . New Agers would constitute the third largest religious denomination in America.[8]

By 2002, Bradley University Religious Studies professor Robert C. Fuller not only verified these findings but did the math and found that an astounding twenty percent of Americans (over forty million people) now embrace the New Age movement.[9] We are no longer talking about the minuscule smattering of spiritual adventurers Spangler referred to in 1965. Something significant, if not pivotal, has indeed occurred!

There are those who might be skeptical of the validity of these statistics. Some may feel they are exaggerated and outlandish—and with good reason. If the New Age is so pervasive, why aren't the outer trappings of it apparent on every street? This is an essential question. One dependable way of validating the size of a movement is through the law of supply and demand. Supply, as a rule, corresponds with demand. Business people, financially, live or die by this rule. A sizable supply of any commodity indicates a large demand; a small supply reflects little demand. It's as simple as that.

The demand for these teachings speaks clearly from the law of the market. For example, the number of shelves devoted to New Age spirituality at sizable national chain bookstores can often reach seventy or eighty shelves. In many cases, this material is rivaling or even outstripping the number of shelves containing Christian books. And in some stores, the various New Age sections correspond in size to the sports sections.

There is also much evidence that various New Age healing practices have moved well beyond trivial numbers. One such method called Reiki came to the United States (from Japan) in the mid 1970s. It took about twenty years for this particular practice to reach 500,000 practitioners. This number is comparable to those who were serving in the entire U.S. Army at that time. By the year 2005, the number skyrocketed to an astonishing *one million* practitioners in just the U.S.![10]

Exactly how did the New Age grow from practically nothing to what it is today in just a few decades? Again, why does its outer structure seem so invisible? Why do so many people still think of the New Age movement as just a fad that is now history? The answers to these questions provide a disturbing glimpse into one of the most ingenious and skillful grassroots religious engineering efforts in human history.

Why Do They Call it New Age?

The *Aquarian Age* or New Age is supposed to signify that the human race is now entering a *golden age*. Many occultists have long heralded the Aquarian Age as a time that would be unparalleled throughout the course of human history. That is why one writer stated, "A basic knowledge of astrological ages is of enormous importance in occult work."[11]

The Age of Aquarius is when we are all supposed to realize that *man is God,* or in the words of one adherent, "A major theme of Aquarius is that *God is within.* The goal of the Age of Aquarius is to bring this idea into meaningful reality" (emphasis mine).[12]

Before we can understand how this goal is being pursued, we must first define New Age spirituality. This definition is not as simple as you might think—as one writer pointed out:

> It's not so much what New Agers believe that sets them apart from other movements . . . but rather how they come by their beliefs.[13]

Many Christian writers use terms such as *pantheism* or *monism* in an attempt to explain what New Agers believe; however, these words alone are rather limiting in conveying the big picture. The best explanation I have come across is from a book titled *The Mission of Mysticism,* which states:

> [O]ccultism [New Ageism] is defined as the science of mystical evolution; it is the employment of the hidden (i.e., occult) mystical faculties of man to discern the hidden reality of nature; i.e., to see God as the *all in all.*"[14] (emphasis mine)

These mystical faculties are the distinguishing mark of this movement—a mystical perception rather than simple belief or faith. A Christian writer once described this movement as *a system of thought* when, in fact, it is more aptly defined as a system of *non-thought.* Meditation teacher Ann Wise explained this by stating:

> A man came to see me once saying that he had meditated for an hour a day every day for twelve years. Although he enjoyed the time he spent sitting, he felt he was missing

something. From talking to other meditators, he felt that he must have been doing something wrong because he had none of the experiences that he had heard others describe. I measured his brainwaves while he was "meditating" and discovered that he had spent those twelve years simply thinking![15]

This is why this particular style of meditation is commonly referred to as *the silence*. This is not silence as being in a quiet environment but inner silence as in an empty mind that opens up the mystical faculties. "The enemy of meditation is the mind," wrote one New Age teacher.[16]

What Exactly is Meditation?

The meditation most of us are familiar with involves a deep, continuous thinking about something. But New Age meditation entails just the opposite. It involves ridding oneself of all thoughts in order to *still* the mind by putting it in the equivalent of pause or neutral. A comparison would be that of turning a fast-moving stream into a still pond. When meditation is employed, stopping the free flow of thinking, it holds back active thought and causes a shift in consciousness. This condition is not to be confused with daydreaming, where the mind dwells on a subject. New Age meditation works as a holding mechanism until the mind becomes thoughtless, empty, and void.

The two most common methods used to induce this thoughtless state are *breathing* exercises, where attention is focused on the breath, and *mantras*, which are repeated words or phrases. The basic process is to focus and maintain concentration without thinking about what you are focusing on. Repetition on the focused object is what triggers the blank mind.

Since mantras are central to this type of meditation, it is important to understand the proper definition of the word. The translation from Sanskrit is *man*, meaning to "think," and *tra*, meaning "to be liberated from."[17] Thus, the word literally means *to escape from thought*. By repeating the mantra, either aloud or silently, the word or phrase begins to lose any meaning it once had. The conscious thinking process is gradually tuned out until an altered state of consciousness is achieved.

It is very difficult for non-mystics to grasp the reality of these practices. The following story is a perfect illustration that this meditation I speak of is not a silly meaningless exercise but is rather a powerful experience that cuts across all religious, cultural, and socioeconomic boundaries.

In a *Life Times* article, a woman described herself as a "skeptic" when she came into contact with mystical practices in 1984. Her skepticism evaporated when she discovered that meditation was "a powerful force":

> The experience began in 1984 when I first learned to meditate. I had read that prayer is talking to God and meditation is listening, so I opened my mind and listened without realizing that meditation is a powerful force.
>
> Soon I began to notice unusual sensations in my body while meditating. It felt like energy flowing through me. In the morning I woke up feeling happy and energetic and filled with a glowing warmth as though I had been sleeping in the sunshine on a sandy beach. Gradually the sensations became stronger and after a while it seemed like electric currents were coursing through my body. My fingers tingled and I felt a slight throbbing in the palms of my hands. I had no inkling of the significance of this energy until one night in a very lucid dream, I was told that I could heal.[18]

Dynamic experiences like this are what New Age mysticism is really all about—not just believing in some doctrine or a faith that is supported by some creed but instead a close personal contact with a powerful *Presence*. The renowned occultist Dion Fortune acknowledged, "shifting the consciousness is the key to all occult training."[19]

The ultimate objective of the meditation effort lies in the concept called the *higher self.* This is thought to be the part of the individual linked to the divine essence of the Universe, the God (or Divine) part of man. The goal is to become attuned with the higher self, thus facilitating the higher self's emergence into the physical realm bringing the practitioner under the guidance and direction of *God*. This connection is referred to in New Age circles as: a*wakening, transformation, enlightenment, self-realization, cosmic consciousness, and superconsciousness.* This is also why an interchangeable term for New Age is *metaphysics*. Metaphysics means that which is beyond the physical realm (the invisible realm) and being intimately connected to those powers not perceived by the ordinary five senses.

The Impact of Practical Mystics vs. Cults

Evangelical scholar David L. Smith correctly assessed the powerful, yet subtle, impact New Age spirituality is having on society when he made the following observations:

> Not since Gnosticism at the dawn of the Christian era has there arisen a philosophy as pervasive and threatening to orthodox Christianity as the New Age movement . . . It would be difficult to find any area of life, which has not been touched or redirected to some degree by the concepts of this movement.[20]

Smith recognizes that, rather than just a small segment, the overall social fabric of society is being impacted. This movement has clearly evolved well past the subculture stage into something much more dynamic and sophisticated. This stunning change has been brought about by the rise of a new breed of mystic—one that presents mysticism as a complement to secular goals and one that is adept at easing the public's natural impulse to reject the strange and unfamiliar. Some examples of this are:

> A prominent, influential speaker and seminar leader, Brian Tracy, promotes the use of the "superconscious mind" (i.e., the higher self), "to improve productivity, performance and output" in the corporate world.[21]

An article in one major Pacific Northwest newspaper features a large color picture of a local university professor in a classic Zen Buddhist meditation pose. He has not joined the Buddhist religion but is trying to reverse his heart condition through Eastern meditation.[22]

A popular morning talk show entices viewers with the promise of "how to get along with your spouse." The show then features popular New Age author Wayne Dyer exhorting viewers to "go into the silence for guidance" when they get angry with their mate[s].[23]

These are just a few examples of what could be called *secular mysticism* or generic mysticism, meditation practiced not for religious reasons but as a tool to improve life. Many Christians have a difficult time comprehending this concept. They have been trained to think in terms of cults such as the Mormons (Church of Jesus Christ of Latter Day Saints) or the Watchtower Society (Jehovah's Witnesses). But these groups are rather limited in their impact because, even if they become sizable, they remain only isolated islands in society. The advantage practical mystics have is that they only have to piggyback a seemingly benevolent meditation method onto whatever programs they are promoting—in other words, they do not have to proselytize people to a dogma, only a practice.

New Age publisher Jeremy Tarcher spoke of this challenge in an interview. Speaking of practical mystics he explained: "They have to learn to present their perceptions in appropriate language and actions that don't arouse fear or resistance."[24]

Because of their success at this effort, one writer declared that interest in meditation was currently *exploding*. This explosion in Western culture is unprecedented and very real.

In the West, mysticism has always been restricted to a tiny fraction of the population (i.e., shamans, esoteric brotherhoods, and small spiritually elite groups). Never before has there been a widespread teaching of these methods to everyone. Now, mysticism pervades the Western world. How did this happen?

The first such book to reach a broad audience was *Creative Visualization* by Shakti Gawain. This book could rightfully be called a practical mystic's bible. Many people can trace their first involvement in metaphysics to this book. Since its publication in 1978, it has sold millions of copies and has influenced the fields of psychology, health, business, and athletics.[25]

The book became so popular because it addresses such topics as creativity, career goals, relationships, better health, and simple relaxation and peacefulness. Who wouldn't want to have all this, especially if all it takes is engaging in a simple practice?

Gawain spells out very clearly what that practice entails. She teaches her readers:

> Almost any form of meditation will eventually take you to an experience of yourself as source, or your higher self . . . Eventually you will start experiencing certain moments during your meditation when there is a sort of "click" in your consciousness and you feel like things are really working; you may even experience a lot of energy flowing through you or a warm radiant glow in your body. These are signs that you are beginning to channel the energy of your higher self.[26]

There had been books like hers before, but those appealed to people already in the New Age subculture. This wasn't true of *Creative Visualization*. This book had just the right secular slant on something inherently spiritual. Gawain believed that one could stay a Jew, Catholic, or Protestant and still practice the teachings of the book. All you were doing was developing yourself, not changing your religion.

Gawain was merely the forerunner of what has become a flood of such books. A more recent book, *The Artist's Way* by Julia Cameron, which is about the "spiritual path to higher creativity,"[27] has sold over *two million* copies.

A good example of this approach was a business in a major West Coast city that sold books, tapes, and videos on *stress reduction*. The owners were very active in their community. Doctors, therapists, and teachers came to them for help. They gave talks to school faculties, major corporations, and all the major hospitals in their city. Their clientele tended to be affluent, well-educated professionals and business people who were interested in personal growth.

Yet, along with stress reduction and self-improvement, another element was subtly present—*spiritual awareness*. One of the owners wrote how she attended a powerful workshop with "Lazaris" and discovered that his techniques were "practical and useful."[28] That does not sound too extraordinary at first glance—however, Lazaris is not a person but a *spirit guide!*

Because of the stereotypes about people who gravitate toward mystical experiences (such as counterculture types), we may tend to assume people associated with these practices have strange personalities or are in other ways offbeat. On the contrary, these individuals are professional, articulate, conservatively dressed, and above all, extremely personable. They are positive and likeable. A newspaper reporter who did an article on one of them told me, "She is one of the most calm, serene persons I have ever met." The reporter added, "People want what she has!"

The health, self-help, and recovery sections of secular bookstores are now saturated with New Age metaphysical books. Christian columnist Terry Mattingly summed up the situation brilliantly when he observed: "The New Age didn't crest, it soaked in . . . It is now the dominant theme in commercial bookstores."[29] If the self-help and personal growth sections of most secular commercial bookstores were examined, the only conclusion to come away with would be that New Age mysticism is the prominent spiritual viewpoint of this country.

A case in point: One day while strolling through a shopping mall, I noticed a New Age bookstore and a secular bookstore just around the corner from each other. Upon examination, it was clear the secular bookstore had far more New Age books than the New Age bookstore did—hundreds more. Moreover, the vast majority were not in the New Age section but in the self-help, health, and other sections. Thus, New Age bookstores have almost been rendered obsolete by the explosion of practical mystic books stocked in traditional bookstores.

This is not an understatement or scare-tactic conjecture. Take a look at book sales for some of the major New Age authors around today. Just the top two, Wayne Dyer and Deepak Chopra, have sold fifty million books between them. James Redfield, the author of *The Celestine Prophecy*, can boast of a staggering *twenty* million books sold, and Neal Donald Walsch, the channeler of *Conversations with God*, a paltry seven million.[30]

The basic message of these books and hundreds of others like them could be reduced to one simple word, a word that cries out a uniform consistent theme—meditate! That is to say, *you're not going to get anywhere in this life unless you get that "click" that Gawain spoke of earlier and to do it, you must meditate.*

If you think the New Age movement is a colorful assortment of strange cults populated by free-spirited aging hippies and assorted odd-balls who are being duped by money-hungry charlatans and egocentric frauds, then think again. We are not dealing with fringe religious groups or chanting flower-children anymore but with a broad-based concerted effort to influence and restructure our whole society.

Modern Day Wizards

The practical mystic surge has also broken open our culture for more exotic forms of spirituality to flourish. Witchcraft, or Wicca as it is more commonly known, has become a contender with some major Christian denominations for the number of adherents. Once obscure and underground, Wicca is now on a roll. Scott Cunningham's book, *Wicca For The Solitary Practitioner*, has sold over 800,000 copies since 1988 and is now in its 37th printing. *The Complete Idiots Guide To* series has put out one book titled *Wicca and Witchcraft* with over 350 pages. It would seem that this one title alone would suffice to reach the intended market. But not so. *The Complete Idiots Guide* series also puts out additional books such as: *Wicca Craft, Spells and Spellcraft, Paganism, Celtic Wisdom,* and *Shamanism*, each with over 300 pages. Add to that list other titles: *Voodoo, Toltec Wisdom, Psychic Awareness* and *Tarot*. This amounts to over 3,500 pages devoted to this subject by *The Complete Idiot's Guide To* series alone.

From a Christian perspective, it becomes obvious this paradigm shift to the public's deeper awareness and greater acceptance of New Age teachings is a very dangerous challenge to Christianity's core message. One mystic proponent made this clear when he noted that meditation "brings with it a curious kind of knowing that there is somebody else there with you; you are not alone."[31] Another woman shared the instructions she received during meditation. Her guide told her: "I love you . . . Stay in my light, my love . . . Trust in me, your Lord."[32]

This, I believe, is a classic example about what Leviticus 19:31 warns:

> Regard not them that have familiar spirits, neither seek after wizards, to be defiled by them: I am the Lord your God.

It is important to note that the word *wizard* in Hebrew means a knowing one. New Age mystic Jacquelyn Small proclaimed, "People who seek spirituality through an inner pathway [meditation] become knowers."[33] In essence, New Agers are wizards!

New Age mysticism reflects the teachings of what were once called the *mystery schools* of antiquity. The mystery religions were so labeled because their teachings were kept hidden from the common people. In fact, the term *occult* originated from the mystery religions because the majority of the people were ignorant of their true meanings. The word occult literally means hidden. The priests and adepts (initiated through various grades or levels) were the ones who gained insight into these hidden truths of the universe. Despite enormous geographical distances and cultural differences, the mysteries all taught the same message: "Happy and blessed one, you have become divine instead of mortal."[34]

When a Christian hears someone claim to be God, he immediately recognizes the pronouncements of Satan: "[Y]e shall be as gods" (Genesis 3:5), and "I will be like the most High" (Isaiah 14:14). The sad thing about this is that these meditative experiences are so real and convincing, and as people often testify, are very beautiful. They experience intense light flooding them, along with a sense of infinite wisdom. In this state, they also experience what many call *ecstasy* and a sense of *unity with everything*.

The late New Age leader Peter Caddy related an incident in which a group of Christians confronted him and tried, as he put it, "to save my soul."[35] He told them to come back and talk to him when they had the same wonderful mystical experiences he had. His point was that these naive Christians had no idea what the mystical life was all about, and if they did, they would want it, instead.

Feelings such as these are common in New Age circles and have hooked many into thinking something this positive *has* to be of God. The truth of the matter is, those who say they have connected with their divinity and are themselves God, sadly, have joined the ranks of those who:

> Professing themselves to be wise, they became fools, And changed the glory of the uncorruptible God into an image made like to corruptible man, and to birds, and fourfooted beasts, and creeping things. (Romans 1:22-23)

One New Age spiritual writer advised her readers:

> When Christians ask if "you believe you are a sinner," respond with, "We have not perfectly realized our divine potential, but are still in the process of unfolding it through meditation and higher states of consciousness."[36]

Swami Muktananda, one of the most admired and respected New Age gurus during the 1970s and early 1980s, claimed to have reached his higher self. Many thought he was the virtual embodiment of the *God-realized* master. He told his disciples:

> Kneel to your own self. Honor and worship your own Being. Chant the mantra always going on within you. Meditate on your own self. God dwells within you as you.[37]

But when Muktananda died in 1983, one of his closest followers revealed that his master "ended as a feebleminded, sadistic tyrant luring devout little girls to his bed every night with promises of grace and self-realization."[38] Without realizing he was echoing the truth of the Bible, the disciple concluded:

> There is no absolute assurance that enlightenment necessitates the moral virtue of a person. There is no guarantee against the weakness of anger, lust and greed in the human soul. The enlightened are on an equal footing with the ignorant in the struggle against their own evil.[39]

Swami Muktananda's "enlightenment" did not translate into personal righteousness. He was just a sinner who mystically perceived he was God.

The Cross vs. The Higher Self

The New Age and Christianity definitely clash on the answer to this question of human imperfection. The former espouses the doctrine of becoming self-realized and united with the universe, which they see as God but in reality is the realm of familiar spirits. On the other hand, the Gospel that Christians embrace offers salvation to humanity through grace (unmerited favor). Romans 3:24 boldly states: "Being justified freely by his grace through the redemption that is in Christ Jesus." In Romans 6:23 we read: "For the wages of sin is death; but the gift of God is eternal life through Jesus Christ our Lord."

This gift is not earned or given as a reward for earnest or good intentions as Scripture clearly states:

> For by grace are ye saved through faith; and that not of yourselves: it is the gift of God: Not of works, lest any man should boast
> (Ephesians 2:8-9)

This Scripture that tackles the issue of pride sharply distinguishes all of man's religions from Christianity. Religion persuades us that man is innately good and, therefore, can earn his way to heaven through human perfectibility or, better yet, through the realization of his own divinity. Christianity emphatically states the opposite view that man needs to humbly recognize his own sinfulness and fallibility, and consequently needs salvation through grace.

The Holy Spirit, through the Scripture, convicts the sinner of his sinful and lost condition and then presents to the despairing and repentant man God's solution—salvation through the sacrificial death and resurrection of Jesus Christ on the Cross: "In whom we have redemption through his blood, the forgiveness of sins, according to the riches of his grace," (Ephesians 1:7) and then:

> [I]f thou shalt confess with thy mouth the Lord Jesus, and shalt believe in thine heart that God hath raised him from the dead, thou shalt be saved. (Romans 10:9)

Salvation is entirely a gift of grace bestowed on whoever believes in Jesus' sacrifice on the Cross as both God and man. Consequently, we must receive Him as Lord and Savior, understanding that it is by grace and grace alone that we are made acceptable in Christ before a holy God. Justification is God's gift to the believer. This saving faith, also a demonstration of God's grace, is more than an intellectual belief in Jesus' death on the Cross but involves committing and entrusting one's life to Jesus as both Lord and Savior—Christ's going to the Cross was a finished work, and we as believers are now complete in Him. Nothing else can be added to this. How totally opposite from New Age thinking is God's plan of salvation!

It all comes down to the preaching of the higher self versus *the preaching of the Cross.* New Agers may say God is synonymous with a person's higher self, and the experience of God can only be discovered by way of meditation. However, the Christian admits his or her sinfulness before a Holy God and remembers he is saved only by the grace and mercy of God through the sacrificial shedding of Christ's blood for his sins.

The message of Jesus Christ reaches out to the lost human race with the love of God who sacrificed His only begotten Son for the Swami Muktanandas of the world. The Bible teaches that man has an inherently rebellious and ungodly nature (which is evident), and his ways are naturally self-centered and evil in the sight of God. The Bible teaches that God is not indifferent to us. The sacrifice of Christ for the ungodly to reconcile us to God reveals the Lord's love toward man.

This explains why Christianity must be steadfast on these issues. If a belief system does not teach the preaching of the Cross, then it is not "the power of God" (1 Corinthians 1:18). If other ways are correct, "then Christ is dead in vain," rendering His shed blood unnecessary and immaterial (Galatians 2:21).

Because of this conflict, we can safely assume that Christianity is the most formidable obstacle to the New Age, standing like a bulwark against this tidal wave of meditation teachers and practical mystics. But, incredibly, as I pointed out in the beginning of this chapter, many of the most successful practical mystics are appearing from within Christendom itself. Ironically, instead of stemming the momentum of New Age spirituality, it is our own churches that may very well be the decisive catalysts to propel this movement into prominence. Certain spiritual practices are becoming entrenched in our churches that, like an iceberg, seem beautiful and impressive on the surface but in reality will cause severe damage and compromise of truth.

The Yoga of the West

One day, I wandered into a secular bookstore to investigate its religion section. The section was divided into two equal parts. To my left was the heading *Spirituality: New Age*. It respectively contained titles reflecting that viewpoint. To my right was the heading, *Spirituality: Judeo-Christian*. In this section, one would expect to find titles reflecting traditional Judeo-Christian concepts. Not so! The basic principles of the New Age movement were represented, with only a few exceptions, in both parts! How is this possible?

Roman Catholic writer William Johnston elaborates more on this in the following paragraph:

> [S]omething very powerful is emerging . . . we are witnessing a spiritual revolution of great magnitude in the whole world . . . the rise of a new school of mysticism within Christianity . . . It is growing year by year.[1]

That bookstore presented a perfect example of this new school of mysticism. Where there had always been a clear difference between Eastern spirituality and Christianity, that line had now become blurred.

Many professing Christians have very little awareness of this rap-
idly growing spiritual revolution. They seem altogether oblivious to
this paradigm shift in spirituality. This is understandable since most
people do not know much of what goes on beyond their own circles.
Historically, and perhaps ironically, God's people have been slow in
responding to the shifts that occur in culture. A consequence of this
naiveté is a growing spillover effect from this phenomenon into the
evangelical church, appealing to those who hunger for ways to walk
closer with God. Many Christians sincerely desire to have more full
and satisfying spiritual lives for themselves and their loved ones. Thus,
it is imperative that Christians come to a clear understanding of just
what *is* the nature of this mystical thinking and why it resonates with
New Age thought.

God *In* All Things?

It was Alice Bailey (the famous occult prophetess who coined the
term New Age) who made this startling assertion:

> It is, of course, easy to find many passages which link the
> way of the Christian Knower with that of his brother in the
> East. They bear witness to the same efficacy of method.[2]

What did she mean by the term "Christian Knower"? The answer
is unmistakable! In the first chapter, we saw how occultism is awakening the *mystical faculties* to see God in everything. In Hinduism, this
is called reaching *samadhi* or enlightenment. It is the final objective
of yoga meditation: God in everything—a force or power flowing
through *all* that exists.

William Johnston believes such an experience exists within the
context of Christianity. He explains:

> What I can safely say, however, is that there is a Christian
> samadhi that has always occupied an honored place in the
> spirituality of the West. This, I believe, is the thing that is
> nearest to Zen. It is this that I have called Christian Zen.[3]

The famous psychologist Carl Jung predicted this system would be the *yoga of the west.* [4]

Christian Zen? Christian yoga? These seem to be oxymorons, like military pacifism or alcoholic sobriety. Christians, conservative ones at least, have always viewed these concepts as heretical and anti-biblical. The word most commonly used for it is *pantheism—all is God.* But when one looks at the *Christian* Zen movement one discovers a similar term, which for all practical purposes, means the same thing. This term is called *panentheism*—God is *in* all things.

A highly respected source, *The Evangelical Dictionary of Theology*, defines panentheism as a worldview that combines "the strengths of classic theism with the strengths of classic pantheism."[5] With panentheism you still have a personal God (theism) coupled with God's pervasive presence in all creation (pantheism). In other words, with panentheism God is both a personality and an all encompassing substance as opposed to God being an impersonal substance that incorporates all of creation as found in pantheism.

The credibility of *A Time of Departing* rests on whether or not panentheism has a legitimate place in orthodox Christianity. This is a vital question because panentheism is the foundational worldview among those who engage in mystical prayer. Ken Kaisch, an Episcopal priest and a teacher of mystical prayer, made this very clear in his book, *Finding God,* where he noted:

> Meditation is a process through which we quiet the mind
> and the emotions and enter directly into the experience
> of the Divine. . . . there is a deep connection between us
> . . . God is in each of us.[6]

Here lies the core of panentheism: God is in everything and everything is in God. The only difference between pantheism and panentheism is *how* God is in everything.

This position of the panentheist is challenging to understand: Your outer personality is not God, but God is still in you as your true identity. This explains why mystics say, *all is one.* At the mystical level, they experience this *God*-force that seems to flow through everything and everybody. All creation has God in it as a living, vital presence. It is just hidden.

The theological implications of this worldview put it at direct odds with biblical Christianity for obvious reasons. Only one true God exists, and His identity is not in everyone. The fullness of God's identity, in bodily form, rests in Jesus Christ and Him only!

Scripture clearly teaches the only deity in man is Jesus Christ who dwells in the heart of the believer. Further, Jesus made it clear not everyone will be born again—having God's Spirit (John 3). Yet the panentheist perceives that all people and everything have the identity of God within them.

> For in him [Christ] dwelleth all the fulness of the Godhead bodily. And ye are complete in him, which is the head of all principality and power.
> (Colossians 2:9-10)

William Johnston again emphasizes, "For God is the core of my being and the core of all beings."[7] This fundamentally eliminates faith in the Gospel as the avenue to reconciliation with God, because God is already there. It effectively leaves out the finished work of Christ as the binding agent and is contrary to the following verses:

> For the preaching of the cross is to them that perish foolishness; but unto us which are saved it is the power of God. (1 Corinthians 1:18)

> Whosoever transgresseth, and abideth not in the doctrine of Christ, hath not God. He that abideth in the doctrine of Christ, he hath both the Father and the Son. (2 John 1:9)

The Bible does reveal, though, that God upholds all things by His powerful Word, but He does not do this by being *the substance of* all things. The Word of God says, "For in him [Christ] we live, and move, and have our being" (Acts 17:28). But this speaks *of Him* as separate from us yet remaining present with us. The belief that God indwells everything is heresy. God will not, and cannot, share His personal essence with anyone or anything outside of the Trinity. Even Christians are only partakers of the Divine Nature and not *possessors* of the Divine Nature. In 2 Peter 1:3-4, it says:

> According as his divine power hath given unto us all things that pertain unto life and godliness, through the knowledge of him that hath called us to glory and virtue:
>
> Whereby are given unto us exceeding great and precious promises: that by these ye might be *partakers of the divine* nature, having escaped the corruption that is in the world through lust. (emphasis mine)

Here the apostle Peter is writing to Christians, not to the world. He acknowledges the *participation* of the believer in conjunction with the work of the Holy Spirit. The word partaker is taken from the Greek word koinonos, which means a sharer (associate), companion, or fellowship partner. In other words, the Christian shares in the promises of the purifying work of the Holy Spirit, being called out and set apart from the corruption of an evil world. Moreover, a partaker or participant is one who has been born again through faith. A possessor, on the other hand, is one who is already in possession of something. In the case of the panentheist and pantheist, the possession they are claiming *is God.* They do not believe a fundamental change is needed, just an awareness of what is already there.

This conclusion becomes quite obvious when we examine such passages as Isaiah 42:8: "I am the LORD: that is my name: and my glory will I not give to another." Creation can *reflect* God's glory (Isaiah 6:3), but it can never *possess* God's glory. For that to happen would mean God was indeed giving His glory to another.

This concept is made crystal clear in William Shannon's book, *Silence on Fire*. Shannon, a Roman Catholic priest, relates the account of a theological discussion he once had with an atheist groom for whom he was performing a wedding ceremony. He told the skeptical young man:

> You will never find God by looking outside yourself. You
> will only find God within. It will only be when you have
> come to experience God in your own heart and let God
> into the corridors of your heart (or rather found God there)
> that you will be able to 'know' that there is indeed a God
> and that you are not separate from God.[8]

This advice is no different from what any New Age teacher would impart to someone who held an *atheistic* point of view. *You want God? Meditate! God is just waiting for you to open up.* Based on Shannon's own mystical beliefs, he *knew* this was the right approach. He alluded to this by explaining that the young man would find enlightenment if he would look in the right place or use the right method.

Those who support this heresy draw the same conclusion of mystical panentheism that author Willigis Jager articulated when he said:

> The physical world, human beings, and everything that
> is are all forms of the Ultimate Reality, all expressions of
> God, all "one with the Father."[9]

He means not all Christians but *all people*. This is nothing less than Hindu samadhi with Christian spray paint. Those in this movement who are honest have no qualms about acknowledging this—as one adherent did so aptly when he confessed, "The meditation of advanced occultists is identical with the prayer of advanced mystics."[10]

Silence—The Language of God?

For many years during my research, I would come across the term *contemplative prayer*. Immediately I would dismiss any thought that it had a New Age connotation because I thought it meant to ponder while praying—which would be the logical association with that term. But in the New Age disciplines, things are not always what they seem to be to untrained ears.

What contemplative prayer actually entails is described very clearly by the following writer:

When one enters the deeper layers of contemplative prayer
one sooner or later experiences the void, the emptiness,
the nothingness . . . the profound mystical silence . . . an
absence of thought.[11]

To my dismay, I discovered this "mystical silence" is accomplished by the same methods used by New Agers to achieve *their* silence—the mantra and the breath! Contemplative prayer is the repetition of what is referred to as a *prayer word* or *sacred word* until one reaches a state where the soul, rather than the mind, contemplates God. Contemplative prayer teacher and Zen master Willigis Jager brought this out when he postulated:

Do not reflect on the meaning of the word; thinking and
reflecting must cease, as all mystical writers insist. Simply
"sound" the word silently, letting go of all feelings and
thoughts.[12]

Those with some theological training may recognize this teaching as the historical stream going back centuries to such figures as Meister Eckhart, Teresa of Avila, John of the Cross, and Julian of Norwich.

One of the most well-known writings on the subject is the classic 14ᵗʰ century treatise, *The Cloud of Unknowing*, written by an anonymous author. It is essentially a manual on contemplative prayer inviting a beginner to:

Take just a little word, of one syllable rather than of two
. . . With this word you are to strike down every kind of
thought under the cloud of forgetting.[13]

The premise here is that in order to really know God, mysticism must be practiced—the mind has to be shut down or turned off so that the *cloud of unknowing* where the presence of God awaits can be experienced. Practitioners of this method believe that if the sacred words are *Christian*, you will get Christ—it is simply a matter of *intent* even though the method is identical to occult and Eastern practices.

So the question we as Christians must ask ourselves is, "Why not? Why shouldn't we incorporate this mystical prayer practice into our lives?" The answer to this is actually found in Scripture.

While certain instances in the Bible describe mystical experiences, I see no evidence anywhere of God sanctioning man-initiated mysticism. Legitimate mystical experiences were always initiated *by* God to certain individuals for certain revelations and was never based on a method for the altering of consciousness. In Acts 11:5, Peter fell into a trance while in prayer. But it was God, not Peter, who initiated the trance and facilitated it.

By definition, a mystic, on the other hand, is someone who uses rote methods in an attempt to tap into their inner divinity. Those who use these methods put themselves into a trance state outside of God's sanction or protection and thus engage in an extremely dangerous approach. Besides, nowhere in the Bible are such mystical practices prescribed. For instance, the Lord, for the purpose of teaching people a respect for His holiness and His plans, instated certain ceremonies for His people (especially in the Old Testament). Nonetheless, Scripture contains no reference in which God promoted mystical practices. The gifts of the Spirit spoken of in the New Testament were supernatural in nature but did not fall within the confines of mysticism. God bestowed spiritual gifts without the Christian practicing a method beforehand to get God's response.

Proponents of contemplative prayer would respond with, *What about Psalms 46:10?* "Be still, and know that I am God." This verse is often used by those promoting contemplative prayer. On the surface, this argument can seem valid, but once the meaning of "still" is examined, any contemplative connection is expelled. The Hebrew meaning of the word is to slacken, cease, or abate. In other words, the context is to slow down and trust God rather than get in a dither over things. Relax and watch God work. Reading the two verses just before Psalms 46:10 puts it in an entirely different light from that proposed by mystics:

> Come, behold the works of the LORD, what desolations
> he hath made in the earth. He maketh wars to cease unto
> the end of the earth; he breaketh the bow, and cutteth

the spear in sunder; he burneth the chariot in the fire. Be
still, and know that I am God: I will be exalted among
the heathen, I will be exalted in the earth.

This isn't talking about going into some altered state of consciousness!

It should also be pointed out that being born again, in and of
itself, is mystical. But it is a direct act of God, initiated by *Him*—the
Holy Spirit has regenerated the once-dead spirit of man into a living
spirit through Christ. Yet, we notice that even in this most significant
of experiences when one is "passed from death unto life" (John 5:24),
God accomplishes this without placing the individual in an altered state
of consciousness.

We can take this a step further by looking at the day of Pentecost
recorded in Acts, chapter 2 where those present were "all filled with
the Holy Ghost" (vs. 4). Notice that they were "all with one accord in
one place" (vs. 1) when the Holy Spirit descended on them. From the
context of the chapter, it is safe to assume this was a lively gathering
of believers engaged in intelligent conversation. Then, when those
present began to speak in other tongues, it was not an episode of
mindless babbling or vain repetition as in a mantra. Rather it was
an event of coherent speech significant enough to draw a crowd who
exclaimed, "we do hear them speak in our tongues the wonderful
works of God" (vs. 11). Other observers who suspected they were
in an altered state of consciousness said, "These men are full of new
wine" (vs. 13). Notice that Peter was quick to correct this group in
asserting that they were all fully conscious. Would it not then stand
to reason that their minds were not in any kind of altered state? Next,
Peter delivered one of the most carefully articulated speeches recorded
in Scripture. This was certainly not a group of men in a trance.

So, through the lens of perhaps the two most meaningful *mystical*
experiences recorded in the New Testament (i.e., being born again
and the outpouring of the Holy Spirit at Pentecost), an altered state
of consciousness was never sought after nor was it achieved. In fact, a
complete search of both Old and New Testaments reveals there were

only two types of experiences sanctioned by God where the recipient is not fully awake—namely dreams and visions—and in each case the experience is initiated by God. Conversely, every instance of a self-induced trance recorded in Scripture is adamantly condemned by God as we see summarized in the following verses:

> When thou art come into the land which the LORD thy God giveth thee, thou shalt not learn to do after the abominations of those nations. There shall not be found among you any one that maketh his son or his daughter to pass through the fire, or that useth divination, or an observer of times, or an enchanter, or a witch. Or a charmer, or a consulter with familiar spirits, or a wizard, or a necromancer. (Deuteronomy 18:9-11)

An examination of the Hebrew meanings of the terms used in the above verses shows that much of what is being spoken of is the invoking of spells. And a spell, used in this context, refers to a trance. In other words, when God induces a trance it is in the form of a dream or a vision. When man induces a trance, it is in the form of a spell or hypnosis.

And remember, nowhere in the Bible is the silence equated with the "power of God," but the "preaching of the cross" (1 Corinthians 1:18) most certainly is!

The Extent of Contemplative Spirituality

While many Christians are still not even aware that a practical Christian mystical movement exists, momentum is picking up, and an obvious surge towards this *contemplative spirituality* has surfaced. Evidence regarding the magnitude of this mystical prayer movement is now within reach of the average person. In 1992, *Newsweek* magazine did a cover story called "Talking to God," which made a clear reference to it. The article disclosed:

> [S]ilence, appropriate body posture and, above all, *emptying the mind* through *repetition* of prayer—have been the practices of mystics in all the great world religions.

And they form the basis on which *most modern spiritual directors* guide those who want to draw closer to God.[14] (emphasis mine)

It is amazing to me how *Newsweek* clearly observed this shift in the spiritual paradigm over fifteen years ago, while many Christians (including most prominent leaders) still live in abject ignorance of this change. Are the teachings of the practical *Christian* mystic actually being assimilated so well that even our pastors are not discerning this shift?

In September 2005, *Newsweek* carried a special report called "Spirituality in America." The feature story, titled "In Search of the Spiritual," is seventeen pages long, and for anyone who thought that a Christian mystical movement did not exist, this article is all the proof needed to show it not only exists but is alive, well, and growing like you wouldn't believe.

The article begins by describing the origin of the contemporary contemplative prayer movement, which began largely with a Catholic monk named Thomas Keating:

> To him [Keating], as a Trappist monk, meditation was second nature. He invited the great Zen master Roshi Sasaki to lead retreats at the abbey. And surely, he thought, there must be a precedent within the church for making such simple but powerful spiritual techniques available to laypeople. His Trappist brother Father William Meninger found it in one day in 1974, in a dusty copy of a 14th-century guide to contemplative meditation, "*The Cloud of Unknowing.*"[15]

The most obvious integration of this movement can be found in Roman Catholicism. Michael Leach, former president of the *Catholic Book Publishers Association*, made this incredibly candid assertion:

> But many people also believe that the spiritual principles underlying the New Age movement will soon be incorporated—or rather reincorporated—into the

mainstream of Catholic belief. In fact, it's happening in the United States right now.[16]

Incorporating it is! And it is assimilating primarily through the contemplative prayer movement.

Contemplative leader Basil Pennington, openly acknowledging its growing size, said, "We are part of an immensely large community . . . 'We are Legion.'"[17] Backing him up, a major Catholic resource company stated, "Contemplative prayer has once again become commonplace in the Christian community."[18]

William Shannon went so far as to say contemplative spirituality has now widely replaced old-style Catholicism.[19] This is not to say the Mass or any of the sacraments have been abandoned, but the underlying spiritual ideology of many in the Catholic church is now contemplative in its orientation.

One of my personal experiences with the saturation of mysticism in the Catholic church was in a phone conversation I had with the head nun at a local retreat center who told me the same message Shannon conveys. She made it clear *The Cloud of Unknowing* is now the basis for nearly all Catholic spirituality, and contemplative prayer is now becoming widespread all over the world.

I had always been confused as to the real nature of this advance in the Catholic church. Was this just the work of a few mavericks and renegades, or did the church hierarchy sanction this practice? My concerns were affirmed when I read in an interview that the mystical prayer movement not only had the approval of the highest echelons of Catholicism but also was, in fact, the *source* of its expansion. Speaking of a meeting between the late Pope Paul VI and members of the Catholic Trappist Monastic Order in the 1970s, Thomas Keating, disclosed the following:

> The Pontiff declared that unless the Church rediscovered the contemplative tradition, renewal couldn't take place. He specifically called upon the monastics, because they lived the contemplative life, to help the laity and those in other religious orders bring that dimension into their lives as well.[20]

Just look at the latest official catechism of the Catholic church to see contemplative prayer officially endorsed and promoted to the faithful by the powers that be. The new catechism firmly states. "Contemplative prayer is hearing the Word of God . . . Contemplative prayer is silence."[21]

I realized just how successfully Pope Paul's admonitions have been carried out when I discovered the following at one popular Catholic bookstore. Many shelves were marked as *spirituality*—the focal point of the entire store. Eighty to ninety percent of the books on those shelves were on mystical prayer. It was clearly the overriding theme.

In response to this turnabout, non-mystic Catholics have become very alarmed at what is happening to their church. What seems to be a glorious renewal to those like Shannon is viewed by other Catholics as a slide into apostasy.

One Catholic layman who is outspoken about this is author Randy England. In his book, *Unicorn In the Sanctuary*, England made plain just how pervasive these practices are in his church. He warned:

> The struggle is difficult. It is more likely than not that your pastor is open to New Age ideas . . . Even Catholics with no interest in New Age practices are becoming accustomed to its concepts; they should be well primed by the time Creation-Centered Spirituality becomes the norm in our churches.[22]

Let there be no mistake about it that a pope was responsible for what Randy England and others like him are witnessing in their church. This is not an aberration—an unwitting wandering from the church but part of the program from the top down.

Contemplative spirituality reaches far beyond the walls of the Catholic church. Mainline Protestant traditions (Episcopalians, United Methodists, Presbyterians, Lutherans, United Church of Christ, etc.) have dived into the contemplative waters too. Their deep tradition of twentieth-century liberalism and sociopolitical activism has left them spiritually dry and thirsting for supernatural experiences. This school of practical mysticism gives them a sense of spirituality while still allowing them a liberal political correctness. Marcus Borg, professor of Religion and Culture at Oregon State University and someone who resonates with mystical spirituality understands the popularity of mystical prayer. He states:

> In some mainline denominations, emerging-paradigm [contemplative] Christians are in the majority. Others are about equally divided between these two ways of being Christian.[23]

A sales person at a bookstore that caters to these denominations once told me the contemplative prayer view has found a large audience in the Protestant mainstream, and many pastors are very open to these practices. She added that some members of the clergy did show resistance, but a clear momentum towards the contemplative direction was nevertheless occurring. An article in *Publisher's Weekly* magazine addressing the move toward contemplative prayer in mainstream religious circles confirmed her observation. One woman in the publishing field was quoted as saying, "[M]any Protestants are looking to satisfy that yearning by a return to the Western contemplative tradition."[24] Another college professor pointed out:

> My students have been typically middle-aged and upper middle class Methodists, Presbyterians, Congregationalists, and Baptists, active in the lay leadership of their churches. To outward appearances, they are quite conventional people. Yet I have found that virtually every one of my students has encountered the new age in one of its many forms and has been attracted by its mystery.[25]

Contemplative spirituality provides a seemingly profound experience of God without having to adhere to a conservative social outlook. It also gives its practitioners comfort to know they draw on a so-called Christian well of tradition. This dilutes any reluctance some might have about the orthodoxy of these practices.

To underscore the scope and reach of the contemplative prayer movement let's look at the numbers put out by an organization called Spiritual Directors International (SDI). On their website this group gives ample evidence of what their practices are. In one national conference, the following was presented:

> This workshop offers an opportunity to study and experience the [spiritual] director's role in a person's move into the beginning and early stages of contemplative prayer, silence, and openness to new sorts of praying.[26]

One of the objectives of SDI is "Tending the holy around the world and across traditions." A 2008 membership list showed 652 Episcopalians, 239 Presbyterians, 239 Methodists, 175 Lutherans, and a whopping 2,386 Roman Catholics; counting another forty or so "traditions," the total was 6648. To show the nature of just what they mean by "across traditions," the list included Buddhist, Gnostic Christian, Hindu, Muslim, Jewish, Siddha Yoga, and even Pagan/Wiccan.*

The Desert Fathers—Borrowing From the East

Catholic priest William Shannon in his book, *Seeds of Peace*, explained the human dilemma as being the following:

> This forgetfulness, of our oneness with God, is not just a personal experience, it is the corporate experience of humanity. Indeed, this is one way to understanding original sin. *We are in God, but we don't seem to know it. We are in paradise, but we don't realize it.*[27] (emphasis mine)

Shannon's viewpoint defines the basic underlying worldview of the contemplative prayer movement as a whole. One can find similar quotations in practically every book written by contemplative authors. A Hindu guru or a Zen Buddhist master would offer

---

*Information taken from the Spiritual Directors International website—"Demographics of our Learning Community."

the same explanation. This conclusion becomes completely logical when tracing the *roots* of contemplative prayer. Let us look at the beginnings of this practice.

In the early Middle Ages, there lived a group of hermits in the wilderness areas of the Middle East. They are known to history as the *Desert Fathers*. They dwelt in small isolated communities for the purpose of devoting their lives completely to God without distraction. The contemplative movement traces its roots back to these monks who promoted the mantra as a *prayer tool*. One meditation scholar made this connection when he said:

> The meditation practices and rules for living of these earliest Christian monks bear strong similarity to those of their Hindu and Buddhist renunciate brethren several kingdoms to the East . . . the meditative techniques they adopted for finding their God suggest either a borrowing from the East or a spontaneous rediscovery.[28]

Many of the Desert Fathers, in their zeal, were simply seeking God through trial and error. A leading contemplative prayer teacher candidly acknowledged the haphazard way the Desert Fathers acquired their practices:

> It was a time of great experimentation with spiritual methods. Many different kinds of disciplines were tried, some of which are too harsh or extreme for people today. Many different methods of prayer were created and explored by them.[29]

Attempting to reach God through occult mystical practices will guarantee disaster. The Desert Fathers of Egypt were located in a particularly dangerous locale at that time to be groping around for innovative approaches to God, because as one theologian pointed out:

> [D]evelopment of Christian meditative disciplines should have begun in Egypt because much of the intellectual,

philosophical, and theological basis of the practice of meditation in Christianity also comes out of the theology of Hellenic and Roman Egypt. This is significant because it was in Alexandria that Christian theology had the most contact with the various Gnostic speculations which, according to many scholars, have their roots in the East, possibly in India.[30]

Consequently, the Desert Fathers believed as long as the desire for God was sincere—anything could be utilized to reach God. If a method worked for the Hindus to reach their gods, then Christian mantras could be used to reach Jesus. A current practitioner and promoter of the Desert Fathers' mystical prayer still echoes the logical formulations of his mystical ancestors:

> In the wider ecumenism of the Spirit being opened for us today, we need to humbly accept the learnings of particular Eastern religions . . . What makes a particular practice Christian is not its source, but its intent . . . this is important to remember in the face of those Christians who would try to impoverish our spiritual resources by too narrowly defining them. If we view the human family as one in God's spirit, then this historical cross-fertilization is not surprising . . . selective attention to Eastern spiritual practices can be of great assistance to a fully embodied Christian life.[31]

Do you catch the reasoning here? Non-Christian sources, as avenues to spiritual growth, are perfectly legitimate in the Christian life, and if Christians only practice their Christianity based on the Bible, they will actually impoverish their spirituality. This was the thinking of the Desert Fathers. So as a result, we now have contemplative prayer. Jesus addressed this when he warned His disciples:

> But when ye pray, use not
> vain repetitions,
> as the heathen do.
> (Matthew 6:7)

It should be apparent that mantra meditation or *sacred word* prayer qualifies as "vain repetition" and clearly fits an accurate description of the point Jesus was making. Yet in spite of this, trusted evangelical Christians have often pronounced that Christian mysticism is different from other forms of mysticism (such as Eastern or occult) because it is focused on Jesus Christ.

This logic may sound credible on the surface, but Christians must ask themselves a very simple and fundamental question: What really makes a practice Christian? The answer is obvious—does the New Testament sanction it? Hasn't Christ taught us, through His Word, to pray in faith in His name and according to His will? Did He leave something out? Would Jesus hold out on His true followers? Never!

Understanding this truth, God has declared in His Word that He does not leave it up to earnest, yet sinful people, to reinvent their own Christianity. When Christians ignore God's instructions in following Him they end up learning *the way of the heathen.* Israel did this countless times. It is just human nature.

The account of Cain and Abel is a classic biblical example of spiritual infidelity. Both of Adam's sons wanted to please God, but Cain decided he would experiment with his own method of being devout. Cain must have reasoned to himself: "Perhaps God would like fruit or grain better than a dead animal. It's not as gross. It's less smelly. Hey, I think I will try it!"

As you know, God was not the least bit impressed by Cain's attempt to create his own approach to pleasing God. The Lord made it clear to Cain that God's favor would be upon him if he *did what is right,* not just what was intended for God or God-focused.

In many ways, the Desert Fathers were like Cain—eager to please but not willing to listen to the instruction of the Lord and do what was right. One cannot fault them for their devotion, but one certainly can fault them for their lack of discernment.

New Age or Christian?

Before writing this book I made sure I could prove, beyond a doubt, that contemplative prayer had not only slipped into the Christian faith, but also prove it *is* an integral part of the New Age movement. In fact, New Agers see contemplative prayer as one of their own practices. Why would both New Agers and Christians claim contemplative prayer as their own? Certainly you will not find the New Age movement promoting someone like Dwight Moody or Harry Ironside, but you will find many instances such as this in which New Age therapist Jacquelyn Small cites contemplative prayer as a gateway to the spirituality to which she belongs. She explains it as:

> A form of Christian meditation, its practitioners are trained to focus on an inner symbol that quiets the mind . . . When practitioners become skilled at this method of meditation, they undergo a deep trance state similar to auto-hypnosis.[32]

The editors of the magazine *New Age Journal* have put together a book titled *As Above, So Below*—which they promote as a handbook on "Paths to Spiritual Renewal," according to their worldview. Along with chapters on shamanism, goddess worship, and holistic health, there is a chapter devoted to contemplative prayer. In it they openly declare:

> Those who have practiced Transcendental Meditation may be surprised to learn that Christianity has its own time-honored form of mantra meditation . . . Reliance on a mantric centering device had a long history in the mystical canon of Christianity.[33]

New Age author Tav Sparks lays out an array of *doorways* in one chapter of his book, *The Wide Open Door*. Again, along with a variety of occult and Eastern practices we find what Sparks calls *Spiritual Christianity*. He says, "The good news is that there are some forms of Christianity today that are alive with spiritual power."[34] He then uses a few contemplative prayer advocates as examples.

Perhaps the most compelling example of all is one by a prominent figure in the contemplative prayer movement itself, Tilden Edwards. Edwards is the founder of the prestigious Shalem Institute in Washington D.C.—a center which turns out spiritual directors from its training programs. In his book, *Spiritual Friend,* Edwards suggests those who practice contemplative prayer and have begun experiencing "spiritual unfolding" and other "unusual experiences," should turn to a book titled *Psychosynthesis* in order to understand the "dynamics" at "certain stages."[35] For the Christian, there is a major problem with this advice. The book Edwards recommends is a book written by a world famous occultist, Roberto Assagioli.

These dynamics for certain stages of "spiritual unfolding" may be desirable by those in tune with occultism, but remember, Edwards is seeking to draw Christians into this form of prayer. Edwards himself puts to rest any pretense that this is *truly* Christian when he openly admits, "This mystical stream [contemplative prayer] is the Western bridge to Far Eastern spirituality."[36]

In answer to the well-meaning but folly-laden attempts of the Desert Fathers and their spiritual descendants, I must refer to the deep observations of Charles Spurgeon who penned:

> Human wisdom delights to trim and arrange the doctrine of the cross into a system more artificial and more congenial with the depraved tastes of fallen nature; instead, however, of improving the gospel carnal wisdom pollutes it, until it becomes another gospel, and not the truth of God at all. All alterations and amendments of the Lord's own Word are defilements and pollutions.[37]

"Christian" Kundalini

M any Christians might have great difficulty accepting the assessment that what is termed Christian mysticism is, in truth, not Christian at all. They might feel this rejection is spawned by a heresy hunting mentality that completely ignores the love and devotion to God that also accompanies the mystical life. To those who are still skeptical, I suggest examining the writings of Philip St. Romain, who wrote a book about his journey into contemplative prayer called *Kundalini Energy and Christian Spirituality.* This title is revealing because kundalini is a Hindu term for the mystical power or force that underlies Hindu spirituality. In Hinduism it is commonly referred to as *the serpent power.*

St. Romain, a substance abuse counselor and devout Catholic lay minister, began his journey while practicing contemplative prayer or *resting in the still point*, as he called it. What happened to him following this practice should bear the utmost scrutiny from the evangelical community—especially from its leadership. The future course of evangelical Christianity rests on whether St. Romain's path is just a fluke or if it is the norm for contemplative spirituality.

Having rejected mental prayer as "unproductive,"[38] he embraced the prayer form that switches off the mind, creating what he described as a mental passivity. What he encountered next underscores my concern with sobering clarity:

> Then came the lights! The gold swirls that I had noted on occasion began to intensify, forming themselves into patterns that both intrigued and captivated me . . . There were always four or five of these; as soon as one would fade, another would appear, even brighter and more intense . . . They came through complete passivity and only after I had been *in the silence* for a while. [39] (emphasis mine)

After this, St. Romain began to sense "wise sayings" coming into his mind and felt he was "receiving messages from another."[40] He also had physical developments occur during his periods in the silence. He would feel "prickly sensations" on the top of his head and at times it would "fizzle with energy."[41]* This sensation would go on for days. The culmination of St. Romain's mystical excursion was predictable—when you do *Christian* yoga or *Christian* Zen you end up with *Christian* samadhi as did he. He proclaimed:

> No longer is there any sense of alienation, for the Ground that flows throughout my being is identical with the Reality of all creation. It seems that the mystics of all the world's religions know something of this.[42]

---

*See page 16.

St. Romain, logically, passed on to the next stage with:

> [T]he significance of this work, perhaps, lies in its potential
> to contribute to the dialogue between Christianity and
> Eastern forms of mysticism such as are promoted in what
> is called New Age spirituality.[43]

Many people believe St. Romain is a devout Christian. He claims he loves Jesus, believes in salvation, and is a member in good standing within his church. What changed though were his sensibilities. He says:

> I cannot make any decisions for myself without the
> approbation of the inner adviser, whose voice speaks so
> clearly in times of need . . . there is a distinct sense of an
> inner eye of some kind "seeing" with my two sense eyes.[44]

St. Romain would probably be astounded that somebody would question his claims to finding truth because of the positive nature of his mysticism. But is this "inner adviser" St. Romain has connected with really God? This is a fair question to ask especially when this prayer method has now spread within a broad spectrum of Christianity.

As articulated earlier in this chapter, this practice has already spread extensively throughout the Roman Catholic and Protestant mainline churches. And it has now crossed over and is manifesting itself in conservative denominations as well—ones that have traditionally stood against the New Age. Just as a tidal wave of practical mystics has hit secular society, so it has also in the religious world. St. Romain makes one observation in his book that I take very seriously. Like his secular practical mystic brethren, he has a strong sense of mission and destiny. He predicts:

> Could it be that those who make the journey to the True
> Self are, in some ways, demonstrating what lies in store
> for the entire race? What a magnificent world that would
> be—for the majority of people to be living out of the True
> Self state. Such a world cannot come, however, unless

hundreds of thousands of people experience the regression of the Ego in the service of transcendence [meditation], and then restructure the culture to accommodate similar growth for millions of others. I believe we are only now beginning to recognize this task.[45]

A book titled *Metaphysical Primer: A Guide to Understanding Metaphysics* outlines the basic laws and principles of the New Age movement. First and foremost is the following principle:

> You are one with the Deity, as is all of humanity . . . Everything is one with everything else. All that is on Earth is an expression of the One Deity and is permeated with Its energies.[46]

St. Romain's statement was, "[T]he Ground [God] that flows throughout my being is identical with the Reality of all creation."[47] The two views are *identical!*

St. Romain came to this view through standard contemplative prayer, not Zen, not yoga but a *Christian* form of these practices. The lights were also a reoccurring phenomenon as one contemplative author suggested:

> Christian literature makes reference to many episodes that parallel the experiences of those going a yogic way. Saint Anthony, one of the first desert mystics, frequently encountered strange and sometimes terrifying psychophysical forces while at prayer.[48]

Unfortunately, this experience was not confined to St. Anthony alone. This has been the common progression into mystical awareness throughout the centuries, which also means many now entering the contemplative path will follow suit. This is not just empty conjecture. One mystical trainer wrote:

> [T]he classical experience of enlightenment as described by Buddhist monks, Hindu gurus, *Christian mystics,*

Aboriginal shamans, Sufi sheiks and Hebrew kabalists is characterized by two universal elements: radiant light and an experience of oneness with creation.[49] (emphasis mine)

Without the mystical connection there can be no oneness. The second always follows the first. Here lies the heart of occultism.

This issue is clearly a serious one to contend with. Many individuals, using terms for themselves like *spiritual director,* are showing up more and more in the evangelical church. Many of them teach the message of mystical prayer.

Interspirituality

The final outcome of contemplative prayer is *interspirituality.* If you have truly grasped the portrait that I have painted throughout this chapter, you have begun to see what this term signifies. The focus of my criticism of mystical prayer must be understood in the light of interspirituality.

Just what exactly *is* interspirituality? The premise behind interspirituality is that divinity (God) is in all things, and the presence of God is in all religions; there is a connecting together of all things, and through mysticism (i.e., meditation) this state of divinity can be recognized. Consequently, this is a premise that is based on and upheld by an experience that occurs during a self-hypnotic trance linking one to an unseen world rather than to the sound doctrine of the Bible.

It is important to understand that interspirituality is a uniting of the world's religions through the common thread of mysticism. Wayne Teasdale, a lay monk who coined the term interspirituality, says that interspirituality is "the spiritual common ground which exists among the world's religions."[50] Teasdale, in talking about this universal church also states:

> She [the church] also has a responsibility in our age to be a bridge for reconciling the human family . . . the Spirit is inspiring her through the signs of the times to open to Hindus, Buddhists, Muslims, Sikhs, Jains, Taoists, Confucians, and indigenous peoples. As *matrix* [a binding

substance], the Church would no longer see members of other traditions as outside her life. She would promote the study of these traditions, seek common ground and *parallel insights.*[51] (emphasis mine)

An article in my local newspaper revealed just how well received interspirituality has become in certain circles. One Presbyterian elder who was described as a "Spiritual Director" made it clear when she said:

> I also have a strong interest in Buddhism and do a sitting meditation in Portland [Oregon] as often as I can. I considered myself ecumenical not only in the Christian tradition, but with *all religions.*[52] (emphasis mine)

Over the course of the last few decades especially there has been a move away from an emphasis on biblical doctrine and a move toward the experiential. Feelings are more important now; and when you include mysticism with this mindset, it is a dangerous combination.

Sound doctrine must be central to this debate because New Ageism has a very idealistic side to it, offering a mystical approach to solve human problems. Everyone would like to have his or her problems solved. Right? That is the practical aspect I wrote about in the last chapter—a seemingly direct route to a happy and fulfilled life. However, one can *promote* the attributes of God without actually *having* God.

People who promote a presumably godly form of spirituality can indeed come against the truth of Christ. Then how can you be assured what you believe and practice *is* of God?

The Christian message has been clear from the beginning—God has sent a *Savior*. If man only had to practice some kind of mystical prayer to gain access to God then the life, ministry, death, and resurrection of Jesus Christ was a fruitless, hollow endeavor.

Sound Christian doctrine comes from the understanding that mankind is sinful, fallen, and separated from God. Man needs a saving work by God! A teaching like panentheism (God is in everybody) cannot be reconciled to the finished work of Christ. How could Jesus be our Savior then? New Age constituents will say He is a model for *Christ consciousness,* but the Bible teaches He is the Savior of mankind. Therefore, panentheism cannot be a true doctrine.

The problem is that many well-intentioned people embrace the teachings of panentheism because it sounds so good. It appears less bigoted on God's part. No one is left out—all are connected to God. There is a great appeal in this message. Nevertheless, the Bible does not teach a universal salvation for man. In contrast, Jesus said:

> Enter ye in at the strait gate: for wide is the gate, and broad is the way, that leadeth to destruction, and many there be which go in thereat: Because strait is the gate, and narrow is the way, which leadeth unto life, and few there be that find it. (Matthew 7:13-14)

Christ's message is the polar opposite of these universalist teachings. Many people (even Christians) today think only a few really bad people will be sent to hell. But in Matthew, the words of Jesus make it clear that this just is not so.

While God sent His Son, Jesus Christ, to die for the sins of the world, He did not say all would be saved. His words are clear that many would reject the salvation He provided. But those who are saved have been given the "ministry of reconciliation" (2 Corinthians 5:18) making an appeal to those who are perishing (2 Corinthians 4:3). The Christian message is not samadhi, Zen, kundalini, or the contemplative silence. It is the power of the Cross!

> For the preaching of the cross is to them that perish foolishness; but unto us which are saved it is the power of God. (1 Corinthians 1:18)

Yes, perishing, and not just unaware of their true self.

In an opinion poll, the startling results describe how Americans actually view God. *Spirituality and Health* magazine hired a reputable pollster organization to gauge the spiritual beliefs of the American public. This national poll revealed that 84 percent of those questioned believed God to be "everywhere and in everything" rather than "someone somewhere."[53] This means panentheism is now the more popular view of God. If true, then a high percentage of evangelical Christians in America already lean towards a panentheistic view of God. Perhaps many of these Christians are fuzzy about the true nature of God.

How could this mystical revolution have come about? How could this perspective have become so widespread? The answer is that over the last thirty or forty years a number of authors have struck a deep chord with millions of readers and seekers within Christendom. These writers have presented and promoted the contemplative view to the extent that many now see it as the only way to "go deeper" in the Christian life. They are the ones who prompt men and women to plunge into contemplative practice. It is their message that leads people to experience the "lights" and the "inner adviser!"

> And no marvel; for Satan himself is transformed into an angel of light. Therefore it is no great thing if his ministers also be transformed as the ministers of righteousness; whose end shall be according to their works. (2 Corinthians 11:14, 15)

Three

Proponents and Visionaries

A friend once related to me a conversation he had with the senior pastor of a respected evangelical church. The pastor shared with him how much he enjoyed the works of one of the figures that will be discussed in this chapter. My friend responded with a substantial concern about the validity of this particular author's practice of mysticism and shared with him what I had discovered about the contemplative prayer movement. On hearing these concerns, the pastor became furious and retorted, "These people [referring to me] just want to tear down everyone; they just want to destroy." He then stormed off in disgust.

This response is quite understandable if you take into account that this pastor obviously perceived something valuable in the writings of this spiritual writer. His respect and admiration for the author automatically rejected anything that resembled criticism. Nevertheless, in spite of this touchiness, the controversy remains valid. Is contemplative spirituality of God or not?

There certainly is a *perceived* presence of God in the contemplative practice as noted by Wayne Teasdale who stated, "[I]n the silence is a dynamic presence. And that's God, and we become attuned to that."[1] But is this presence really God? Based on the criteria put forth in the previous chapter, it may not be God they are attuned to at all but rather the "dynamic presence" of familiar spirits. The problem with addressing this issue is that the proponents of these practices appear to be devout and virtuous. Scripture warns:

> Beloved, believe not every spirit, but try the spirits whether they are of God: because many false prophets are gone out into the world. (1 John 4:1)

With this in mind, I fully realize any critical approach to these writers must be very sensitive. It is my intention to show civility and grace on this issue toward those individuals whose teachings and practices my research demonstrates are in error. However, if my findings are correct, such errors can open a person to a realm that leads to spiritual disaster. Scripture continually warns us to test and prove what is or is not from God. I do not want to provoke readers into a witch-hunt but rather to godly vigilance and discernment.

These issues are of vital importance! I personally know of people who, in the context of wanting to explore Christianity at a deeper level, have become full-blown New Agers by reading and practicing what some of the following authors have promoted. There may be some good in what these writers say, but it is also true that a little leaven can indeed leaven the whole lump (Galatians 5:9). What I am saying may appear controversial, but please keep in mind what New Age writer Marilyn Ferguson discovered: 31 percent of New Agers she quizzed said it was "Christian mysticism" that got them involved.[2] Now let's look at what some of these authors say.

M. Scott Peck (1936-2005)

Over the past couple of decades, on the New York Times bestseller list, one title has consistently stood out: *The Road Less Traveled,* by the late Dr. M. (Morgan) Scott Peck. *LIFE* magazine called it a "national institution" and compared its selling power to that of the Bible.[3] That may not be an overstatement considering the book has sold millions of copies and profoundly influenced tens of millions of people. The prestigious *Wall Street Journal* resounded that *The Road Less Traveled* was "Brilliant in its insistence that there is no distinction between the process of achieving spiritual growth and achieving mental growth."[4]

In the self-help sections of many large bookstores, M. Scott Peck usually receives almost half a shelf devoted to his books. His influence remains substantial and enduring. The remarkable chord Peck has struck with so many readers is his no-nonsense approach to life's problems. He proposes how one should tackle adverse situations head on with the goals being both psychological and spiritual growth. But what does spiritual growth mean to Peck? Well, we can learn this by the very statement he poses to his readers: "I have said that the ultimate goal of spiritual growth is for the individual to become as one with God." He then makes this bold proclamation: "It is for the individual to become totally, wholly God."[5] In familiar New Age fashion he believes "these concepts" have been promoted in the past "by Buddha, by Christ, by Lao-Tse, among many others."[6]

Many of Dr. Peck's admirers would be highly offended seeing the much-decried title *New Age* associated with his name. Some may say, "Well, he was a Buddhist when he wrote the book, but now he is a Christian; besides, there are so many useful ideas in his book that don't conflict with Christianity." However, to get an idea of the kind of "Christianity" Peck has espoused, from the time of his baptism on March 9, 1980 to the present, consider the following facts:

1. In an interview with *New Age* magazine, Peck revealed that *The Road Less Traveled* was dropped on him from God, and that there are "an enormous number of people who have a passion for God, but who are fed up to the gills with fundamentalism." The interview also divulged that Peck moved from "Eastern mystical religions toward Christian mysticism [contemplative prayer]."[7]

2. Mystical prayer is also the basis for Peck's spirituality. He noted the necessity of it in his book, *A World Waiting To Be*

Born: "This process of emptying the mind is of such importance it will continue to be a significant theme . . . It may help to remember, therefore, that the purpose of emptying the mind is not ultimately to have nothing there; rather it is to make room in the mind for something new, something unexpected, to come in. What is this something new? It is the voice of God."[8] Peck also conveys the notion that Jesus was "an example of the Western mystic" who "integrated himself with God."[9] He added that Jesus' message to us was to "cease clinging to our lesser selves" and find "our greater true selves."[10] Contemplative prayer, he believes, "is a lifestyle dedicated to maximum awareness."[11] It might interest you to know that former Vice President Al Gore has his endorsement on the book's back cover. He praises it as being "extremely important" and an "invaluable guide," stating the book's teachings have given us "powerful new reasons for hope."[12]

3. *The Coming of the Cosmic Christ,* is a book in which New Age leader/Episcopal priest Matthew Fox puts forth the idea that "mysticism" should become the praxis around which all the world's religions can unite—something he calls "deep ecumenism." The "cosmic Christ," Fox explains, is the "I AM in every creature" and Jesus is someone "who shows us how to embrace our own divinity."[13] Peck thoroughly endorses Fox's statements with his comment on the back cover, that Fox is offering "values and practice required for planetary salvation."[14] This praise is revealing since Fox advocates there should be a "shift away from the historical Jesus" and more attention given to the "cosmic Christ."[15] I am certain Peck would not give such an endorsement to a manuscript he had not read or did not totally agree with.

Perhaps the best source for finding Scott Peck's spiritual mindset is an audiocassette titled: *Further Along the Road Less Traveled*. Peck gives a lecture of his personal views on the New Age movement. In it he reveals:

- "I spent 20 years in Zen Buddhism which prepared me for Christianity."[16]
- "Zen Buddhism should be taught in every 5th grade class in America."[17]
- "Christianity's greatest sin is to think that other religions are not saved."[18]
- "The New Age movement can get flaky but is potentially very [g]odly and its virtues are absolutely enormous."[19]
- If the New Age can reform society rather than just adversely challenge it then it can be "extremely holy and desperately needed."[20]
- He himself presents the question to his audience: "Is Scott Peck a New Ager?" and then answers "yes" and adds that he is "proud to be listed as an Aquarian Conspirator."[21]
- He says his Foundation for Community Encouragement is "very much a New Age organization."[22]

It is not surprising then, that in his book about the New Age movement, *Heaven on Earth*, secular journalist Michael D' Antonio saw Scott Peck as "becoming the Billy Graham of the New Age" and that he was "a major New Age leader."[23]

Thomas Merton (1915-1968)

What Martin Luther King was to the civil rights movement and what Henry Ford was to the automobile, Thomas Merton is to contemplative prayer. Although this prayer movement existed centuries before he came along, Merton took it out of its monastic setting and made it available to, and popular with, the masses. But for me, hands down, Thomas Merton has influenced the Christian mystical movement more than any person of recent decades.

Merton penned one of the most classic descriptions of contemplative spirituality I have ever come across. He explained:

> It is a glorious destiny to be a member of the human race,
> . . . now I realize *what we all are*. . . . If only they [people]
> could all see themselves as they really are . . . I suppose
> the big problem would be that we would fall down and

worship each other. . . . At the center of our being is a point
of nothingness which is untouched by sin and by illusions,
a point of pure truth. . . . This little point . . . is the pure
glory of God in us. It is in everybody. [24] (emphasis mine)

Notice how similar Merton's description is to the occultic definition of the higher self.

In order to understand Merton's connection to mystical occultism, we need first to understand a sect of the Muslim world—Sufis,
who are the mystics of Islam. They chant the name of Allah as a
mantra, go into meditative trances and experience *God in everything*.
A prominent Catholic audiotape company now promotes a series of
cassettes Merton did on Sufism. It explains:

> Merton loved and shared a deep spiritual kinship with the
> Sufis, the spiritual teachers and mystics of Islam. Here he
> shares their profound spirituality.[25]

In a letter to a Sufi Master, Merton disclosed, "My prayer tends very
much to what you call fana."[26] So what is fana? *The Dictionary of Mysticism
and the Occult* defines it as "the act of merging with the Divine Oneness."[27]

Merton saw the Sufi concept of *fana* as being a catalyst for Muslim unity with Christianity despite the obvious doctrinal differences.
In a dialogue with a Sufi leader, Merton asked about the Muslim
concept of salvation. The master wrote back stating:

> Islam inculcates individual responsibility for one's actions
> and *does not* subscribe to the doctrine of atonement or the
> theory of redemption.[28] (emphasis mine)

To Merton, of course, this meant little because he believed that
fana and contemplation were the same thing. He responded:

> Personally, in matters where dogmatic beliefs differ, I think
> that controversy is of little value because it takes us away
> from the *spiritual realities* into the realm of words and ideas

> . . . in words there are apt to be infinite complexities and
> subtleties which are beyond resolution. . . . But much more
> important is the sharing of the *experience of divine light* . . .
> It is *here* that the area of fruitful dialogue exists between
> Christianity and Islam.[29] (emphasis mine)

Merton himself underlined that point when he told a group of contemplative women:

> I'm deeply impregnated with Sufism.[30]

And he elaborated elsewhere:

> Asia, Zen, Islam, etc., all these things come together in
> my life. It would be *madness* for me to attempt to create
> a monastic life for myself by excluding all these. I would
> be less a monk.[31] (emphasis mine)

When you evaluate Merton's mystical worldview, it clearly resonates with what technically would be considered traditional New Age thought. This is an inescapable fact!

Merton's mystical experiences ultimately made him a kindred spirit and co-mystic with those in other Eastern religions also because his insights were identical to their insights. At an interfaith conference in Thailand he stated:

> I believe that by openness to Buddhism, to Hinduism,
> and to these great Asian [mystical] traditions, we stand a
> wonderful chance of learning more about the potentiality
> of our own Christian traditions.[32]

Please understand that contemplative prayer *alone* was the catalyst for such theological views. One of Merton's biographers made this very clear when he explained:

> If one wants to understand Merton's going to the East it
> is important to understand that it was his rootedness in

his own faith tradition [Catholicism] that gave him the
spiritual equipment [contemplative prayer] he needed to
grasp the way of wisdom that is proper to the East.[33]

This was the ripe fruit of the Desert Fathers. When you borrow
methods from Eastern religion, you get their understanding of God.
There is no other way to put it. It does not take being a scholar to
see the logic in this.

Merton's influence is very strong in the Catholic church and
mainline Protestant denominations, and it is starting to grow in evangelical circles. While many Christians are impressed with Merton's
humility, social consciousness, and piety, his intellectual dynamism
is also a powerful draw. But sadly, Merton's heresies neutralize his
qualities. He revealed the true state of his soul to a fellow monk prior
to his trip to Thailand where his life ended by accidental electrocu-
tion. Before he left, he confided to his friend, "I am going home
. . . to the home I have never been in this body."[34] I do not believe
Merton was talking about a premonition of his death but rather was
professing the East to be his true spiritual home.

This is not a thoughtless assertion. Virtually all Merton scholars
and biographers make similar observations. One Merton devotee
wrote, "The major corpus [body] of his writings are embedded in the
central idea, experience and vision of the Asian wisdom."[35]

Henri Nouwen (1932-1996)

An individual who has gained popularity and respect in Christian
circles, akin to that of Thomas Merton, is the now deceased Catholic
theologian Henri Nouwen. Like Merton, Nouwen combines a strong
devotion to God with a poetic, comforting, yet distinctly intellectual
style that strikes a strong and sympathetic chord with what could be
called Christian intelligentsia. Many pastors and professors are greatly
attracted to his deep thinking. In fact, one of his biographers revealed
that in a 1994 survey of 3,400 U.S. Protestant church leaders, Nouwen
ranked second only to Billy Graham in influence among them.[36]

Nouwen also attracts many lay people who regard him as very inspirational. One person told me that Nouwen's appeal could be compared to that of motherhood—a warm comforting embrace that leaves you feeling good. Despite these glowing attributes, several aspects of Nouwen's spirituality have earned him a place in this book.

Unfortunately, this widely read and often-quoted author, at the end of his life, stated in clear terms that he approached God from a universalistic view. He proclaimed:

> Today I personally believe that while Jesus came to open the door to God's house, all human beings can walk through that door, whether they know about Jesus or not. Today I see it as my call to help every person claim his or her own way to God.[37]

Nouwen's endorsement of a book by Hindu spiritual teacher Eknath Easwaran, teaching mantra meditation, further illustrates his universalistic sympathies. On the back cover, Nouwen stated, "This book has helped me a great deal."[38]

Nouwen also wrote the foreword to a book that mixes Christianity with Hindu spirituality, in which he says:

> [T]he author shows a wonderful openness to the gifts of Buddhism, Hinduism and Moslem religion. He discovers their great wisdom for the spiritual life of the Christian . . . Ryan [the author] went to India to learn from spiritual traditions other than his own. He brought home many treasures and offers them to us in the book.[39]

Nouwen apparently took these approaches seriously himself. In his book, *The Way of the Heart*, he advised his readers:

> The quiet repetition of a single word can help us to descend with the mind into the heart . . . This way of simple prayer . . . opens us to God's active presence.[40]

But what God's "active presence" taught him, unfortunately, stood more in line with classic Hinduism than classic evangelical Christianity. He wrote:

> Prayer is "soul work" because our souls are those sacred centers where *all is one* . . . It is in the heart of God that we can come to the full realization of the *unity of all that is*.[41] (emphasis mine)

It is critical to note here that Nouwen did not say all Christians are one; he said "all is one," which is the fundamental panentheistic concept of God—the God in everything unites everything. Like Thomas Merton, it was Nouwen's intent to make mystical prayer a pervasive paradigm within all traditions of Christianity. He felt the evangelical church had many admirable qualities but lacked one vital one: mysticism. He sought to remedy this by imploring, "It is to this silence [contemplative prayer] that we all are called."[42]

One of the most classic examples I've ever encountered that reveals Nouwen's spiritual mindset is from his autobiographical book, *Sabbatical Journey*. In it, he speaks glowingly of his encounter with author and lecturer, Andrew Harvey, in April of 1996. Nouwen exclaimed, "I had the deep sense of meeting a soul friend [mentor]."[43]

What makes this comment so revealing about Nouwen's belief system is that Harvey is a world-renowned advocate of *interspirituality* through mysticism. He has written thirty books on this subject, one of which bears the following declaration that sums up the meaning of this term:

> When you look past the different terminologies employed by the different mystical systems, you see clearly that they are each talking about the same overwhelming truth—that we are all *essentially children of the Divine* and can realize that identity with our Source here on earth and in a body.[44] (emphasis mine)

It is important to note here that Andrew Harvey is one of about two dozen members of the Living Spiritual Teachers Project. The project's main goal is to promote mysticism as a bridge to interspirituality. Members include Catholic and Buddhist nuns and monks as well as Zen masters and the bestselling New Age author, Marianne Williamson.

A skeptic might respond with the comeback that Nouwen liked Harvey as a person, but didn't necessarily agree with his views. Nouwen himself put this possibility to rest when he said:

> Before driving home, Michael, Tom and I had a cup of tea at a nearby deli. We discussed at some length the way *Andrew's mysticism* had touched us.[45] (emphasis mine)

Thomas Keating and Basil Pennington (1931-2005)

In the book *Finding Grace at the Center*, written by these two Catholic monks, the following advice is given:

> We should not hesitate to take the fruit of the age-old wisdom of the East and "capture" it for Christ. Indeed, those of us who are in ministry should make the necessary effort to acquaint ourselves with as many of these Eastern techniques as possible.
>
> Many Christians who take their prayer life seriously have been greatly helped by Yoga, Zen, TM and similar practices, especially where they have been initiated by reliable teachers and have a solidly developed Christian faith to find inner form and meaning to the resulting experiences.[46]

Thomas Keating and Basil Pennington have taken their Christianity and blended it with Eastern mysticism through a contemplative method they call *centering prayer*.

I met a woman who once enthusiastically told me that in her church "we use a mantra to get in touch with God." She was referring to centering prayer. It is quite accurate to say centering prayer groups are flourishing today. Moreover, many times those who embrace it are the most active and creative people in the congregation. Christian peers often see these advocates as bringing a new vitality to the church.

Keating and Pennington have both authored a number of influential books on contemplative prayer thus advancing this movement greatly. Pennington essentially wrote a treatise on the subject called *Centering Prayer* while Keating has written the popular and influential classic, *Open Mind, Open Heart,* and both are major evangelists for contemplative prayer. Keating preaches, "God's first language is silence."[47] He taught 31,000 people in 1991 alone how to "listen to God."[48] Often hundreds of people in a single seminar will be taught how to "center."

To show how well respected Keating is, when *Newsweek* did its 2005 feature article titled "In Search of the Spiritual," they chose him to begin the piece. Using the term "worldwide phenomenon" to describe the success of his movement, *Newsweek* recounted:

> Twice a day for 20 minutes, practitioners find a quiet place to sit with their eyes closed and surrender their minds to God. In more than a dozen books and in speeches and retreats that have attracted tens of thousands, Keating has spread the word to a world of "hungry people, looking for a deeper relationship with God."[49]

Tilden Edwards and Gerald May (1940-2005)

If the contemplative prayer movement has a major alma mater, it would be the Shalem Institute (for Spiritual Formation) located in Washington D.C. The Shalem Institute is one of the bastions of contemplative prayer in this country and has trained thousands of spiritual directors since its inception in 1972. To understand the interspiritual proclivities in the contemplative prayer movement, I invite you to take a good look at this organization. Founded by an Episcopal clergyman, the Reverend Tilden Edwards, Shalem's mission is to spread the practice of mystical prayer to Christianity as a whole.

Dr. Edwards himself makes no effort to hide his interspiritual approach to Christianity. One example was a workshop he did titled *Buddhist Contributions to Christian Living.* He promises that if one wants to live in the *divine Presence,* then consider that:

> Some Buddhist traditions have developed very practical
> ways of doing so that many Christians have found
> helpful . . . offering participants new perspectives and
> possibilities for living more fully in the radiant gracious
> Presence through the day.[50]

An individual who had a particularly large influence in the Christian counseling field is the late psychiatrist and author Gerald May. May, who passed away in 2005, was also a cofounder and teacher at the Shalem Institute. Again, as with the other proponents named in this chapter, one finds a direct affinity between May and Eastern mysticism.

In the front of his book, *Simply Sane*, he states upfront: "The lineage of searching expressed herein arises from scriptures of the world's great religions." He then gives thanks to two Tibetan Buddhist lamas (holy men) and a Japanese Zen Master for their "particular impact" on him.[51]

The influence of Eastern spirituality is also depicted in his book, *Addiction and Grace*, which is considered to be a classic in the field of Christian recovery. In this book, May conveys that "our core . . . one's own center . . . is where we realize our essential unity *with one another with all God's creation*"[52] (emphasis mine).

Of course the method for entering this "core" is the silence, which May makes obvious when he explains:

> I am not speaking here of meditation that involves
> guided imagery or scriptural reflections, but of a more
> contemplative practice in which one just sits still and
> stays awake with God.[53]

May is even more upfront about his Eastern metaphysical views in his book, *The Awakened Heart*, where he expounds on the "cosmic presence" which he explains is "pervading ourselves and all creation."[54]

One might defend May by saying he was just speaking of God's omnipresence. But May was firmly in the mystical panentheistic camp. There can be no mistaking his theological underpinnings when May revealed his meaning of "cosmic presence" in such statements as:

It is revealed in the Hindu greetings *jai bhagwan* and *namaste* that reverence the divinity that both resides within and embraces us all.[55]

Like M. Scott Peck, May started with Zen Buddhism back in the 1970s. He was still in tune with it some thirty years later when he wrote the foreword to a book called *Zen for Christians*. In it, he wrote: "I wish I'd had this book when I began to explore Buddhism. It would have made things much easier."[56]

Morton Kelsey (1917-2001)

Morton Kelsey was an Episcopalian priest and a popular writer among certain Christian thinkers. His most influential book, *Other Side of Silence: The Guide to Christian Meditation* has influenced tens of thousands. One publication stated that his book, *Companions on the Inner Way: The Art of Spiritual Guidance* was a "favorite among spiritual directors."[57] Where contemplative prayer has lead Kelsey is apparent in his pronouncement that:

> You can find most of the New Age practices in the depth of Christianity. . . . I believe that the Holy One lives in every soul.[58]

Kelsey had a close relationship with author Agnes Sanford, a renowned panentheist who wrote *The Healing Light*. Sanford, in turn, has influenced a number of authors who have had an impact in Christian circles.

Kelsey was a significant promoter of mysticism within the traditional denominations. He asked the question:

> How can the Christian community meet the religious needs of modern men and women pointed up by the New Age—needs that are not now being met by most Christian churches?

> Each church needs to provide classes in forms of prayer.
> This is only possible if seminaries are training pastors in
> prayer, contemplation and meditation, and group process.
> . . . The church has nothing to fear from the New Age
> when it preaches, teaches, and heals.[59]

Matthew Fox

The individual most often spoken of as being the proponent of
New Age mysticism within Christianity is writer and Episcopalian priest
Matthew Fox. His popular books, *Original Blessing* and *The Coming of the
Cosmic Christ*, are primers for what he calls *creation-centered spirituality*,
which is nothing more than simple panentheism with a glorified title.

Fox has a sizable following in both Catholic and mainline Protestant circles, although he has not generated near the enthusiasm or
respect of Thomas Merton or Henri Nouwen. Yet Fox manifests the
same God-in-everything view and aligns with Eastern religion as did
Merton and Nouwen:

> Divinity is found in all creatures. . . . The Cosmic Christ
> is the "I am" in every creature.[60]

Fox believes that mysticism is essential to humanity in saying:

> Without mysticism there will be no "deep ecumenism,"
> no unleashing of the power of wisdom from *all* the
> world's religious traditions. Without this [mysticism] I am
> convinced there will never be global peace or justice since
> the human race needs spiritual depths and disciplines,
> celebrations and rituals to awaken its better selves.[61]

Fox coined the term "deep ecumenism," which is a synonym
for interspirituality. As the name implies, this would be a unity that
goes well beyond the surface level to the mystical core of all religions.

Fox founded a school to teach these principles to a wide number
of students. It was called the University of Creation Spirituality but
is now known as the more exotic sounding Wisdom University.

Sitting at the Wrong Table

Scores of books and writings by similar authors and teachers of contemplative prayer have been written, but it would be redundant to profile them all. Basically, these authors echo Thomas Merton, and in understanding Merton, we can understand the whole movement. It is essential to see that although Merton and his proponents have an apparent devotion to God and a strong commitment to moral integrity, they have attempted to marry biblical principles to a mysticism that is, through the Desert Fathers, derived from Eastern religions.

I recall coming out of an interspiritual center once where the creed was all religions are one. I thought to myself, *I'm sure I am viewed as someone who gets up and smugly cries out, "only my religion is true!"* It's true that I've come to this conclusion, yes, but why? Simply put, because the prophets and apostles of *my religion* made that unmistakably clear. None of the biblical champions of God were interspiritualists—absolutely none! Paul, the apostle, illustrated this in the following account:

> And when the people saw what Paul had done, they lifted up their voices, saying in the speech of Lycaonia, The gods are come down to us in the likeness of men. And they called Barnabas, Jupiter; and Paul, Mercurius, because he was the chief speaker. Then the priest of Jupiter, which was before their city, brought oxen and garlands unto the gates, and would have done sacrifice with the people.
>
> Which when the apostles, Barnabas and Paul, heard of, they rent their clothes, and ran in among the people, crying out, And saying, Sirs, why do ye these things? We also are men of like passions with you, and preach unto you that ye should turn from these vanities unto the living God, which made heaven, and earth, and the sea, and all things that are therein: Who in times past suffered all nations to walk in their own ways. (Acts 14: 11-16)

Paul said this because he knew that these other gods were not God at all—only Jesus Christ could be worshiped, only He died for humanity's sins. Needless to say, other faiths do not embrace this. Hindu and Buddhist *karma* and Islamic *submission* are only, at best, futile, vain human efforts.

In contemplative-promoting literature, one can find numerous statements that either belittle or actually condemn the gospel message of Jesus Christ. Here are two examples:

> Unfortunately, over the course of the centuries, this [Christianity] has come to be presented in almost legal language, as if it were some sort of transaction, a deal with God; there was this gap between us and God, somebody had to make up for it—all that business. We can drop that. The legal metaphor seems to have helped other generations. Fine. Anything that helps is fine. But once it gets in the way, as it does today, we should drop it.[62]

> The fundamentalist continually waves one or two out-of-context gospel passages in front of us, stretching them beyond all valid interpretation and meaning. Thus the quotation "No one comes to the Father except through me" (John 14:6) is often used to declare that no one except the Christian can attain to God-or for that matter be "saved." *This we know is nonsense.* When the Divine Mother gathers up her harvest during the decades ahead, the chaff of fundamentalism will be separated from the good wheat of the new consciousness and left by the wayside.[63] (emphasis mine)

Interspiritualists look with great distain on the concept that God is confined to one religion. One statement that demonstrates this repugnance was made by an Anglican bishop. He maintains:

> The problem with exclusivism is that it presents us with a god from whom we need to be delivered rather than the living God who is the hope of the world. The exclusivist god is narrow, rigid, and blind. This god pays no attention to the sanctity and personal holiness of people outside the

Christian fold. This god takes no loving and parental pride in the lives of great spiritual teachers who spoke of other paths to truth, figures like Moses, Siddartha [Buddha], Mohammed, and Gandhi. . . . Such a god is *not worthy of honour, glory, worship, or praise.* This god offers no hope for a world deeply divided along religious lines, a world crying out for peace and reconciliation.[64] (emphasis mine)

At this point, we must return to what the apostle Paul said: "Ye cannot drink the cup of the Lord, and the cup of devils: ye cannot be partakers of the Lord's table, and of the table of devils [i.e., pagan mysticism]" (1 Corinthians 10:21).

No longer is the contemplative movement confined to just the Roman Catholic church and mainline Protestant camps. With a sincere desire to find a deeper walk with God many conservative, evangelical Christians are now exploring and embracing the spirituality of those individuals I have just profiled. This pursuit oddly covers the whole gamut of evangelical Christianity from charismatic to Baptist. Only the most discerning and biblically grounded Christians seem aware of the dangers of the contemplative prayer movement. A lack of discernment or a misleading view of Scripture can open the doors to becoming a *contemplative* evangelical. The list of these evangelicals is growing, and you may be surprised who is involved in swiftly moving the evangelical church toward a new mystical paradigm.

All scripture is given by inspiration of God and is profitable for doctrine, for reproof, for correction, for instruction in righteousness. (2 Timothy 3:16)

Four

Evangelical Hybrids

One afternoon in February of 1994, I visited the youth pastor of a large evangelical church in my community. I shared with him my discoveries about the New Age effect on our society—especially regarding the practical mystic element. He then confided in me that a notable Christian author and speaker would be conducting a seminar at his church the following November. He had read the man's first book, and he disclosed to me how an uneasy feeling about this author still lingered. The author's name was Richard Foster. The youth pastor asked me to check out Foster to see what I could learn about him. I agreed to do so.

Although I knew the name Richard Foster, I knew little else about him. But when I examined a copy of his popular book, *Celebration of Discipline* and discovered eleven references to Thomas Merton throughout the book, I immediately suspected a connection. This would not have surprised me if I had read Foster's own words in the book beforehand:

> [W]e should all without shame enroll as apprentices in the school of contemplative prayer.[1]

After reading his book, I suspected Foster would promote contemplative prayer during his talk at the upcoming conference, resulting in numerous attendees seeking out a local contemplative prayer center. Alarmed, the youth pastor and I made an appointment with the senior pastor and two other staff members to express our concerns and show them some examples of what the contemplative prayer movement taught. They listened readily, and the senior pastor said he planned to discuss these issues personally with Foster in a phone conversation.

Later, after that conversation took place, the senior pastor came away from it feeling fully satisfied nothing was erroneous about Foster's agenda. Foster told him *Christian* mystics who were not schooled in the East developed the contemplative tradition. Foster also acknowledged some individuals in this movement had crossed over into Eastern thought, and Thomas Merton had been *shaped* by these ideas. Foster admitted he did not know exactly where Merton stood theologically when he died but believed we could still learn from him without *going in all the directions he went*. After this exchange, the senior pastor ended all discussion with us on the matter—Foster was coming!

In-Depth

Once I recognized Foster had passed the test before a sharp senior pastor, I began to study his teachings. I discovered he was the founder and head of an organization called Renovaré, from the Latin word meaning *renewal*. The goal of this group, as stated in their material, is to provide the evangelical church with a "practical strategy" for growing spiritually. "An army without a plan will be defeated,"[2] states one of Renovaré's promotional materials. Renovaré provides that plan or as they refer to it: "practical training for transformed living."[3]

For the next eight months, I studied Foster's work, focusing on his promotion of contemplative prayer. Foster became a riddle; his statement of faith and other writings seem clearly evangelical in nature, making it understandable why he has struck a chord with so many learned Christian readers. On the other hand, he also avidly endorses a practice that leads to a mystical panentheistic understanding of God.

For example, Foster openly quotes Merton on the virtues and benefits of contemplative prayer putting forth the view that through it God "offers you an understanding and light, which are like nothing you ever found in books or heard in sermons."[4] But when one digs deeper and finds what exactly this "understanding" is, it casts a very dubious light on Foster's judgment. Listen to a few statements from some of the mystics whom Foster sees as examples of contemplative spirituality:

- [T]he soul of the human family is the Holy Spirit.[5]— **Basil Pennington**
- I saw that God is in all things.[6]—**Julian of Norwich**
- My beloved [God] is the high mountains, and the lovely valley forests, unexplored islands, rushing rivers.[7]—**John of the Cross**
- Here [the contemplative state] everything is God. God is everywhere and in all things.[8]—**Madam Guyon**

The point is this—*their* silence and Foster's silence are identical, as he makes notably clear. By using them as models, Foster tells us to *follow them* because they have experienced *deep union with God*—and if you also want this, you must go into their silence.

But if this is the case, then Foster's promotion of these mystics brings into play a difficult problem for him. Panentheism was the fruit of their mysticism. This mysticism led them to believe as they did, and Foster cannot distance himself from this fact. Consequently, to promote them as the champions of contemplative prayer, he is also, wittingly or not, endorsing their panentheism. What he endorses is a bundled package. You can accept both or reject both, but you cannot have one without the other.

To absolve these mystics of fundamental theological error, Foster has to also defend panentheism. Therefore, the evangelical church must come to a firm consensus on panentheistic mysticism. Contemplative prayer and panentheism go together like a hand in a glove—to promote one is to promote both. *They are inseparable!* Further, when one looks at Foster's method of entering this silence, it casts his teachings in a very questionable light.

When Foster speaks of the *silence*, he does not mean external silence. In his book, *Prayer: Finding the Heart's True Home*, Foster recommends the practice of breath prayer[9]—picking a single word or short phrase and repeating it in conjunction with the breath. This is classic contemplative mysticism. In the original 1978 edition of *Celebration of Discipline*, he makes his objective clear when he states, "Christian meditation is an attempt to empty the mind in order to fill it."[10]

In *Prayer: Finding the Heart's True Home*, he ties in a quote by one mystic who advised, "You must bind the mind with one thought."[11]

The advice recounts Anthony de Mello's remarks in his contemplative prayer classic, *Sadhana: A Way to God*. His approach was virtually identical to Foster's:

> To silence the mind is an extremely difficult task. How hard it is to keep the mind from thinking, thinking, thinking, forever thinking, forever producing thoughts in a never ending stream. Our Hindu masters in India have a saying: one thorn is removed by another. By this they mean that you will be wise to use one thought to rid yourself of all the other thoughts that crowd into your mind. One thought, one image, one phrase or sentence or word that your mind can be made to fasten on.[12]

I once related Foster's *breath prayer* method to a former New Age devotee who is now a Christian. She affirmed this connection when she remarked with astonishment, "That's what I did when I was into ashtanga yoga!"

The goal of prayer should not be to *bind the mind* with a word or phrase in order to induce a mystical trance but rather to use the mind to glory in the grace of God. This was the apostle Paul's counsel to the various churches: "Study to shew thyself approved" (2 Timothy 2:15) and "we pray always" (2 Thessalonians 1:11) as in talking to God with both heart and mind.

What Foster presents, focuses not on one subject but on one thought. Prayer is a sequence of thoughts on a spiritual subject.

Keeping the mind riveted on only one thought is unnatural and adverse to true reflection and prayer. Simple logic tells us the repeating of words has no rational value. For instance, if someone called you on the phone and just said your name or one phrase over and over, would that be something you found edifying? Of course not; you would hang up on him or her. Why would God feel otherwise? And if God's presence is lacking, what *is* this presence that appears as light during meditation and infuses a counterfeit sense of divinity within?

The Seminar

With my new understanding of Foster, I attended the seminar in November to witness his public speaking on these issues. Foster seemed charming, winsome, and gifted in speech. His oratorical skills reminded me of a Shakespearean actor on stage. His program mixed serious oratory, music, and humor in just the right doses. However, his message conveyed that today's Christians suffer from spiritual stagnation, and consequently need something more. The following are a few examples:

- There is a hunger . . .
- We have become barren within . . .
- We are floundering . . .
- People are trying rather than training.

Foster alluded to a remedy for this problem with such statements as:

- We need a way of moving forward . . .
- We need a plan to implement the Great Commission . . .
- We need a simple mechanism . . .
- This might be new or frightening, but you are being drawn.[13]

After the seminar ended, curious about what he meant by these statements, I approached Foster and politely asked him, "What do you think of the current Catholic contemplative prayer movement?" He appeared visibly uncomfortable with the question, and at first seemed evasive and vague.

He then replied, "Well, I don't know, some good, some bad (mentioning Matthew Fox as an example of the bad)." In defense, he said, "My critics don't understand there is this tradition within Christianity that goes back centuries." He then said something that has echoed in my mind ever since that day. He emphatically stated, "Well, Thomas Merton tried to awaken God's people!" I realized then Foster had waded deep into Merton's belief system.

This statement regarding Merton seemed paradoxical because earlier that morning Foster made a concerted effort to convince the audience he himself most certainly had no New Age sympathies. He told the 650 people assembled that he taught people to "hear the voice of Jehovah" and not the "loose, nutty kind of a thing" of the New Age.[14] But it is precisely this alignment with Merton that undermines Foster's claim to being mystically attuned to the God of the Bible. Merton expressed views such as, "I see no contradiction between Buddhism and Christianity . . . I intend to become as good a Buddhist as I can."[15]

It is essential to really understand *why* Merton said things like this in order to understand why the contemplative prayer movement presents such a potential danger to evangelical Christian churches. Merton's conversion was spiritual, not social or political, as clearly revealed in one of his biographies:

> His [Merton's] change of mind with regard to the higher religions was not the result of tedious comparison and contrast or even concerted analysis. It was an outgrowth of his experience with the Absolute [God].[16]

In other words, Merton found Buddhist enlightenment in contemplative prayer.

Richard Foster has written of Merton's mystical prayer in sparkling terms, saying, "Thomas Merton has perhaps done more than any other twentieth-century figure to make the life of prayer widely known and understood."[17] Foster considers Merton's book, *Contemplative Prayer*, "a must book"[18] He also states, "Merton continues to inspire countless men and women,"[19] and credits his books as being filled with "priceless wisdom for all Christians who long to go deeper in the spiritual life."[20]

This is the same Merton who "quaffed [drank] eagerly from the Buddhist cup in his journey to the East."[21] Yet how could Merton be a co-mystic with Eastern religions, and Foster engage in the same method as Merton, and come out on the opposite end of the spectrum? The answer may lie in some of the places I have found Foster's books being offered.

During a trip across the country, I stopped to research at the world headquarters for the Unity School of Christianity, a New Age metaphysical church located in the suburbs of Kansas City, Missouri. In their bookstore under *authors A-Z* (a who's who of New Age writers), I found no less than *five* of Foster's titles. A number of New Age bookstores also carry his books, under the headings of *mysticism*.

After seeing *Celebration of Discipline* at one New Age bookstore (a store operated by devotees of a famous Hindu swami), I asked the store's book buyer what he thought of Foster. "He is wonderful," the man enthusiastically replied. "His views on prayer are absolutely wonderful." I then asked if he knew Foster was considered a conservative Christian in many circles. His reply was intriguing: "Well, if he was a fundamentalist he wouldn't be sold at a bookstore like this one." He ended the conversation with further praise of Foster.

Perhaps the most unsettling example of all is in a book titled *The Miracle of Prayer*. This book could not be any more blatantly New Age in viewpoint, filled with occult concepts and references. Yet under suggested reading, in the back of the book, Foster's book, *Prayer: Finding the Heart's True Home* is recommended.[22]

Why do these obvious New Agers sell and promote Foster's books? The answer is unmistakable: the silence! New Agers recognize their form of prayer when they see it. They know where the silence leads. They *know* what Foster means when he advises:

> Every distraction of the body, mind, and spirit must be
> put into a kind of suspended animation before this deep
> work of God upon the soul can occur.[23]

If Foster heard the "voice of Jehovah," as he claims, wouldn't God have placed a warning upon his heart and mind that Merton taught harmful theology and convicted Foster not to champion him?

Although Foster may be sincere and well meaning, he has unfortunately drawn on a tradition the Bible does not present or condone. When he made an appeal from Scripture to support the credence of the contemplative prayer practice all he could find was Psalm 62:1, a verse that refers to being still and attentive to God. But this passage is certainly not suggesting that one go *beyond thought* by a sacred word or focusing on the breath. If that were the case, it would be taught throughout Scripture.

A Christian supporter of Foster once defended him by claiming that Foster is teaching Christians nothing more than what the apostle Paul experienced on the road to Damascus—a direct experience of God's presence. This may sound legitimate on the surface, but if you look at certain criteria, a far different picture emerges.

First of all, as I stated in chapter two, Paul did not use a method in this situation. There was no *prayer word* or *breath prayer* that propelled him into God's presence; it was a spontaneous action of God. Paul did nothing to bring on his experience. If he had, it certainly would have been referenced in the text as an important catalyst.

Secondly (and most importantly), Paul never wrote of a method in his letters to the various churches. He spoke of various spiritual gifts, but these were not based on any sort of technique that was taught. These gifts were bestowed by God as He saw fit. On that account, Foster can certainly back up a mystical element in the Bible, but he cannot back up *his* mysticism from the Bible. Unfortunately, he has instructed multitudes that:

> God has given us the Disciplines of the spiritual life as a means of receiving his grace. The Disciplines allow us to place ourselves before God so that he can transform us.[24]

I would like to impress on anyone going in this direction, the words of Solomon who gravely warned:

> Every word of God is pure: he is a shield unto them that
> put their trust in him. Add thou not unto his words, lest he
> reprove thee, and thou be found a liar." (Proverbs 30:5-6)

The apostle Paul also wrote, "For I have not shunned to declare unto you all the counsel of God" (Acts 20:27). In light of these statements, if you can find the silence (i.e., sacred words, going beyond thought) anywhere in Paul's writings to the church, I will humbly apologize to Richard Foster. I would like to note at this point that in the first edition of *A Time of Departing*, I presented a similar challenge, and no one to date has sent me a response—no one has found any refutation, not from Paul's writings nor from the entirety of the Word of God.

Just how influential has Foster become in Christian circles? For certain, his effect on the evangelical church cannot be overestimated. In a 1993 poll by *Christianity Today*, the magazine revealed that Foster's book, *Prayer: Finding the Heart's True Home*, was the number one most popular book with its readers.[25] Astoundingly, this is the same book that well-known New Ager Rosemary Ellen Guiley has on her suggested reading list in the back of her book, *The Miracle of Prayer*.

Christianity Today also showed Foster's famous book, *Celebration of Discipline* as number *three* on a list of books that its readers voted having "the most significant impact on their Christian life, other than the Bible."[26] Foster beat out the likes of Oswald Chambers, John Calvin, John Bunyan, and A.W. Tozer, who were also on the list. In fact, a recent edition of *Celebration of Discipline* states on the back cover that it has sold over *one million copies* over the last twenty years. That figure is astounding when you consider it is a nonfiction how-to book on spirituality. This type of book generally appeals to only a very limited segment of Christian readership.

Without a doubt, Foster has generated a vast and dedicated following in the evangelical church. Any charge that he is promoting a pseudo-Christian mysticism is bound to generate a storm of controversy. However, this issue should not be taken lightly—much is at stake here. During the period I was working on this revised edition of *A Time of Departing*, I received an e-mail from a pastor who is connected with a very well-known and highly regarded Christian ministry. He had read my book and thought it was informative and valuable to the extent where I clearly identified the influence of *outright Eastern mysticism* within Christianity. He would see open references to Buddhism in certain persons' writings as being a valid target for my argument. But when it came to my critique of the Christian mystical tradition and Richard Foster, he used words and phrases such as: "misrepresents, selective, doesn't prove, imbalanced, and assumes." He quotes from the 1988 edition of *Celebration of Discipline* where Foster says what he is teaching is filling the mind not emptying the mind. This pastor also quotes where Foster expounds a more conventional interpretation of what meditation is. In addition, he believes one can't "destroy" all of Foster's works just on one point.

I welcome letters like this because they give me a chance to make clear just what the issues are. I give careful attention to the views of someone who has an honest objection to what I am saying.

First, *both* Eastern and Christian mysticism (i.e. contemplative prayer) are trying to fill the mind after emptying it first. This is what Foster said of Christian meditation in the first edition of *Celebration of Discipline*. He took it out in later editions but that is what it still remains. In the recent editions he still says that thoughts should be put in "suspended animation" which is what emptying the mind is all about. In all these other religions you just don't empty the mind to have it empty, you always fill it with your desired end such as the Buddha nature, Brahman, Allah, Ein Sof, and so on, yet the process is always to create a void and then experience the end result.

This man wrote me saying he felt Thomas Merton took contemplative prayer to a "dangerous, unbiblical place" but my response to that is it was the other way around; it was this western tradition that took Merton to a dangerous place. Do you remember what William Shannon said of Merton? "[H]e had to find the East in the West before he could discover the East in itself."[27] In others words, he found the essence of Sufism and Buddhism in contemplative prayer.

Spiritual director Jan Johnson in her book, *When the Soul Listens: Finding Rest and Direction in Contemplative Prayer*, is a perfect example of an evangelical Christian who endorses and promotes this practice. She leaves no doubt about what this type of prayer entails:

> *Contemplative prayer*, in its simplest form, is a prayer in which you still your thoughts and emotions and focus on God Himself. This puts you in a better state to be aware of God's presence, and it makes you better able to hear God's voice, correcting, guiding, and directing you.[28]

Johnson's explanation of the initial stages of contemplative prayer leaves no doubt that "stilling" your thoughts means only one thing; she explains:

> In the beginning, it is usual to feel nothing but a cloud of unknowing. . . . If you're a person who has relied on yourself a great deal to know what's going on, this *unknowing* will be unnerving.[29]

Brennan Manning (1934-2016)

A former Catholic, Brennan Manning authored such popular titles as the *Ragamuffin Gospel* and *The Signature of Jesus*. His admirers include people such as Max Lucado, Amy Grant, and Michael Card. He too has struck a serious chord in the evangelical community.

His appeal was easy to understand when one heard Manning in person. His manner was very genuine and down-home. Many admired him for his passionate and dynamic character.

When he related how his mother mistreated him as a young child you cannot help but feel his pain deeply. However, despite all his admirable qualities and devotional intensity, he taught contemplative prayer as a way to God.

Manning devotes an entire chapter to contemplative prayer in his popular book, *The Signature of Jesus*. He compares traditional evangelical practice with the advantages and virtues of contemplative prayer. He gives his readers the impression they are really missing out on God's love if they ignore this method of prayer. In fact, he calls this chapter "Grabbing Aholt [a hold] of God." He makes it very obvious this is "the goal of contemplative prayer."[30] In the back of *Ragamuffin Gospel,* one finds M. Basil Pennington. Manning strongly supports Pennington's book, *Centering Prayer,* and states Pennington's methods will provide us with "a way of praying that leads to a deep living relationship with God."[31]

That is the crux of the matter. Does contemplative prayer lead to a deeper life with God? Did it for Pennington? Does it for Manning? Many think, perhaps, that Manning has the right answer to this question. Popular Christian author and editor-at-large of *Christianity Today,* Philip Yancey, endorsed Manning to all his own readers proclaiming, "I consider Brennan Manning my spiritual director in the school of grace."[32]

Grabbing Aholt of Who?

Taking a closer look at "Grabbing Aholt of God," one comes eyeball to eyeball with none other than Thomas Merton. There is a quote from Merton's good friend, David Steidl-Rast, three from John Main (*way of the mantra*), a very revealing one from Merton himself and the following one from Merton's biographer, William Shannon:

> During a conference on contemplative prayer, the question was put to Thomas Merton: "How can we best help people to attain union with God?" His answer was very clear: We must tell them that they are already united with God. "Contemplative prayer is nothing other than 'coming into consciousness' of what is already there."[33]

Merton was referring here to his pure glory-of-God-in-everybody worldview. He is not just speaking of Christians. His universalism elsewhere repudiates that fact. Therein lies the heart of this issue; when Manning invites Christians to grab "aholt" of God—it is the god of Merton they are grabbing for! But Manning is such a likeable man with such an impressive spiritual flair, few bother to look under the surface and see where his affections really lie.

Behind Manning's charisma lie some troubling connections. For example, Manning favorably quotes a Catholic monk, Bede Griffiths, in two of his books, *Abba's Child* and *Ruthless Trust*. Griffiths, like Merton, "explored ways in which Eastern religions could deepen his prayer."[34] Griffiths also saw the "growing importance of Eastern religions . . . bringing the church to a new vitality."[35]

A few years ago, Manning spoke at a church in my hometown. After the meeting, I asked him about his connection with Griffiths. He told me, "I have been reading him for years going all the way back to *The Golden String*" (the autobiography of Griffiths). This book has been around for about forty years, so it is clear Griffiths has influenced Manning for many years. When I also asked Manning which books on prayer he liked, he recommended Thomas Keating's, *Open Mind, Open Heart*, a well-known primer on the practice of centering prayer, which projects a panentheistic view of God.

The June 2004 issue of *Christianity Today* had a four-page article about Manning and his influence. The first few paragraphs featured an impressive list of Christian luminaries and their quotes on the positive impact Manning had on their spiritual lives. Included were members of the rock super group U2.

This article backs up some of what I am saying here in this book, such as the following statements:

- "['T]he vast majority of my ministry is in the evangelical world.'"
- "In order to hear from God, Manning himself retreats to silence and solitude."
- "It takes him about 20 minutes he says, to come to a state of inner stillness."[36]

Changing Trends in American Spirituality

R ichard Foster and Brennan Manning both have had a widespread impact on evangelicals with their enormously popular books and seminars. In all probability, at least one copy of either author's books can be found in nearly every evangelical church in America. The rise in popularity of these two authors is attributed to two major social trends that have occurred over the last twenty years.

The first trend that has captivated American spirituality is an openness to explore the formerly novel or exotic—especially if couched in terms that speak to Christian devotion. A strong appeal exists for many to involve themselves in *cutting-edge spirituality*. People are seeking spiritual experiences that leave behind the humdrum of dry intellectualism and stale institutionalism. These seekers are quick to jump on a bandwagon that promises spiritual refreshment and innovation.

The second trend is the *quick-fix* mentality that permeates our modern culture. People in past generations put up with life's frustrations, whereas today we see an inclination to seek out, seemingly surefire approaches that promise clear results. Our own era has nurtured a strong reliance on pragmatism. No longer is truth determined by what God has said to be true, but rather, by what works (what is practical). The question that drives many to determine truth is, "Will it make me feel good about myself?" However, for the Christian, we are not to live by what *feels good* but rather by what *is* good. We must stand by the apostle Paul's caution to the Thessalonians:

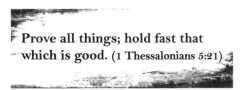

Prove all things; hold fast that which is good. (1 Thessalonians 5:21)

Bridging the Gap

One of the most common objections made by the defenders and admirers of Foster and Manning is that they are not really teaching Eastern mysticism, because their focus and attention is on the God of Christianity; they argue that their focus is for people to walk more closely with Jesus, not Shiva or Buddha, thus the teachings are westernized even though the practices are identical to the East. On the surface this may seem like a valid defense, but listen to the founder of the top contemplative prayer school in America (Shalem Institute), and see why this defense is precarious at best: Tilden Edwards explains, "This mystical stream [contemplative prayer] is the Western bridge to Far Eastern spirituality."[37]

This means that, regardless of intent, Western mysticism, due to its common practices with the East, produces a passage into the understanding of Eastern spiritual concepts. Thus, if you practice Western yoga or pray the mantra, you go into the same trance as the East; if you open yourself, through this trance, to the Western spirit world, you end up in the same demonic realm or with *gods* of the East; then, if you open yourself to the demonic realm, you enter into the same realm of consciousness as the East where all is One and everyone and everything is seen as God—hence panentheism; finally, if you embrace panentheism, the Gospel loses its significance, and each individual feels persuaded to find his or her own way to God. What begins as a seemingly innocent "Jesus Prayer" becomes a rejection of the Gospel. In other words, you can call a practice by any other name, but it is the same practice, hence the same results. For example, if you were to jump off a cliff with the intent to fly saying the word "fly, fly, fly" as you jump off and someone else jumped off the same cliff with the intent to hit the bottom saying "fall, fall, fall" as he jumps off, in either case both will hit the bottom. Unfortunately, this is exactly what is happening in contemplative prayer, although the intent may be to honor Christ.

In a similar manner, *guilt by promotion (or guilt by proxy)** provides us with a legitimate reason for examining who Foster and Manning regard as role-models for their practices, for you cannot promote someone without, in effect, embracing his teachings and beliefs.

For example, when Manning quotes from (and even recommends in one interview)[38] William Shannon's book, *Silence on Fire,* one would expect to find a common ground somewhere between the two of them. Yet *Silence on Fire* contains nothing that would inspire a

---

*Guilt by promotion or proxy is a much more powerful premise than guilt by association. Wheras the latter shows connection through merely association, guilt by promotion or proxy shows endorsement and actual support and encouragement.

true evangelical. In fact, it is filled with universalist statements that would offend anyone with doctrinally-sound evangelical sensibilities. One portion states, "[T]here is a oneness in God that unites all women and men . . . The goal of all true spirituality is to achieve an awareness of our oneness with God and with all of God's creation."[39]

So, where is the common ground that causes Manning to see Shannon as a co-mystic? If we can find no other reasonable answer, we must conclude that Manning may have already crossed Tilden Edwards so-called bridge between contemplative prayer and Eastern spirituality. At best, if he is unaware of the teachings of the one he promotes, he is misleading thousands of Christians who are now reading Shannon's heretical book. But realistically speaking, for Manning to have read *Silence On Fire*, he would clearly see where this practice led Shannon. So, to promote him at all, means he, at best, ignored Shannon's heresies. What makes it worse is that Shannon's heresies clearly stem from contemplative prayer and Manning *still* advocates this practice. What causes Manning to promote such people as Shannon, Griffiths, and Keating? We must look at the objectives of the "powers" and "spiritual hosts" (Ephesians 6:12) that are against the preaching of the Cross.

As Christians, we often forget that familiar spirits are *fallen* angels, once created to minister as messengers and worshipping spirits for God. They know how to sound spiritually positive, and they know how to communicate God's truths. But, as the Bible states, they are on a mission to deceive "if it were possible, even the elect" (Mark 13:22) and come as "ministers of righteousness" (2 Corinthians 11:15). This explains why God has given every Christian the Holy Spirit and His living Word to discern what is of God and what is not. When we go beyond the teachings of Scripture into man's tradition (as Manning and Foster have done), we are indeed treading upon dangerous ground.

Dr. Rodney R. Romney, former Senior Pastor of the First Baptist Church of Seattle is a person frequently quoted as an example of a New Age Christian. He very candidly revealed what was conveyed to him in his contemplative prayer periods. The "source of wisdom" he was in contact with told him the following:

> I want you to preach this oneness, to hold it up before
> the world as my call to unity and togetherness. In the end
> this witness to the oneness of all people will undermine
> any barriers that presently exist.[40]

Could this be a familiar spirit speaking here? Jesus Christ did not teach that all people are one. There are the *saved* and the *unsaved*. And Jesus Christ is the catalyst for this distinction. But the spirit who spoke to Dr. Romney also revealed something else of vital importance. It declared, "Silence is that place, that environment where I work."[41]

Please pay attention to this! God does not work in *the silence*— but familiar spirits do. Moreover, what makes it so dangerous is that they are very clever. One well-known New Ager revealed what his guiding (familiar) spirit candidly disclosed:

> We work with all who are vibrationally sympathetic;
> simple and sincere people who feel our spirit moving, but
> for the most part, only *within the context of their current
> belief system.*[42] (emphasis mine)

The term "vibrationally sympathetic" here means those who suspend thought through word repetition or breath focus—inward mental silence. *That* is what attracts them. *That* is their opening. *That* is why Tilden Edwards called this the "bridge to far Eastern spirituality," and this is what is being injected into the evangelical church!

In *The Signature of Jesus*, Manning teaches how to suspend thought. He instructs his readers methodically:

> [T]he first step in faith is to stop thinking about God at
> the time of prayer.[43]

> [C]ontemplative spirituality tends to emphasize the need
> for a change in consciousness . . . we must come to see
> reality differently.[44]

> Choose a single, sacred word . . . repeat the sacred word
> inwardly, slowly, and often.[45]

[E]nter into the great silence of God. Alone in that silence, the
noise within will subside and the Voice of Love will be heard.[46]

If one could draw a spiritual tree of both Manning's and Foster's
mystical heritage it would look like this: from India—to Alexandria—
to the Desert Fathers—to Thomas Merton—to them; and now,
through them and others like them—to you. What it *should* look like
is: from the triune God—to His holy prophets and apostles—to you.
Very simple! That, my friend, is the decisive factor of this controversy.

I am aware that Foster and Manning both say things that would
stir the heart of any Christian. But the issue here is one of mysticism. Is their mysticism legitimate? Biblical meditation and prayer,
as found abundantly in the book of Psalms, is not to stop thinking
about God but rather to think intently on God and to direct all our
thoughts toward God. The following statement by William Shannon
quoting Merton leaves an inescapable conclusion:

> The contemplative experience is neither a union of separate
> identities nor a fusion of them; on the contrary, *separate
> identities disappear* in the All Who is God.[47] (emphasis mine)

In essence, he is saying there is only one big identity—God. This
is more in tune with *core shamanism* than Christianity, yet Manning
embraces Shannon. In Leviticus 19:31, God says "I am the LORD your
God." Only God possesses God's identity. Any other teaching is heretical.

I challenge the Christian community to look at the facts sur-
rounding the contemplative prayer movement and see its connection
to New Age occultism and Eastern mysticism. Just because a writer
is emotionally stirring, sincere, and uses biblical language does not
necessarily mean he or she advocates sound, biblical truths. A good
example is Catholic devotion to Mary, the mother of Jesus. Most of
those who practice this would be very likable, devout people. But is
Mary-devotion biblically advocated or grounded? The same principle
applies to Foster and Manning. Is contemplative prayer biblical, or is
it actually spiritual treason and mere tradition?

For those who hold to the authoritative view of the Bible, these errors can readily be seen. After one pastor became aware of the issues covered in this chapter he made the keen observation, "How can Foster and Manning receive spiritual nourishment from people who throw out the Great Commission?" He summed up in this one observation the whole controversy with the men I have just profiled. How can a Christian leader like Manning recommend Thomas Keating's book on centering prayer when Keating says things like:

> In order to guide persons having this experience [divine oneness], Christian spiritual directors may need to dialogue with Eastern teachers in order to get a fuller understanding.[48]

In effect, Keating is stating that Christian leaders must turn to Hindus and Buddhists to better understand the result of centering prayer. In addition, how can Foster feel the way he does toward Thomas Merton when Merton shared a spiritual kinship with Buddhists and Sufis who have rejected the "word of reconciliation" (II Corinthians 5:19)?

These are hard questions that *need* to be answered! And if they cannot be effectively answered, then maybe we shouldn't "enroll in the school of contemplative prayer" or expect to hear the "Voice of Love" in the silence.

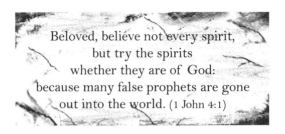

Beloved, believe not every spirit,
but try the spirits
whether they are of God:
because many false prophets are gone
out into the world. (1 John 4:1)

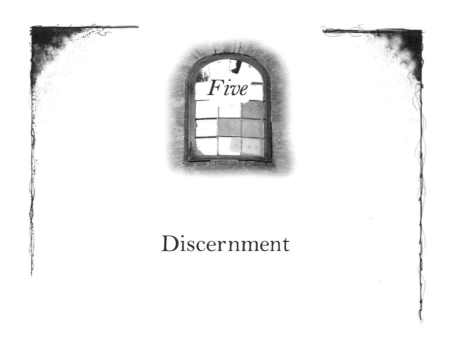

Five

Discernment

A Christian mom I know had been researching the New Age for some time and felt she must share the information with others. She recognized how New Age thought had saturated our society, and wanting to alert others, she organized a seminar series at her church. After the seminars, many people approached her to say thanks for a job well done. However, some of the parents were unconcerned and told her they did not have to worry about such things because they did not yet have children of high school age.

This naive response is all too common among evangelicals today. When they hear the term New Age many tend to equate it with wayward teens dabbling in Ouija boards or astrology. And though we most certainly do have our children to be concerned about, no age group is immune from being influenced by New Age spirituality. In fact, it is often middle-age Christians who are open to the upscale side of metaphysics, and some of the most educated and well-read people show the most interest.

A vast number of Christians feel they are safe from being misled, simply because they have been professing Christians for so long. This is not the case at all. Considering today's spiritual and social climate, both adults and young people desperately need keen spiritual discernment, hence my motivation in writing this book as an aid to this difficult task. As we move closer to the return of Christ, Scripture makes clear reference to the deluding spirits that will manifest themselves with increased intensity and effectiveness.

The Chicken Soup Phenomenon

In recent years, a series of high profile, immensely successful books (120 million sold) have impacted the lives of many Christians. They are the *Chicken Soup for the Soul* books by Jack Canfield and Mark Victor Hansen. Although these books are filled with seemingly charming and uplifting stories, Canfield's New Age spirituality is quite disturbing from a Christian viewpoint. In understanding the foundational views of these two authors, one must ask, "Can a corrupt tree bring forth good fruit" (Luke 6:43)?

In 1981, in the *Science of Mind* magazine, an interview revealed Canfield was no less than a teacher of the highly occultic "psychosynthesis" method developed by a direct disciple of Alice Bailey (see Bailey's clear occultism and birthing of the term *New Age* in chapter two). In some of his most recent writings, Canfield openly reveals he had his "spiritual awakening" in a yoga class in college where he felt God "flowing" through all things.[1] Hence, Canfield also promotes many occult writers.

In order to draw a conclusion on the spiritual persuasions of the *Chicken Soup for the Soul* authors take a look at one particular book they both enthusiastically endorse. The book is called *Hot Chocolate for the Mystical Soul*, compiled by Arielle Ford. Its format is identical to that of the *Chicken Soup for the Soul* series—101 stories by different authors on a particular theme.

Ford's book permeates with Eastern and New Age metaphysical content. A panoply of psychics, mediums, astrologers, channelers, and especially Hindu mystics present a wide array of stories. One such story is about a psychic who writes of her abilities.[2] Another story in the book is about a Hindu holy man who manifests "holy ash" out of thin air.[3] Yet another involves a man who claims to be the reincarnation of the apostle Paul and writes that the message of Jesus is "God dwells within each one of us [all humanity]."[4]

Co-author of the *Chicken Soup for the Soul* series, Mark Victor Hansen, agreed with Ford's book so wholeheartedly that he wrote the foreword. Listen to a few excerpts from this foreword, which reveal Hansen's view:

> [E]nlightening stories will inspire you. They will expand your awareness . . . you will think in new exciting and different ways . . . You will be renewed through the tools, techniques and strategies contained herein . . . May your mystical soul be united with the mystical magical tour you've been wanting and waiting for."[5]

Jack Canfield echoes this praise on the back cover by stating, "They [the stories in the book] will change your beliefs, stretch your mind, open your heart and expand your consciousness."[6]

In March 2005, Canfield came out with his book, *The Success Principles*. As can be expected, one of these *success principles* is about meditation. Canfield relates, "I attended a meditation retreat that permanently changed my entire life."[7] Canfield does a superb job of integrating metaphysics with the needs of business creativity. He emphasizes:

> As you meditate and become more spiritually attuned, you can better discern and recognize the sound of your higher self or the voice of God speaking to you through words, images, and sensations.[8]

These books are selling like hotcakes in some evangelical bookstores because they are *positive*. If someone would have told me fourteen years ago that such books would someday be selling in Christian bookstores, I would have said they were nuts—no way!

Sadly, other such books have seeped into Christian bookstores. In one store, Sara Ban Breathnach's book *Simple Abundance, A Daybook of Comfort and Joy*, was spotted under a sign, which read,

"For Devotions." In this book she informs her readers we are all "asleep to our divinity."[9] Yet, in spite of her obvious connection to the New Age, I have been told that women's prayer groups at evangelical churches have ordered this book in bulk!

Creeping New Age

If you are wondering at this point why these authors and their teachings are *creeping* past many Christians, then maybe the definition of *creeping* might help. The term means: slowly advancing at a speed that is not really apparent until you look back over a long time period. For instance, creeping inflation is not noticed in the short term, but when one looks back over twenty to thirty years, it is shocking. A meal that cost two dollars in 1970 now may cost eight dollars—however, the increase moved so slowly that the impact was diminished.

This same kind of movement has happened within our society and has gradually become mainstream. What was once seen as flaky is normal today—even useful. This trend is impacting evangelical Christianity at only a slightly lesser degree than secular society. The reason for the slight variance is that many, perhaps most, Christians have not yet grasped, or come to terms with, the *practical mystic* approach that New Age proponents have already incorporated into the secular world, as well as Christianity.

A mystical pragmatism is growing particularly fast through various New Age healing techniques. One such procedure is called Reiki (pronounced ray-key), a Japanese word that translates to *Universal Life Energy* or *God energy*. It has also been referred to as the *radiance technique*. Reiki is an ancient Tibetan Buddhist healing system, rediscovered by a Japanese man in the 1800s, that only recently has come to the West.

The Reiki technique consists of placing the hands on the recipient and then activating the energy to flow through the practitioner and into the recipient. One practitioner describes the experience in the following way:

> When doing it, I become a channel through which this
> force, this juice of the universe, comes pouring from

my palms into the body of the person I am touching, sometimes lightly, almost imperceptibly, sometimes in famished sucking drafts. I get it even as I'm giving it. It surrounds the two of us, patient and practitioner.[10]

What is this "juice of the universe?" The answer is an important one, given by a renowned Reiki master who explains:

> A Reiki attunement is an initiation into a sacred metaphysical order that has been present on earth for thousands of years . . . By becoming part of this group, you will also be receiving help from the Reiki guides and other spiritual beings who are also working toward these goals.[11]

While this is not widely advertised, Reiki practitioners depend on this "spirit guide" connection as an integral aspect of Reiki. In fact, it is the very foundation and energy behind Reiki. One Reiki master who has enrolled hundreds of other masters spoke of her interaction with the spirit guides:

> For me, the Reiki guides make themselves the most felt while attunements are being passed. They stand behind me and direct the whole process, and I assume they also do this for every Reiki Master. When I pass attunements, I feel their presence strongly and constantly. Sometimes I can see them.[12]

A Christian's initial response to this information might be, "So what? I don't travel in those circles, so it does not concern me." This nonchalant viewpoint would be valid except for the fact that Reiki is currently growing to enormous proportions and in some very influential circles. (It may even be in your local hospitals, schools, and youth organizations.) It is essential to know that many nurses, counselors, and especially massage therapists use Reiki as a supplement to their work. It is often promoted as a *complementary* service.

Even more significant are the numbers involved in this practice. Examine the following figures to catch just a glimpse of the growing popularity of Reiki. In 1998, there were approximately 33,000 Reiki listings on the Internet. Today that number, on some search engines, constitutes over 22,000,000 listings. In just ten years, that number increased almost 700 fold! As I said in the first chapter of this book, there are now over one million Reiki practitioners in the U.S. One Reiki master delightfully noted this surge of interest when he stated:

> Over the years, there has been a shift in the belief system of the general public, allowing for greater acceptance of alternative medicine. As a result, we are seeing a growing interest in Reiki from the public at large. People from all backgrounds are coming for treatments and taking classes.[13]

One very revealing statistic involves Louisville, Kentucky, where 102 people were initiated into Reiki in just a single weekend.[14] This denotes a large number of people are drawn to Reiki in the Bible belt, traditionally a conservative part of America.

It is important to understand the way in which Reiki is presented to the public at large. Despite its underlying metaphysical foundation, when one reads the literature put out by Reiki practitioners it is not at all apparent. One Reiki master who runs a day spa repeatedly uses words like *comfort* and *nurture* in her brochure. Reiki is something that will give you pleasure. Another woman who is a professional counselor tells her potential clients that Reiki will give them *deep relaxation* and *reduce pain*. Again and again these same themes emerge from promotional literature on Reiki—relaxation, well-being, reduce illness, reduce stress, balance your mind, etc. How can one say that Reiki is bad when it claims to help people?

The reason for this level of acceptance is easy to understand. Most people, many Christians included, believe if something is spiritually positive then it is of God. A pastor friend of mine recounted a situation in which a Christian, who had some physical problems, turned to Reiki for comfort. When this pastor advised the man that Reiki fundamentally opposed the Christian faith he became furious and responded with the following defense, "How can you say this is bad when it helped me?" That is why I titled this chapter "Discernment."

To discern is to "try the spirits" (1 John 4:1). If something is of God it will conform to the very cornerstone of God's plan to show His grace through Christ Jesus and Him alone (Ephesians 2:7). Reiki, as I defined earlier, is based on the occult view of God.

This assessment of Reiki is beyond question. Every Reiki book I have ever seen is chock full of pronouncements that back up the point I am trying to make. In *The Everything Reiki Book*, the following clears up any doubt about Reiki's incompatibility with Christianity:

> During the Reiki attunement process, the avenue that is opened within the body to allow Reiki to flow through also opens up the psychic communication centers. This is why many Reiki practitioners report having verbalized channeled communications *with the spirit world.*[15] (emphasis mine)

What is even more disturbing is that the Reiki channeler may not even have control over this "energy" as the following comment shows:

> Nurses and massage therapists who have been attuned to Reiki may never disclose when Reiki starts flowing from their palms as they handle their patients. Reiki will naturally "kick in" when it is needed and will continue to flow for as long as the recipient is subconsciously open to receiving it.[16]

Another such method is *Therapeutic Touch*. Like Reiki, it is based on the occultic *chakra* system, portrayed as the seven *energy centers* in the body aligned with spiritual forces. The seventh chakra identifies with the God-in-all view. Therapeutic Touch is widely practiced by nurses in clinics and hospitals. It is seen as a helpful and healing adjunct to nursing care.

If the connection between Reiki healing and other metaphysical practices can be seen, then we more fully understand why the following quote is one of the most powerful statements as to the true nature of contemplative prayer. A Reiki master in the course of promoting the acceptance of this method relayed:

Anyone familiar with the work of . . . or the thought of
. . . [she then listed a string of notable New Age writers
with Thomas Merton right in the center of them] will
find compatibility and resonance with the theory and
practices of Reiki.[17]

Reiki comes from Buddhism, and as one Merton scholar wrote,
"The God he [Merton] knew in prayer was the same experience that
Buddhists describe in their enlightenment."[18]

This is why it is so important to understand the connection
between the writings of Richard Foster and Brennan Manning with
Merton. Promotion indicates attachment, and attachment indicates
common ground. Something is terribly wrong when a Reiki master
and two of the most influential figures in the evangelical church today
both point to the same man as an example of their spiritual path.

Stress Reduction

Overstressed people are looking for new avenues to better their health.
Stress is believed to be one of the leading causes of illness in America
today. Millions of people suffer from disorders such as headaches, in-
somnia, nervousness, and stomach problems because of excess tension
in their lives. In response to this situation, an army of practitioners has
come forward to teach *relaxation skills* and *stress-reduction techniques*
to the affected millions. One newspaper article reported:

> Once a practice that appealed mostly to mystics and
> occult followers, meditation now is reaching the USA's
> mainstream . . . The medical establishment now recognizes
> the value of meditation and other mind-over-body states
> in dealing with stress-related illness.[19]

When we compare meditation techniques used in stress reduction with the type of meditation used in New Age spirituality, it is
easy to see these practices as basically the same. Both methods use
either the breathing technique or mantra exercises to still the mind.

Unknown to most people, a blank mind in a meditative state is all that is necessary for contact with a *spirit guide*.

An example of this is found in John Randolph Price, founder of the Quartus Foundation and initiate of the December 31 World Healing Day Meditation. Price became involved in New Age metaphysics through just such a meditative encounter. He reveals:

> Back when I was in the business world, the American Management Association put out a little book on meditation, which indicated that meditation was a way to attain peace of mind and reduce stress in a corporate environment. So I decided I'd try it ... I discovered how to come into a new sphere of consciousness. Consciousness actually shifts, and you move into a *realm you may not have even known existed.*[20] (emphasis mine)

As one meditation teacher explains:

> It is more than a stress reducer. It is the vehicle all religions use to *impart the esoteric knowledge* of their own mystical tradition.[21] (emphasis mine)

Thus, many people have unwittingly become New Agers by simply seeking to improve their physical and mental health through meditation. Two examples on this issue are comments made by two authors who honor the higher self view of man, Joan Borysenko and Ann Wise. Borysenko, a medical doctor, revealed:

> I originally took up secular meditation for its medical benefits and in time discovered its deeper psychological and spiritual benefits.[22]

Ann Wise, who works in the corporate field to improve decision-making abilities for business people, makes an identical observation:

> Those who initially participate in this work purely for enhancements to their productivity in the corporate world

are often startled and pleased by what one VP called "the value and inevitable focus on spirituality that evolved from the work." . . . I often find that individuals who began brainwave training [meditation] for a specific, objective purpose also become quickly interested and involved in seeking higher levels of spiritual consciousness.[23]

Here lies the basic message of *A Time of Departing*. The silence is really all the same. It transcends context. Whatever the format in which it is placed, from stress reduction to contemplative prayer, it inevitably leads to a certain spiritual perception, but one that contradicts the Gospel and nullifies the Cross as essential to salvation.

According to a *Time* magazine cover story on the popularity and acceptance of meditation in mainstream society:

Ten million American adults now say they practice some form of meditation regularly, twice as many as a decade ago. . . . In fact, it's becoming increasingly hard to avoid meditation. It's offered in schools, hospitals, law firms, government buildings, corporate offices and prisons.[24]

The article also said that so many meditation centers were opening in the Catskill Mountains that it was going from being called the "Borscht Belt" to the "Buddhist Belt." Meditation is here to stay and now has the official sanction of society. If you tell a co-worker that you meditate, except maybe in a blue collar setting, it will not raise eyebrows. The article backed this up by the following observation:

In a confluence of Eastern mysticism and Western science, doctors are embracing meditation not because they think it's hip or cool but because scientific studies are beginning to show that it works, particularly for stress-related conditions.[25]

Yoga

This new spiritual awareness is often discovered in a popular practice known as yoga. This Eastern technique was so in vogue that in 1992,

Newsweek magazine proclaimed, "The Boomers Turn to Yoga!"[26] The article spoke of the sharp rise of interest in this practice and the increased demand for it. By 1998, *USA Weekend's* supplement indicated the trend was still going strong:

> Yoga is finding itself in an unusual position these days. Finally shaking its reputation as a 1960s remnant, the body-bending practice has become a staple in some surprising circles . . . Today, more than 6 million Americans practice yoga, and the numbers are growing.[27]

It should be no surprise that the *baby boomers* and their offspring have embraced yoga because a pivotal moment in their history pointed them in this direction 36 years ago. One yoga publication reveals:

> Swami Satchidananda won himself a permanent place in the hearts of Baby Boomers when he presided as spiritual mentor at Woodstock in 1969, and taught an entire generation to chant "Om."[28]

In an article in *What is Spirituality* magazine,* by 2005 the number of yoga adherents had indeed grown to an astounding twenty million regular practitioners.

What has propelled this tidal wave of interest is a sincere desire for greater fitness and a sense of well-being and calmness. Most people would have only a vague sense that yoga had anything to do with religion. They would say things like "I do yoga for my back pain," or "I think it's a great way to relieve stress."

I would like to invite these folks to stop by their local bookstore, go to the fitness section, and examine more closely the finer points of yoga. The actual meaning of the word yoga might surprise them. It does not mean stretch or bend as many might think. The word stands for "union" as in hooking up with something. And in this case, that something is spiritual in nature. In the majority of these yoga

---

*From the December 05-February 06 issue.

fitness books, terms like *samahdi, chakras, kundalini* and *namaste* fill the pages. Each of these terms, as any yoga teacher would openly acknowledge, reflects the man-is-god spiritual viewpoint. Namasté, for example, means *the god in me greets (or salutes) the god in you.*

In a September 2005 issue of *Time* magazine, an article titled "Stretching for Jesus" paints a vivid portrait of what I am talking about in this book. In the article, the word "Jesus" is presented as the mantra. One pastor explained, "Yoga is just another way to pray." The article reports that *Christian yoga* is a "fast-growing movement" and that "a slew of books and videos are about to hit the market."[29]

In the article, Professor Tiwari at the Hindu University of America said that "Yoga *is* Hinduism." I wonder what the average Hindu would think if he or she knew that Christians are trying to incorporate yoga into their own lives and call it nothing but exercise. I would imagine that most Hindus would find that to be rather amusing, if not downright insulting.

I can clearly understand this position because one yoga teacher spoke of "yoga's potency"[30] in the context of mysticism. She told the story of one client when he first came to learn yoga: "I don't want to hear anything about philosophy or meditation. I'm just very stiff from sitting and typing 10 hours a day, and I want to loosen up." But this attitude changed, "Within a year . . . he was meditating, doing pranayama, and signing up for workshops on the *Yoga Sutras* [scriptures]."[31] She concluded, "Ultimately, yoga 'workouts' just may be the way that mysticism sneaks in the back door of American culture."[32]

The Guru of Self-Help

Without question, the most influential practical mystic today is talk show host Oprah Winfrey. Her predominantly female audience, numbering in the tens of millions, looks to her as the source of spiritual inspiration—even more so than church, in many cases.

I realize speaking critically of someone as warm and caring as Oprah might stir angry emotions in many of her viewers. Nonetheless, please keep in mind that with Oprah, as with the others I have written about, her obvious good qualities are not the issue here. While I might admire Oprah as a person, I am gravely concerned about what she promotes.

Somewhere during her career, Oprah read a book titled *Discover The Power Within You* by Unity minister Eric Butterworth. In line with Unity teaching, the book expounded on the *Divinity of Man* as perceived through mystical practice. Oprah embraced these views so earnestly that she advocated:

> This book changed my perspective on life and religion. Eric Butterworth teaches that God isn't "up there." He exists inside each one of us, and it's up to us to seek the divine within.[33]

Her talk show has launched many New Age authors into national super-stardom—authors such as Marianne Williamson, Sarah Ban Breathnach, Iyanla Vanzant, and Cheryl Richardson.

One such author propelled into prominence by Oprah, with regard to New Age teaching, is Gary Zukav. Zukav became a regular guest on the Oprah show following his first appearance in October of 1998. Afterwards, his book titled *The Seat of the Soul* became a constant fixture at the top of the New York Times bestseller list for an astounding two years!

The Seat of the Soul, pure and simple, is a spiritual primer or manual for New Age thought. It has gained such popularity even though it lacks the elements that have traditionally attracted a wide readership (i.e., novels, biography, scandal, health, etc.). The book's basic message is, "Dwell in the company of your nonphysical Teachers and guides [spirit guides]."[34]

The Seat of the Soul has struck a resonant chord with an enormous number of people. The notion of "nonphysical guides and teachers" is now considered perfectly acceptable by a vast number in the reading public. When such a book is embraced by so many for so long it means the New Age is already here. Clearly, our society is not heading toward the cliff concerning New Age spirituality—we are already over it!

Oprah's 2005 book, *Live Your Best Life*, highlights various areas of her philosophies. In the chapter on spirituality there is a story about

Spiritual Energy. In it, there is a positive reference to a Reiki master who supports Oprah's view that "we [humanity] are all interrelated."[35] This underlies Winfrey's spirituality, that ALL IS ONE. Despite her charming personal manner, there is little doubt her viewers and readers are still being fed a consistent diet of New Age spirituality.

If some readers are angered that I would be critical of someone as nice as Oprah, then what I have to say next regarding someone even nicer still will really be upsetting. How about being critical of someone whose very name has become a metaphor for niceness? How about calling into question the most trusted person of recent decades?

Author Wayne Muller (who is not the person I'm alluding to) has written a book titled *Sabbath*. Muller is clearly in tune with all the other interspiritualists profiled in chapter three of *A Time of Departing*. His book is dedicated to Henri Nouwen whom Muller refers to as "my teacher" and nearly every page thereafter reflects this fact. The Holy Spirit and the "Buddha Nature" are presented as being synonymous. The 23rd Psalm is quoted in conjunction with quotes from the *I Ching*. One paragraph in particular with a direct reference to Henri Nouwen reflects the entire book's theme:

> If we surrender fully into Sabbath time, we can slowly move from a life so filled with noisy worries that we are deaf to the gifts and blessing of our life, to a life in which we can listen to God, Jesus, and all the Buddhas and saints and sages and messengers who seek to guide and teach us.[36]

In Muller's book, *Sabbath*, which according to Muller is another term for meditation or contemplative prayer, is an endorsement. This endorser I speak of is none other than the beloved Fred Rogers, who was the host of *Mr. Roger's Neighborhood*, the popular kids show on public television for decades. Fred Rogers says of Muller's book:

> In *Sabbath*, Wayne Muller gives us the license, the encouragement to take that single mindful breath which puts our busy lives in perspective and helps restore our souls.[37]

Fred Rogers obviously read the book and found its interspiritual tone acceptable. This is a clear example that having a nice friendly personality does not necessarily mean that one has a gospel-oriented understanding.

The New Age Christian—An Accepted Oxymoron

All this popularity with meditative mysticism presents a very new and perplexing challenge for evangelical Christianity. We are beginning to encounter the *New Age or Aquarian Christian.* This new term describes someone who remains in his or her home church and professes the Christian faith but has also incorporated various aspects of the New Age or Aquarian mindset into his or her life. New Age author David Spangler was very optimistic about the possibility of this integration when he wrote, "The point is that the New Age is here . . . it builds itself and forms itself in the midst of the old."[38]

What has fueled the momentum of this trend is the buffet-style dining approach that has become a hallmark of American religious sensibilities in the last twenty years—you take what you want and leave the rest. Americans are picking and blending religions as if they were ordering espressos: pick your espresso blend, but you still get coffee—pick your spiritual path, but you still get God. Whatever suits your spiritual tastes, you bring together. The result is hybrid New Age spirituality.

I recall a conversation once with a woman in a coffee bar. We chatted on spiritual subjects, and her comments led me to believe she was an evangelical Christian. Towards the end of our friendly conversation she dropped a bombshell on me when she blurted-out, "Well, *we all* have the Christ consciousness!"

In another incident, a local pastor shared with me how a woman he had long known as a strong solid Christian was almost swept up by New Age thinking. Her young adult son had been addicted to drugs and went through a drug rehabilitation program. In the process, his counselor introduced him to New Age spirituality. He, in turn, shared it with his mother, giving her a book to read titled *Conversations With God* (a New Age bestseller).

Incredibly, she found herself being swayed by the book's arguments and began to doubt whether or not her evangelical Christianity was indeed the only way to God. Her desire to see her son aligned with God left her mind open in welcoming the possibility that various mystical paths were equally genuine in finding God. It took this pastor nearly two hours to help this woman understand the error of her thinking. Keep in mind this woman was a solid and devoted Christian who had been living her Christian faith for decades. If these Christians can be swayed, what about people who are even more vulnerable to what is going on in the larger culture?

The New Age message has such a positive ring that it is necessary to look behind the appealing facade to see what is *actually* there. If one goes to a massage therapist who does Reiki one should know the true nature of that practice. If your doctor wants you to meditate, you should know the spiritual dangers of non-biblical meditation. As the world moves further into becoming a full-fledged mystical society, it will become increasingly difficult to escape the ideas and practices described in this chapter. Christians must become aware of what is happening in order to make informed choices about things that may adversely affect them spiritually. In addition, many of our friends, family members, and co-workers will be seeking spiritual solutions to the uncertainties of our society and the world in which we live as a whole. The following account brings this point home like no other. A Christian in Georgia e-mailed me with the following story:

> At work a colleague who is a deacon at the local Baptist church was telling me about his visits to a local woman for "Therapeutic Massage." He said she used "some kind of Indian technique." I asked him if it was Reiki and he said "Yeah that's it. She's a Reiki practitioner." I told him what I had read in your book about Reiki and he got defensive. He said, "I don't care what it is as long as it works." I was floored. I said, "You are a deacon. How can you make such a statement?" He said, "There are several deacons at my church that believe in Reiki." I pleaded with him to

do some research on the subject and I sent him an email with quotes off some sites that promote Reiki. Later he told me he could see where I was coming from but that as long as he didn't believe in the spiritual aspect of it, he didn't see why he shouldn't participate in it. I was surprised that there was a Reiki practitioner in the middle of rural Bible Belt America. I guess nothing should shock me anymore.[39]

One book on the Chakra* system clearly shows:

> Many people who have open crown chakras have had a profound spiritual experience in which their usual sense of being separate and apart falls away and there is a feeling of being at One with All and Everything. There is a profound sense of merging. . . . There is, in essence, a feeling that All of This Is God, and I Am a part of all of this so I, too, Am God.[40]

This concept of course, has its source in the spirit world. The "Reiki News" provides this evidence:

> Imagine my surprise during my first Reiki class when I observed the astral images of *guides and healing spirits* pouring forth bright shimmering rays of healing energy at the hands of novice practitioners.[41] (emphasis mine)

Interest in Reiki and other mystical practices are accelerating to such a degree that most people will come face to face with this sooner or later. One popular counselor made the following assessment regarding the growing momentum of New Age practical mysticism:

> We cannot overstate how profoundly their impact is being felt in education, business, medicine, and psychotherapy. It is safe to say that the prevailing religion in America . . . is no longer Christianity but is instead New Age.[42]

---

* What Reiki is based on.

It would not surprise me if the majority of people in America have a family member or close friend who does mantra meditation, practices yoga, has either encountered Reiki or Therapeutic Touch, or is an avid fan of the Oprah Winfrey show. How could anyone possibly conceive that any of these seemingly benign or even helpful methods or talk shows might have a connection to Satan or that which is against God? A brother in Christ whom I met for coffee one day gave me the answer to that question: He referred to the Scripture in which Eve took of the fruit, and while it had the appearance of something good, the results of her partaking were detrimental.

> And when the woman saw that the tree was good for food, and that it was pleasant to the eyes, and a tree to be desired to make one wise, she took of the fruit thereof, and did eat, and gave also unto her husband with her; and he did eat. (Genesis 3:6)

Secondly, and just as important, what actually constitutes that which is satanic? Virtually everyone in Christendom equates that term, *satanic*, with things dark and sinister. However, the Bible paints a far different picture of Satan—one that fits the New Age movement perfectly. Satan said, "I will be like the Most High" (Isaiah 14:14). He did not say he would *be* the Most High; he said he would be *like* the Most High. The word "like" here means to *correspond to*. How could Satan accomplish this mission?

It is important to understand that Satan is not simply trying to draw people to the dark side of a good versus evil conflict. Actually, he is trying to eradicate the gap between himself and God, between good and evil, altogether. When we understand this approach it helps us see why Thomas Merton said everyone is already united with God* or why Jack Canfield said he felt God flowing through *all* things. All means all—nothing left out. Such reasoning implies that God has given His glory to all of creation; since Satan is part of creation, then he too shares in this glory, and thus is "*like the Most High.*"

---

*See page 83.

Contrary to this belief of good and evil merging and man or creation becoming "like the most High," man and God can only be brought together through the Cross. If the all-is-one view were true, then salvation through a Redeemer would become unnecessary and Jesus' death on the Cross would be rendered altogether futile and pointless. In order for the Cross to make *any* sense, there must be a separation between God's perfect nature and Man's sin nature. We know Satan has only one enemy—the Cross; he knows that without it no human being can be restored to God.

The Bible says the message of the Cross is the power of God, and while there *are* two opposing spiritual realms, God has always and will always, prevail. Satan can never thwart God's ultimate plan. And yet, today's Western society is enticed by practical mystics who deny, by their own proclamations, God's plan of eternal salvation. Will the majority of mankind come to believe that all is one and there is no line to be drawn in the sand regarding good and evil? The Bible admonishes, "Woe unto them that call evil good, and good evil" (Isaiah 5:20).

Yet, such a plan now exists and will shape future events—events that will alter the course on which millions will advance.

> For the preaching of the cross is to them that perish foolishness; but unto us which are saved it is the power of God. (1 Corinthians 1:18)

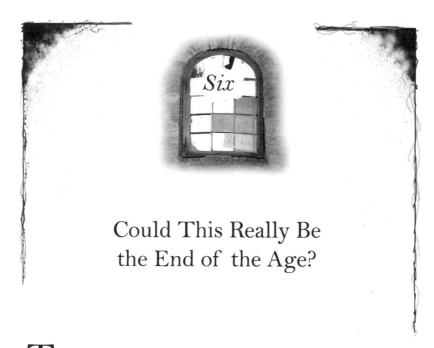

Could This Really Be
the End of the Age?

Throughout my Christian life I have periodically heard fellow Christians suggest we are in *the last days*. Often these comments were initiated from current cases of violent crimes, sexual perversions, war, or natural disasters. Since I knew history had repeatedly encountered these calamities, such predictions of Christ's imminent return rang hollow.

However, in 1984 I had an unexpected encounter that changed my entire outlook. A newfound friend educated me about the New Age movement and its end-times implications. After a period of investigation, I came to believe this could very well be the time period the book of Revelation showcases. Instead of a vague and obscure manifestation of prophecy, I saw something distinct and pervasive happening in our churches and society. And incredibly enough, this shift has been predicted from both sides of the struggle.

Christians must remember that the authenticity of Christianity itself is predicated upon its prophecies coming to pass. Jesus Christ, the apostle Paul, and various apostles and prophets of the Old and New Testaments make clear and direct references to particular events occurring in the future. If these events are only fantasies, then everything else could be deemed equally fictitious as well. I believe current trends authenticate Jesus Christ's and the apostle Paul's prophetic claims regarding the end of the age. Upon examination of the evidence, it becomes clear that the course our society (and our churches) is taking has been foretold by the apostolic writings.

The apostle Paul spoke of the "day of the Lord" in reference to "the times and seasons" in the fifth chapter of I Thessalonians. He describes how God will intervene swiftly and without delay. Paul states:

> But of the times and the seasons, brethren, ye have no need that I write unto you. For yourselves know perfectly that the day of the Lord so cometh as a thief in the night.
>
> For when they shall say, Peace and safety; then sudden destruction cometh upon them, as travail upon a woman with child; and they shall not escape.
>
> But ye, brethren, are not in darkness, that that day should overtake you as a thief. Ye are all the children of light, and the children of the day: we are not of the night, nor of darkness. Therefore let us not sleep, as do others; but let us watch and be sober. (1 Thessalonians 5:1-6)

Paul is saying the end of the age will come upon the world like a thief in the night. In other words, it will actually *sneak up* on people. Then interestingly, the apostle contrasts two groups: "But ye, brethren [followers of Christ] are not in darkness [people of ignorance], that that day should overtake you as a thief. [unaware]" (v.4). Here, Paul is saying believers in Christ will have the information (Scripture) available to them to prepare for "that day."

Those who walk in the light can see both where they are going and what is coming up ahead. Paul then warns against spiritual slumber and drunkenness, which could lead to a person being overtaken by that day, unaware: "Therefore let us not sleep, as do others; but let us watch and be sober" (v. 6). The word sober means *be alert* or *aware*. If we are instructed to watch and be aware, there must be something to watch for—otherwise, Paul's admonition would be useless. But who and what are we to watch for?

The Coming One

In the early twentieth century, a figure who would have a major impact on the Western esoteric movement came out of the occultic Theosophical Society. The actual coining of the very term *New Age* has been attributed to her writings. Her name was Alice Ann Bailey.

Born Alice LaTrobe-Bateman, in Manchester, England on June 16, 1880, she grew up as a society girl and enjoyed all the privileges of the British upper class. Being very religious, Alice met and married a man who later became an Episcopal minister. In time, they moved to the United States. When Alice's husband became physically abusive toward her, she fled from him and settled with her three children in Pacific Grove, California.

Alice was greatly comforted when she met two other English women living in Pacific Grove. These women introduced her to theosophy, which seemed to provide answers to her questions concerning why such misfortune had befallen her. Alice, then 35, was about to have her life changed forever. Later, in her unfinished autobiography, she wrote:

> I discovered, first of all, that there is a great and divine Plan . . . I discovered, for a second thing, that there are Those Who are responsible for the working out of that Plan and Who, step by step and stage by stage, have led mankind on down the centuries.[1]

In 1917, Alice moved to Los Angeles and began working for that plan at the Theosophical Society headquarters where she met Foster Bailey, a man who had devoted his life to occultism. She divorced her estranged husband and married Bailey in 1920. Alice had her first contact with a voice that claimed to be a master in November of 1919. Calling himself the Tibetan, he wanted Alice to take dictation from him. Concerning this, Alice wrote:

I heard a voice which said, "There are some books, which it is desired, should be written for the public. You can write them. Will you do so?"[2]

Alice felt reluctant at first to take on such an unusual endeavor, but the voice continued urging her to write the books. At this point in time Alice experienced a brief period of intense anxiety in which she feared for her health and sanity. One of her other spirit "masters" finally reassured her she had nothing to fear and she would be doing a "really valuable piece of work."[3] The "valuable work" Alice was to do ended up lasting thirty years. Between 1919 and 1949, by means of telepathic communication, Alice Bailey wrote nineteen books for her unseen mentor.

To occultists, the significance of the Alice Bailey writings has heralded anticipation of the appearance of a *World Healer and Savior* in the coming Aquarian Age (the astrological age of enlightenment and peace). This savior would unite all mankind under his guidance. Bailey termed him the "Coming One." This person was not to be the Lord Jesus Christ, of whom Christians await the return, but an entirely different individual who would embody all the great principles of occultism, chiefly the *divinity and perfectibility of man*. One of Bailey's followers wrote:

> The reappearance of the Avatar [world teacher], by whatever name he may be known, has been prophesied in many religions as well as in the esoteric [occult] tradition. A major manifestation is expected in connection with the Aquarian age.[4]

Interestingly, the apostle Paul declared one called "the man of sin" and "the son of perdition" would also proclaim himself to be *God* (2 Thessalonians 2:3,4). I believe this coming Aquarian *messiah* will be the son of perdition spoken of by Paul in 2 Thessalonians. Furthermore, I am convinced the New Age movement is his spiritual platform. Too many things fit together for this to be just mere coincidence. Therefore, we must watch for the restructuring of our world by those who are preparing the way for his arrival and identity to be revealed.

Daniel 8:23 states this man will be a master of dark sayings. In Hebrew, this translates as one skilled in cunning and ambiguous speech. The world will see him as one who is distinguished and spiritually brilliant. Keep this in mind as you read the following description:

> The coming one will not be Christian, a Hindu, a Buddhist, not an American, Jew, Italian or Russian—his title is not important; he is for all humanity, to unite all religions, philosophies and nations.[5]

The only one who could bring this about is the one who fits the description mentioned in Daniel. This explains the all-out effort by the New Age, which is saturating our society with meditation right now. When this man comes forward, all those who are in touch with their higher self, those who are *awakened* will clearly recognize him as their unifier and give him their allegiance. He will have a ready-made constituency (many in key positions) to help him reconstruct society. This will be the final culmination of the paradigm shift.

A disciple of the Indian guru Rajneesh made this keen observation, illustrating the potential power of this deception and the hypnotic influence of this "Coming One":

> Something had happened to Rajneesh that made him unlike other men. He had undergone some change— enlightenment, the rising of kundalini [serpent power]— and his being had been altered in palpable [noticeable] ways. The change in him in turn affected his sannyasins [disciples] and created a persistent and catalyzing resonance between them.[6]

What was the nature of the resonance? The Bible predicts the Antichrist and the false prophet will perform lying wonders (Revelation 13). Alice Bailey described the work of her New Age *Christ* very explicitly:

The work of the Christ (two thousand years ago) was
to proclaim certain great possibilities and the existence
of great powers. His work when He reappears will be to
prove the fact of these possibilities and to reveal the true
nature and potency of man.[7]

The following is another powerful example of what this could
mean. A Hindu spiritual teacher named Sri Chinmoy demonstrated
an ability to lift 7000 pounds with one arm. Twenty spectators wit-
nessed this and recorded it by photograph and video. He attributed
his impressive ability to *meditation power* and admits that without it
he could not lift sixty pounds.[8] What had most likely enabled him
to do this was the power of familiar spirits giving him (and those
observing this) the impression this was done through the power of
his higher self. This is what the Bible means by *lying wonders*. The
"man of sin" (the "Coming One") will do this on a vast scale. He
will seem to work great miracles to convince humanity we all have
this great power, or as Bailey called it, potency, within us.

An American woman with a secular worldview took a trip to
Brazil to study a Brazilian New Age *healer*. The impact he had on
her was quite remarkable. She recounted:

> Instantly my body felt as though it were filled with
> white light and I became weak in my knees and I
> started swaying. Soon, I became unable to stand, and
> someone helped me to sit in a chair. Thereafter, I felt
> extreme heat beating down into my head, particularly on
> the left side. All during this experience, I was completely
> conscious and my body was filled with waves of ecstasy.
> I had heard about and visualized white light before, but
> had never experienced being totally infused with it. I
> immediately made an association to the healing power of
> Jesus Christ, and had no doubts that this was the nature
> of the energy being transmitted to me.[9]

If this healer could do something of this nature on one woman, could
not someone, such as the Antichrist, who really had the power of

occultism behind him, do the same thing on a much grander scale? He could in essence *Reiki* the entire world.

Mystery Babylon

Familiar spirits (fallen angels) will not just mislead a few individuals; they will deceive the whole world into embracing a new system. Satan (whose name means adversary) will be the power behind the "Coming One"—the great Antichrist. The origin of the Antichrist's religious system is clearly revealed by the apostle John in Revelation 17:5:

> And upon her forehead was a name written, Mystery, Babylon the Great, the Mother of Harlots and Abominations of the Earth.

Another word for Babylon in the Old Testament was Chaldea. The Chaldeans were renowned for their use of metaphysical arts. They began the first mystery schools. Daniel 4:7 says: "Then came in the magicians, the astrologers, the Chaldeans, and the soothsayers." This Mystery Babylon, then, would be the original source or mother of what is now New Age metaphysics.

Thus, when the apostle John identifies the Antichrist's spiritual format, he is making reference to the city and the people that first spawned occultism in ancient times. All of the other mystery schools flowed out of Babylon, teaching essentially the same thing—the higher self. John saw it as one unbroken line throughout history culminating in the Antichrist's rule with hundreds of millions being given over to familiar spirits. Luke, who wrote the book of Acts, gave us an account of this activity as the first century believers were daily confronting spirits not of God:

> But there was a certain man, called Simon, which beforetime in the same city used sorcery, and bewitched the people of Samaria, giving out that himself was some great one: To whom they all gave heed, from the least to the greatest, saying, This man is the great power of God.

> And to him they had regard, because that of long time he
> had bewitched them with sorceries. (Acts 8:9-11)

Simon was a man whose activities appeared good; otherwise the people would not have declared, "this man is the great power of God." But the truth of the matter is, he wasn't of God—he just appeared to be. Fortunately for Simon, he repented from his Chaldean practice, and he and those with him were saved.

Simon's conversion (like all conversions) was a huge threat to the mystical agenda. Hence, it is easy to see why the coming of the Gospel to the town of Ephesus was a great hindrance to the practice of occultism. Once the people understood they had been deceived by what appeared to be spiritual truth, they repented and liberated themselves of all their collections of mystical recipes. The following describes this dramatic event:

> And many that believed came, and confessed, and shewed
> their deeds. Many of them also which used curious arts
> brought their books together, and burned them before all
> men: and they counted the price of them, and found it
> fifty thousand pieces of silver. So mightily grew the word
> of God and prevailed. (Acts 19:18-20)

The magical or metaphysical arts flew out their door when the Gospel of Christ came in. The two were not only incompatible but totally opposite. Further, what the new believers burned equaled the wages of 150 men for one year. The Ephesian believers gave up their wealth and mystical formulas for the truth found only in Jesus Christ. Unfortunately, the opposite is happening in the world today!

There is another account in Scripture that highlights what I am trying to say. It is found in Acts 16:16-19:

> And it came to pass, as we went to prayer, a certain damsel
> possessed with a spirit of divination met us, which brought
> her masters much gain by soothsaying: The same followed

Paul and us, and cried, saying, These men are the servants of the most high God, which shew unto us the way of salvation. And this did she many days. But Paul, being grieved, turned and said to the spirit, I command thee in the name of Jesus Christ to come out of her. And he came out the same hour. And when her masters saw that the hope of their gains was gone, they caught Paul and Silas, and drew them into the marketplace unto the rulers.

Such events in Scripture illustrate several things critical to understanding the nature and aim of familiar spirits:

The spirit was the source of her power, not some latent faculty inherent in her human makeup. When it left, her ability left with it.

The spirit was accurate to a high degree. Otherwise she would not have brought her masters "much gain." Deception often occurs when there is 99 percent truth and just 1 percent falsehood. It only takes a little leaven or white lie to leaven or taint the greater lump, which is truth.

Paul and the spirit were *not on the same side*; all was not *one* here. This is quite evident due to the fact that he cast it out of her. Most important of all, the spirit tried to identify or associate itself with God by open acknowledgment. It was crafty when it followed Paul and Silas, for it was proclaiming the truth: "These men show us the way of salvation." This reveals that *Mystery Babylon* and its spirit guide legions will try to appear as being on God's side. Today, many of these types of occurrences are already happening in the name of Christianity.

Coming In His Name

I believe the Bible contains an important passage, which clearly indicates a change of times and seasons may indeed be at hand. In Matthew 24:3-5, which is a chapter dealing with the tribulation period, Jesus spoke these words to His disciples concerning the signs of His coming and the end of the age:

> And as he sat upon the mount of Olives, the disciples came unto him privately, saying, Tell us, when shall these things be? and what shall be the sign of thy coming, and of the end of the world?

> And Jesus answered and said unto them, Take heed that no man deceive you. *For many shall come in my name,* saying, I am Christ; and shall deceive many. (emphasis mine)

I have heard two interpretations of Jesus' reply. The first interpretation asserts various individuals will claim to be the returning, incumbent Jesus Christ. The other view says a number of messiah figures will appear and gather followers to themselves in a similar fashion to cult leader Jim Jones or Bhagwan Shree Rajneesh, the guru leader who set up his idea of utopia in Oregon. I now believe neither of these interpretations encompass the bigger picture. It is in light of numerous New Age statements that Matthew 24 takes on new significance.

A basic tenet of New Age thinking is that of the *Master Jesus.* Adherents to this idea believe during the unrecorded period of His life, Jesus traveled to various occult centers and mystery schools in such places as Tibet, India, Persia, and Egypt; at these places this same Jesus learned the metaphysical secrets of the ages. Therefore, they claim this Jesus spent seventeen years of travel on a pilgrimage of higher consciousness. According to this viewpoint, Jesus of Nazareth became the Master Jesus, one who allegedly gained mastery over the physical world by becoming one with his higher self.

This is how the New Age interprets the word *Christ.* The word comes from the Greek word *kristos,* which means the anointed. New Agers believe this means being anointed or in touch with the higher self or divine nature. In other words, to be anointed is to be enlightened.

Since New Agers believe Jesus was completely in tune with his higher self, this made him a *Christ.* It is, they believe, a state of awareness and a spiritual condition rather than a title. For that reason, anyone who is in full attunement with his or her *divine essence* is also a *Christ.*

After reading innumerable such statements that promote this *Christ consciousness,* I took a closer look at Matthew 24:5. What I found astounded me! The Greek word for *many* in this verse is *polus,* which means a very great or sore number. The word may actually be saying that millions upon millions of people are going to claim deity for themselves. The Greek words for "come in my name" mean they shall come claiming to represent what Jesus alone personifies by misusing His name and mistaking His true identity.

In summary, Matthew 24:5 is saying a great number of people will come claiming to represent what He (Jesus) represents but will be in fact deceiving people. In light of Jesus' warning ("many shall come in my name"), consider the following remarks taken from two New Age sources:

> Jesus was one soul who reached the state of Christ Consciousness; there have been many others. He symbolized the blueprint we must follow . . . The way is open to everyone to become a Christ by achieving the Christ Consciousness through walking the same path He walked. He simply and beautifully demonstrated the pattern.[10]

> The significance of incarnation and resurrection is not that Jesus was a human like us but rather that *we are gods like him*—or at least have the potential to be. The significance of Jesus is not as a vehicle of salvation but as a model of perfection. [11] (emphasis mine)

New Agers claim Jesus is a model of what the New Age or Aquarian person is to become. These statements could be called *coming in His name* or *claiming to represent what He represents.*

The remainder of verse five in Matthew, chapter 24, reveals the warning of Jesus that they will actually say: "I am Christ." Again, we find a multitude of statements by New Agers that confirm the admonition of Jesus. Here are some examples:

This World Leader . . . is supposed to represent the new Aquarian Age and establish the Oneness of all mankind—one religion . . . In the Aquarian Age, you will not need the outer saviour, for you will be able to learn how to reach the inner Christ Consciousness . . . The Saviour of the New Age will be a channel through which all Cosmic Truth will come.[12]

The Christ is You. You are the one who is to come—each of you. Each and everyone of you![13]

Christhood is not something to come at a point in the future when you are more evolved. Christhood is—right now! I am the Christ of God. *You are the Christ of God.*[14] (emphasis mine)

It is not surprising to find those in the contemplative prayer camp who also subscribe to this view. Contemplative author John R. Yungblut, former Dean of Studies at the Quaker Meditation Center at Pendle Hill in Pennsylvania, echoes a similar notion:

[W]e cannot confine the existence of the divine to this one man [Jesus] among men. Therefore we are not to worship the man Jesus, though we cannot refrain from worshiping the source of this Holy Spirit or Christ-life which for many of us has been revealed primarily in this historical figure.[15]

Willigis Jager, who ironically, titled his book, *Contemplation: A Christian Path,* stated the same perception of Christ's role to humanity:

Salvation will now be nothing other than a realization of the fact that "the kingdom of God is within you" . . . This is the Good News Jesus proclaimed to humanity. The kingdom is *already within all of us.*[16] (emphasis mine)

Although many contemplative authors still maintain a traditional view of Christology, enough subscribe to the New Age model to where there is cause for grave concern.

There is also a movement flourishing in Jewish circles, which parallels the contemplative spirituality of Catholics and Protestants. Based on the Kabbalah, the Jewish mystical text, this version of contemplative prayer is spreading like wildfire through Judaism. Take a look at any section on Judaism at a local bookstore and you will find it saturated with books on this subject.

One such book, *New Age Judaism* (written by meditation teacher Melinda Ribner), is typical of such titles. Ribner explains:

> Many people will be surprised to find that Judaism is fundamentally aligned with what we think of today as the New Age. Many of the beliefs and practices we associate with the New Age are not new but are part of kabbalah, the Jewish mystical tradition. . . . Though this knowledge has been mostly closeted throughout time, kabbalah is becoming increasingly popular and available today.[17]

Ribner echoes the view of mystical Judaism when she emphasizes:

> Though the term "Messiah" refers to an actual person, Judaism believes that the Messiah is within the consciousness of every person. We all carry the sparks of Messiah within us. Though we await a person who will embody this consciousness and unite the world, we each have to develop this consciousness ourselves. . . . Thus, when a sufficient number of people have developed a consciousness of spiritual unity, the rest of mankind will be uplifted.[18]

Israel itself is ripe for this type of spirituality. One recent book, *The Israelis* by Donna Rosenthal, said that according to a Gallup-Israel survey, sixty percent of all Israelis are attracted to mysticism. In fact, *Reiki News* magazine reported there to be 6,000 Reiki healers in Israel. That is a very large number for such a small country.[19]

One Kabbalah proponent, Rabbi Phillip Berg, has opened fifty "Kabbalah Centres" around the world to spread its message to the masses. According to his literature, this organization has guided 3.9 million people into this mystical practice. His center in Tel Aviv alone has drawn in thousands of students. In addition, there is an entire publishing company devoted to the Kabbalah, Jewish Lights Publishing, with scores of titles on the subject. Their most prominent author is Rabbi Lawrence Kushner, who has reached a wide audience of readers.

This is significant to the prophecies in Matthew, chapter 24 because the mystic Jews also refer to the higher states they enter into as the "messianic consciousness."[20] So, in effect, this state of being, according to their view, makes one a messiah, or in the Greek language, a christos or a *christ.*

The Great Apostasy

In light of the many who will be coming in Christ's name, I also believe the Alice Bailey *prophecies* can provide further insight into what the apostle Paul called in 2 Thessalonians the *falling away.* Bailey eagerly foretold of what she termed "the regeneration of the churches."[21] Her rationale for this was obvious:

> The Christian church in its many branches can serve as a St. John the Baptist, as a voice crying in the wilderness, and as a nucleus through which world illumination may be accomplished.[22]

In other words, instead of opposing Christianity, the occult would capture and blend itself with Christianity and then use it as its primary vehicle for spreading and instilling New Age consciousness! The various churches would still have their outer trappings of Christianity and still use much of the same lingo. If asked certain questions about traditional Christian doctrine, the same answers would be given. But it would all be on the outside; on the inside a contemplative spirituality would be drawing in those open to it.

In wide segments of Christendom, this has indeed already occurred. As stated earlier, Thomas Keating alone taught 31,000 people mystical prayer in one year. People are responding to this in large numbers because it has the external appearance of Christianity but in truth, is the diametric opposite—what a skillful spiritual delusion! Could this possibly be the *falling away* Paul speaks of?

Note this departure is tied in with the revelation of the "man of sin." If he is indeed Bailey's "Coming One," then both Paul's prophecy and Bailey's *prophecy* fit together perfectly—but indisputably from opposite camps and perspectives.

> Let no man deceive you by any means: for that day shall not come, except there come a falling away first, and that man of sin be revealed, the son of perdition.
>
> (2 Thessalonians 2:3)

This is very logical when one sees, as Paul proclaimed, that they will fall away to "the mystery of iniquity" (2 Thessalonians 2:7). The word mystery in Greek, when used in the context of evil (iniquity), means hidden or occult!

Could this *revitalization* of Christianity fit in with Bailey's "new and vital world religion"[23]—a religion that would be the cornerstone of the New Age? Such a religion would be the spiritual platform for the New Age "Coming One." This unity of spiritual thought would not be a single one-world denomination but would have a unity-in-diversity, multicultural, interfaith, ecumenical agenda. Thomas Merton made a direct reference to this at a spiritual summit conference in Calcutta, India when he told Hindus and Buddhists, "We are already one, but we imagine, we are not. What we have to recover is our original unity."[24]

One can easily find numerous such appeals like Merton's in contemplative writings. Examine the following:

> The Christian is not to become a Hindu or a Buddhist, nor a Hindu or Buddhist to become a Christian. But each must assimilate the spirit of the others.[25]—**Vivekananda**

> It is my sense, from having meditated with persons from many different [non-Christian] traditions, that in the silence we experience *a deep unity*. When we go beyond the portals of the rational mind into the experience, there is only *one God to be experienced*. [26] (emphasis mine)—**Basil Pennington**

> The new ecumenism involved here is not between Christian
> and Christian, but between Christians and the grace of other
> intuitively deep religious traditions.[27]—**Tilden Edwards**

I observed this "new ecumenism" in a syndicated article featured in one regional Catholic newspaper. The article proclaimed that the "word of God" can also be found in Eastern religions. A Catholic retreat master offered the notion that "today Catholics have an obligation to seek God in other traditions."[28]

This is not just an isolated commendation or admonition. It is what I refer to as *Mertonization* (remaining in the religion you already are in but being aligned with Eastern mysticism), which is exactly Merton's dream fulfilled: mystical unity within religious diversity. In effect that one-world religion is already here!

Satan's plan has always been to deceive people into believing they can become like God, and God has given Satan the freedom to carry out his diabolical plans, with certain powers to recruit humans in attempting to complete it. While Scripture clearly tells us that Satan is the father of lies, it is not inconceivable that Satan would reveal these things to whomever he wishes for the purpose of attaining his goals. I believe Alice Bailey may be one of those through whom he chose to lay out his master plans. Therefore, Bailey's predictions could indeed be more than just the fanciful meanderings of an overactive imagination. When the depth and intricate detail of her work is studied, it cannot be dismissed as trivial. One author made the following keen observation regarding this point:

> Alice Bailey's gigantic corpus of wisdom could not
> have been invented by human minds; the teachings are
> undoubtedly superhuman in origin.[29]

In a manner of speaking, I consider Alice Bailey as an *apostle* of New Age occultism, and her writings as mystical *revelations*. She is telling the world the path it will be taking and how it is going to be done—in essence, a combined manifesto and blueprint. The fact that much of what she predicted has indeed actually happened gives even greater credence that her work really could be the design for the one Paul called "the son of perdition."

"Rethinking" the Gospel

Various church statements reflect Bailey's dark prophecies that speak to the "revitalization" of the churches. Even now a recent Catholic dictionary states: "Current ideas about mysticism underscore that it is for the many, not just a chosen few."[30] An article in *America*, a national Catholic magazine, shows the result of this mysticism in regard to evangelization. The article, titled *Rethinking Mission in India*, states the *spirit* is active in Hinduism as much as Christianity and therefore both religions "are co-pilgrims on the way to fulfillment."[31] The significance of this is clearly revealed in the following view from the same article:

> Any claims to superiority are damaging. Religions need not be compared. All we are expected to do is to serve man by revealing to him the love of God made manifest in Jesus Christ.[32]

What is happening here is a complete turnaround regarding the meaning of evangelization. In truth, if you want to reveal to man the love of God, made manifest in Jesus Christ, you proclaim the *blood of Christ* for salvation! Yet, it is vital to note the article says this "love of God" is "indissolubly linked to contemplation."[33]

The April 26th, 2002 edition of the PBS series "Religion and Ethics Newsweekly" also reveals the findings of a national poll conducted by them and *U.S. News & World Report* magazine. The findings speak for themselves. According to their poll, 80 percent of Americans consider themselves Christians, and 77 percent of these do not believe their religion is the only one that is true, saying that "all religions have elements of truth."[34]

This means that, if this poll is accurate, only one out of every four Christians in the country believes that Christianity has the corner on presenting the way to heaven and salvation.

The view that Christianity is not the only religion that offers salvation fits the Merton/Nouwen notion of salvation rather than the one the apostles of the New Testament held. While other religions may have some good elements to them, what the other religions lack is a *Savior*, who is the Lord Jesus Christ.

The poll also showed that 70 percent of all Christians believe that those in other religions should not be actively reached for Jesus Christ—that they should be left alone. In effect this means 70 percent are saying Jesus is *my* way but your way (e.g., the higher self, the Buddha nature) is equally fine.

It's not that much of a step further to start seeing Jesus as a model rather than a Savior, one of many manifestations of God rather than the *only* manifestation of God.

For those who are still skeptical of a world-mysticism that could become pervasive, I suggest they carefully reflect on the words of popular seminar leader, John Gray, a T.M. practitioner and author of the bestseller, *Men Are From Mars, Women Are From Venus*. He has revealed how easily and quickly people are moving into the mystical realm:

> I lived as a monk in the mountains of Switzerland for nine years to experience my inner connection to God. Now, when I teach meditation, I see people progressing light-years faster than I did. Within a few weeks, they begin to experience the current of energy flowing in their fingertips. Ninety percent of the people who learn to meditate at my seminars have this experience in one or two days. To me, this is extremely exciting.

> Throughout history this has never happened. To have such an immediate experience was unheard of. The great mystics and saints of our past had to spend years waiting to have a spiritual experience, and now practically anyone can experience the current of energy.[35]

Some day, and it could be soon, the Lord will allow the man of lawlessness to emerge. In the mean time, the world is opening its arms to wholly embrace a spirituality that will exist under the umbrella of mysticism. The correlating theme will be—we are all One. When the man of lawlessness does rise to power with a one-world economy and political base, he will seduce many into searching for their own *Christ consciousness* rather than the Messiah, Jesus Christ.

Seven

Seducing Spirits

I once heard a radio interview with Richard Foster that revealed the high regard in which many influential evangelicals hold him. The talk show host made his own admiration obvious with such comments to Foster as, "You have heard from God . . . this is a message of enormous value," and in saying Foster's work was a "curriculum for Christ-likeness." I found this praise especially disturbing after Foster stated in the interview that Christianity was "not complete without the contemplative dimension."[1] Of course, my concern was that Foster's *curriculum* would result in Thomas Merton-likeness instead.

When I look ahead and ponder the impact of this book, unquestionably there are some very sobering considerations. The contemplative prayer movement has already planted strong roots within evangelical Christianity. Many sincere, devout, and respected Christians have embraced Thomas Merton's vision that:

> The most important need in the Christian world today is this inner truth nourished by this Spirit of contemplation . . . Without contemplation and interior prayer the Church cannot fulfill her mission to transform and save mankind.[2]

A statement like this should immediately alert the discerning Christian that something is wrong. It is the Gospel that saves mankind, not the silence. When Merton says "save," he really means *enlighten*. Remember, Merton's spiritual worldview was panentheistic oneness.

Some will see this book as divisive and intolerant—especially those who share Merton's view of the future. Pastors may be set at odds with one another and possibly with their congregations; friends, and even family members may be divided on the issues of contemplative spirituality. Nevertheless, having weighed the pros and cons of writing this book, I am prepared to receive the inevitable responses from fans of these contemplative mentors. And although I sincerely feel goodwill toward those I have critiqued, I am convinced the issues covered in this book are of vital importance, leaving me compelled to share them regardless of the cost.

After taking an honest look at the evidence, the conclusion is overwhelming that contemplative prayer is not a spiritually-sound practice for Christians. The errors of contemplative spirituality are simple and clear for the following three reasons:

- It is not biblical.
- It correlates with occult methods (i.e., mantra, vain repetition).
- It is sympathetic to Eastern mystical perceptions (God in every thing; all is One—Panentheism).

These are well-documented facts, not just arbitrary opinions. Furthermore, the contemplative prayer movement is uniform, indicating a link to a central source of knowledge. Based on the above facts, we know what that source is.

The apostle Paul warns us of seducing spirits in his first letter to Timothy:

> Now the Spirit speaketh expressly, that in the latter times some shall depart from the faith, giving heed to seducing spirits, and doctrines of devils.
> (1 Timothy 4:1)

The operative word here is "deceiving" or *seducing* which means to be an *imposter* or to *mislead*. It is plain to see a real delusion is going on or, as Paul called it, a seduction. How then can you tell if you are a victim yourself? It is actually not that difficult.

The doctrines (instructions) of demons—no matter how nice, how charming, how devoted to God they sound—convey that everything has Divine Presence (all is One). This is clear heresy—for that would be saying Satan and God are one also (i.e., "I [Lucifer] will be like the Most High," Isaiah 14:14). If what Henri Nouwen proclaimed is true when he said, "[W]e can come to the full realization of the unity of all that is,"[3] then Jesus Christ and Satan are also united. *That* is something only a demonic spirit would teach!

An even more subtle yet seductive idea says: Without a mystical technique, God is somehow indifferent or unapproachable. Those of you who are parents can plainly see the falsehood of this. Do your children need to employ a method or engage in a ritual to capture your full attention or guidance? Of course not! If you love your children, you will care for and interact with them because you are committed to them and want to participate with them. The same is true of God's attention towards those He has called his own.

And, we must not forget the most decisive indication of the Deceiver's handiwork: the belief or doctrine in question will undermine the uniqueness of Jesus Christ as both God and man and His atoning work on the Cross. The apostle John brings out this distinction with clarity in his first letter:

> Hereby know ye the Spirit of God: Every spirit that confesseth that Jesus Christ is come in the flesh is of God: And every spirit that confesseth not that Jesus Christ is come in the flesh is not of God: and this is that spirit of antichrist, whereof ye have heard that it should come; and even now already is it in the world. (1 John 4:2-3)

It is evident then, that the whole idea of a *Christ consciousness* where we all have divinity, is completely unbiblical in that it negates who Jesus was and what He came to do.

The central role of a shepherd is to guide and direct the sheep. The sheep know the voice of their Master by simply following Him in faith (John 10:14-18). The Shepherd does not expect or desire the sheep to perform a method or religious technique to be close to Him. He has already claimed them as His own. Remember! Religiosity is *man's* way to God while Christianity is *God's* way to man. Contemplative prayer is just another man-inspired attempt to get to God.

When we receive Christ, we receive the Holy Spirit—thus we receive God. Christians do not have to search for some esoteric technique to draw closer to God. The fullness of God has already taken residency in those who have received Christ. The Christian's response is not to search for God through a method but simply to yield his or her will to the will of God.

When looking at principles like these, Paul's warning becomes clear. A seduction will not work if we are wise to the ways of the seducer.

Christians must not be led purely by their emotions or a particular experience; there must be ground rules. A popular saying is: "You can't put God in a box." That is correct in some ways, but it's not true if the box is the Bible. God will not work outside of what He has laid down in His message to humanity.

The answer to the contemplative prayer movement is simple. A Christian is complete in Christ. The argument that contemplative prayer can bring a fuller measure of God's love, guidance, direction, and nurturing is the epitome of dishonor to Jesus Christ, the Good Shepherd. It is, in essence, anti-Christian.

The late Dr. Paul Bubna, President of the Christian and Missionary Alliance, wrote in an article, "Purveyors of Grace or Ungrace":

> Knowing Christ is a journey of solid theological understanding. It is the Holy Spirit's illuminating the Scriptures to our darkened minds and hearts that give birth to the wonder of unconditional love.[4]

The contemplative message has seriously maligned this wonderful work of God's grace and the sanctifying work of the Holy Spirit.

The Holy Spirit is the one who guides the Christian into all truth. Those who have the Holy Spirit indwelling them do not need the silence. It is one thing to find a quiet place to pray (which Jesus did) but quite another to go into an altered state of consciousness (which Jesus never did). The Christian hears the voice of Jehovah through the Holy Spirit, not through contemplative prayer. Again, Jesus made it clear He is the one who initiates this process, not man:

> If ye love me, keep my commandments. And I will pray the Father, and he shall give you another Comforter, that he may abide with you for ever; Even the Spirit of truth; whom the world cannot receive, because it seeth him not, neither knoweth him: but ye know him; for he dwelleth with you, and shall be in you. (John 14:15-17)

Scripture instructs us to "try the spirits" (1 John 4:1). Let's test them, using Richard Foster's teachings. In his book, *Celebration of Discipline,* Foster devotes a number of pages to what he calls the *biblical basis* for this form of prayer. He makes reference to many instances throughout the Bible where God talked to people,—in other words, encounters between man and Divinity. But Foster then jumps straight into contemplative prayer, leading the reader to think this is how it is done when, in fact, he has not really presented a biblical basis for using the repetition of sacred words at all. He looks to the contemplative mystics to legitimize his teachings when he writes:

> How sad that contemporary Christians are so ignorant of the vast sea of literature on Christian meditation by faithful believers throughout the centuries! And their testimony to the joyful life of perpetual communion is amazingly uniform.[5]

That is the problem. The contemplative authors *are* "amazingly uniform." Even though they all profess a love for God and Jesus, they have each added something that is contrary to what God conveys in His written Word.

Contemplative mystic John R. Yungblut penned the following observation that rings true for almost all such contemplative practitioners. He concludes:

> The core of the mystical experience is the apprehension of unity, and the perception of relatedness. For the mystics the world is one.[6]

Panentheism is the bedrock of the contemplative prayer movement; therefore, the establishment of whether or not it is biblically valid is imperative.

Foster also believes, as discussed earlier in this chapter, that God's ability to impact the non-contemplative Christian is limited. Foster expresses:

> What happens in meditation is that we create the emotional and spiritual space which allows Christ to construct an inner sanctuary in the heart.[7]

But as I stated, the Trinity already has an inner sanctuary in every Christian. It is being in Christ (via the Holy Spirit) that allows every believer to receive guidance and direction.

Furthermore, when Richard Foster cites someone like Sue Monk Kidd as an example of what he is promoting (as he does in his book *Prayer: Finding the Heart's True Home)*, it is reasonable to expect that if you engage in Foster's prayer methods, you will become like his examples.

Monk Kidd's spirituality is spelled out clearly in her book *When the Heart Waits*. She explains:

> There's a bulb of truth buried in the human soul [not just Christian] that's "only God" . . . the soul is *more than something to win or save.* It's the seat and repository of the inner Divine, the God-image, the truest part of us.[8]
> (emphasis mine)

Sue Monk Kidd, an introspective woman, gives a revealing description of her spiritual transformation in her book *God's Joyful Surprise: Finding Yourself Loved.* She shares how she suffered a deep hollowness and spiritual hunger for many years even though she was very active in her Baptist church.[9] She sums up her feelings:

> Maybe we sense we're disconnected from God somehow. He becomes superfluous to the business at hand. He lives on the periphery so long we begin to think that is where He belongs. Anything else seems unsophisticated or fanatical.[10]

Ironically, a Sunday school co-worker handed her a book by Thomas Merton, telling her she needed to read it. Once Monk Kidd read it, her life changed dramatically.

What happened next completely reoriented Sue Monk Kidd's worldview and belief system. She started down the contemplative prayer road with bliss, reading numerous books and repeating the sacred word methods taught in her readings.[11] She ultimately came to the mystical realization that:

> I am speaking of recognizing the hidden truth that we are one with all people. We are part of them and they are part of us . . . When we encounter another person . . . we should walk as if we were upon holy ground. We should respond as if God dwells there.[12]

One could come to Monk Kidd's defense by saying she is just referring to Christians and non-Christians sharing a common humanity and the need to treat all people well. Yet, while respecting humanity is important, she fails to distinguish between Christians and non-Christians thereby negating Christ's imperative, "Ye must be born again" (John 3:7), as the prerequisite for the indwelling of God. Her mystical universalism is apparent when she quotes someone who advises that the Hindu greeting namaste, which translates, *I honor the god in you*, should be used by Christians.[13]

Monk Kidd, like Merton, did not join a metaphysical church such as the Unity Church or a Religious Science church. She found her spirituality within the comfortable and familiar confines of a Baptist church!

Moreover, when Monk Kidd found her universal spirituality she was no teenager. She was a sophisticated, mature family woman. This illustrates the susceptibility of the millions like her who are seeking seemingly novel, positive approaches to Christian spiritual growth. Those who lack discernment are at great risk. What looks godly or spiritually benign on the surface may have principles behind it that are in dire conflict with Christianity.

Since the original edition of *A Time of Departing* came out, two major discoveries have come to my attention. First, Sue Monk Kidd has become a widely known author. She has written a bestselling book titled *The Secret Life of Bees,* which has sold millions of copies. Her latest book, *The Mermaid Chair,* is also on the bestseller list. Secondly, and perhaps more importantly, I found even more profound evidence that my conclusions about her worldview were right. It seems that just a few years after she had written the book I've quoted, she wrote another book on spirituality. This one was titled *The Dance of the Dissident Daughter.* If ever there was a book confirming my message in *A Time of Departing,* this book is it.

In her first and second books, Monk Kidd was writing from a Christian perspective. That is why the back cover of *God's Joyful Surprise* was endorsed by *Virtue, Today's Christian Woman,* and (really proving my point) *Moody Monthly.* But with her third and fourth book, Monk Kidd had made the full transition to a spiritual view more in tune with Wicca than with Christianity. Now she worships the Goddess Sophia rather than Jesus Christ:

> We also need Goddess consciousness to reveal earth's holiness. . . . Matter becomes inspirited; it breathes divinity. Earth becomes alive and sacred. . . . Goddess offers us the holiness of everything.[14]

There is one portion in Monk Kidd's book *The Dance of the Dissident Daughter* that, for me, stands out and speaks right to the heart of this issue. I want my readers to grasp what she is conveying in the following account. No one can lightly dismiss or ignore the powers behind contemplative prayer after reading this narrative:

> The minister was preaching. He was holding up a Bible. It was open, perched atop his raised hand as if a blackbird had landed there. He was saying that the Bible was the sole and ultimate authority of the Christian's life. The *sole* and *ultimate* authority.
>
> I remember a feeling rising up from a place about two inches below my navel. It was a passionate, determined feeling, and it spread out from the core of me like a current so that my skin vibrated with it. If feelings could be translated into English, this feeling would have roughly been the word *no!*
>
> It was the purest inner knowing I had experienced, and it was shouting in me *no, no, no!* The ultimate authority of my life is not the Bible; it is not confined between the covers of a book. It is not something written by men and frozen in time. It is not from a source outside myself. *My ultimate authority is the divine voice in my own soul.* Period.[15]

If Foster uses these kinds of mystics as contemplative prayer models without disclaimers regarding their universalist beliefs (like Sue Monk Kidd), then it is legitimate to question whether or not he also resonates with the same beliefs himself. At the Foster seminar I attended, a colleague of his assured the audience that when they were in this altered state, they could just "smell the gospel." Based on the research of this movement, what you can smell is not the Gospel but the Ganges![16]

Merton or the Holy Spirit

Two authors from Great Britain portrayed a stunningly clear picture of New Age spirituality. They explained:

> [T]he keynote of it appears to be a movement for synthesis
> derived from an understanding of the underlying unity
> behind all things and the sense of oneness that this brings.
>
> This oneness of all life is the crux of the New Age
> movement.[17]

M. Basil Pennington defined the contemplative spiritual worldview in his book *Thomas Merton My Brother*. He related:

> The Spirit enlightened him [Merton] in the true synthesis
> [unity] of all and in the harmony of that huge chorus of
> living beings. In the midst of it he lived out a vision of a
> new world, where all divisions have fallen away and the
> divine goodness is perceived and enjoyed as present in
> all and through all.[18]

The first viewpoint describes God as the oneness of all existence. In Merton's new world, God is perceived as being present
"in all and through all." It certainly appears that the same spirit
enlightened both parties. The only difference was Merton's revelation worked in a Christian context just as Alice Bailey predicted.
Unfortunately, this context is now commonplace in Catholic
circles, becoming so in mainline Protestant churches, and being
eagerly explored and embraced by an ever-increasing number of
evangelical Christians.

Evangelical leaders now debate whether such spiritual truths as
resting in God are the same as contemplative silence. Based on these
presented documentations, I believe contemplative prayer has no
place in true Christianity. Scripture clearly teaches that with salvation comes an automatic guidance system—the Holy Spirit. Lewis
Sperry Chafer, in his outstanding book *Grace: The Glorious Theme*,
spells out this truth with crystal-clear clarity:

> It is stated in Romans 5:5 that "the Spirit is given to us."
> This is true of every person who is saved. The Spirit is

the birth-right in the new life. By Him alone can the character and service that belongs to the normal daily life of the Christian be realized. The Spirit is the "All-Sufficient One." Every victory in the new life is gained by His strength, and every reward in glory will be won only as a result of His enabling power.[19]

Show me a scripture in the Bible in which the Holy Spirit is activated or accessed by contemplative prayer. If such a verse exists, wouldn't it be the keynote verse in defense of contemplative prayer?

None exists!

I want to emphasize in this chapter what I believe cuts through all the emotional appeal that has attracted so many to teachers like Foster and Manning and really boils the issue down to its clearest state.

In his book *Streams of Living Water*, Richard Foster emanates his hoped-for vision of an "all inclusive community" that he feels God is forming today. He sees this as "a great, new gathering of the people of God."[20]

On the surface, this might sound noble and sanctifying, but a deeper examination will expose elements that line up more with Alice Bailey's vision than with Jesus Christ's. Foster prophesies:

> I see a Catholic monk from the hills of Kentucky standing alongside a Baptist evangelist from the streets of Los Angeles and together offering up a sacrifice of praise. I see a people.[21]

The only place in "the hills of Kentucky" where Catholic monks live is the Gethsemane Abbey, a Trappist monastery. This also, coincidentally, was the home base of Thomas Merton.

Let me explain this significant connection. In the summer of 1996, Buddhist and Catholic monks met together to dialogue in what was billed the "Gethsemane Encounter."[22] David Steidl-Rast, a Zen-Buddhist trained monk and close friend of Thomas Merton, facilitated this event.

During the encounter, presentations on Zen meditation and practice from the Theravedan Buddhist tradition were offered.[23] One of the speakers discussed the "correlation of the Christian contemplative life with the lives of our Buddhist sisters and brothers."[24]

For these monks and the Baptist evangelist to be "a people," as Richard Foster says, someone has to change. Either the monks have to abandon their Buddhist convictions and align with the Baptists, or the Baptists have to become contemplative style Baptists and embrace the monks' beliefs. That is the dilemma in Foster's "great gathering of God."

David Steidl-Rast once asked Thomas Merton what role Buddhism played in his going deeper into the spiritual life. Merton replied quite frankly: "I think I couldn't understand Christian teaching the way I do if it were not in the light of Buddhism."[25]

Did Merton mean that in order to understand what Christianity really is, you have to change your consciousness? I believe that is exactly what he meant. Once he personally did that through contemplative prayer, Buddhism provided him with the explanation of what he experienced. But again the catalyst was *changing his consciousness*. This is what I am warning Christians about. Contemplative prayer is presenting a way to God identical with all the world's mystical traditions. Christians are haplessly lulled into it by the emphasis on seeking the Kingdom of God and greater piety, yet the apostle Paul described the church's end-times apostasy in the context of a *mystical* seduction. If this practice doesn't fit that description, I don't know what does.

You don't have to change your consciousness to grab "aholt" of God. All you need is to be born-again. What Steidl-Rast and the other Gethsemane monks should have been telling Buddhists is, "Behold the Lamb of God, which taketh away the sin of the world" (John 1:29).

In his book, *Ruthless Trust*, Brennan Manning mentions that Sue Monk Kidd eventually came under the mentorship of Dr. Beatrice Bruteau who authored the book *What We Can Learn From the East*. Since that title is self-explanatory, it's easy to understand why Dr. Bruteau would write the preface to a book like *The Mystic Heart* by Wayne Teasdale. In the preface, she touts that a universal spirituality based on mysticism is going to save the world.

It seems that all these people want a better world. They do not seem like sinister conspirators like those out of a James Bond film. Yet, it is their *niceness* that rejects the reality of the fundamental separation between Man and God. It is their sense of compassion that feeds their universalism. It is idealism that makes Manning so attractive and causes him to say that Dr. Bruteau is a "trustworthy guide to contemplative consciousness."[26]

The irony of this is that Manning is completely correct in his statement—Dr. Bruteau *is* a reliable guide to contemplative awareness. She has founded two organizations, the Schola Contemplationis (school for contemplation) and the very Christian sounding Fellowship of the Holy Trinity. With the latter, she is promoted as "a well-known author and lecturer on contemplative life and prayer."[27] Both of these organizations incorporate Hindu and Buddhist approaches to spirituality. This should come as no surprise because Bruteau also has studied with the Ramakrishna order, which is named after the famous Hindu swami Sri Ramakrishna.

The Ramakrishna order is dedicated to promoting the vision of Sri Ramakrishna. He was known for his view that all the world's religions were valid revelations from God if you understood them on the mystical level. He was an early proponent of interspirituality. According to the book, *Wounded Prophet*, Henri Nouwen even viewed him in a favorable light and esteemed him as an important spiritual figure.

Sue Monk Kidd became enamored with contemplative spirituality while attending a Southern Baptist church. We could possibly dismiss that and say she was just an untaught member of the laity who was spiritually lacking in discernment. Maybe her spiritual dryness was a result of her not being grounded firmly enough in the faith. But what about the leaders and pastors whom so many look up to and who are considered trusted individuals in the church? Surely they are able to discern what is spiritually unsound. It seems safe to make this assumption. Right? Unfortunately, this is no longer the case.

Eight

"America's Pastor"

In the fall of 2002, at the same time the first edition of *A Time of Departing* was released, another book came on the scene. This second book gained almost overnight fame, and before too long, *The Purpose Driven Life* had become a household name. Rick Warren captured the heart and soul of millions of Americans (the majority in evangelical Christianity) like no one else had ever done. His books are seen as blueprints of the Christian life not just for millions but tens of millions worldwide. In fact, *The Purpose Driven Life* has sold over thirty million copies, and that number continues to climb. This means that practically every Christian family in America has at least one copy in their home.

The question you may be asking right now is, "Why is Rick Warren included in a book that is covering New Age interspirituality and exposing the dangers of contemplative prayer? Are you saying that Rick Warren is heading in that direction too? Not America's pastor! Surely not." If that were the case, we'd hear about it from Christian leaders. Right?

On the contrary, some of the leaders I have trusted over the past many years have wholeheartedly endorsed Warren's Purpose Driven teachings. The late pastor Adrian Rogers was just such a leader. Rogers wrote of *The Purpose Driven Church* (Warren's first book) in the most vibrant terms. Of it he said, "This book is on the must-read list for every pastor."[1]

And Adrian Rogers isn't the only one. In fact, it appears that most Christian leaders support Warren, with only a small number who do not. And this support has cut across nearly every denominational and religious partition. From Southern Baptist (Warren's own denomination) to Pentecostal to Lutheran to Jewish to Catholic, countless leaders and pastors have given their unwavering support and endorsement to Warren and his Purpose Driven program.

In my book, I have tried to lay out a concise and well-documented explanation of contemplative prayer—its history, its makeup, and its technique. I have also illustrated with one example after another just how widespread and pervasive contemplative spirituality really is. If indeed Rick Warren is promoting contemplative prayer, as I believe he is, this guarantees that contemplative prayer will be promoted on an enormous scale. Through Rick Warren, Richard Foster's vision could enter fully into mainstream evangelicalism both in North America and around the world; and with the unprecedented following and support Warren has gained, we could be heading towards a crisis in the church that might possibly lead to the falling away that the apostle Paul warns about.

Contemplative Prayer—"a Hot Topic"

Rick Warren believes that his "Purpose Driven paradigm" is an essential element and the heartbeat of the church. Of it, he says:

> Personal computers have brand names. But inside every pc is an Intel chip and an operating system, Windows. . . . The Purpose Driven paradigm is the Intel chip for the 21st-century church and the Windows system of the 21st-century church.[2]

Warren also believes Purpose Driven has helped to put evangelical Christianity on a path that will lead to a second "reformation" and a great *spiritual awakening*:

> I believe that we are possibly on the verge of a new
> reformation in Christianity and another Great Awakening
> in our nation . . . The signs are everywhere, including the
> popularity of this book.[3]

In an interview, Warren stated:

> I'm looking for a second reformation. The first reformation
> of the church 500 years ago was about beliefs. This one is
> going to be about behavior. The first one was about creeds.
> This one is going to be about deeds. It is not going to be
> about what does the church believe, but about what is
> the church doing.[4]

Many who adhere to the Purpose Driven movement see great hope
in its message. With Warren's proposed *global P.E.A.C.E. Plan,* that
hope extends far beyond the borders of Christianity, and Warren has
been seen as someone who can solve the major dilemmas the world
faces! Yet the danger is that this agenda could serve as a platform for
promoting a global spirituality that compromises the Gospel.

In February of 2003, my publisher sent a copy of *A Time of Departing* to Rick Warren with the hopes of alerting him to the dangers of
contemplative spirituality. At the time, we knew nothing about how
far Warren had already traveled down that road. We had actually
hoped to warn him of what I saw sweeping the church. A couple of
weeks after sending the book, he sent a card, which read:

> Just a note to say thanks for the copy of *A Time of
> Departing* by Ray Yungen. It definitely will be a useful
> addition to my personal library and resource in my
> studies. I agree this is a hot topic. Sincerely, Rick Warren

While his response was vague, it seemed clear by his note he
had recognized contemplative spirituality as an item of relevance
in Christianity today. The question then was, on which side of the
fence was he standing?

As I have carefully shown in this book, contemplative spirituality is a belief system that is a bridge to interspirituality and thus a denial of the message of the Cross. And we know by Scripture that we cannot serve both man and God. Rick Warren is either for or against contemplative prayer. Which one is it? It cannot be both.

We can begin to find the answer to this question by turning to Warren's first book *The Purpose Driven Church*. In that book, Warren praises a number of parachurch movements he believes God has "raised up" to remedy a "neglected purpose" in Christianity. One of these he mentions is the *spiritual formation movement,* which promotes contemplative prayer through the "Spiritual Disciplines." Warren names Richard Foster and Dallas Willard as leaders of this movement.[5]

I believe I can document that Warren does indeed embrace the spiritual formation movement, of which he writes that this movement has a "valid message for the church"[6] and has "given the body of Christ a wake-up call."[7] What this means is that Warren, leader of this "New Reformation," has landed on the side of the contemplative prayer (i.e., spiritual formation) movement. In order to prove this to be true, it is essential to examine Warren and his ministry. In so doing, you may also come to the conclusion, as I have, that the Purpose Driven paradigm could very well be providing an avenue not for a new reformation and spiritual awakening from God but rather for a descent into spiritual apostasy.

Purpose Driven: Mystics, Monks, and Breath Prayers

The vast majority of people who read Warren's books feel his approach to Christianity is articulate and refreshing. Furthermore, they see some of his statements, such as the one below, as proof beyond measure that he is a staunch defender of the faith:

> Every human being was created by God, but not everyone is a child of God. The only way to get into God's family is by being born again into it. But there is one condition: faith in Jesus. The Bible says, "You are all children of God through faith in Christ Jesus."[8]

However, a growing number of believers see Warren in a very different light, as someone who has sold out Christianity by using high-tech marketing methods and a watered-down gospel—one that de-emphasizes sin and repentance and promotes sensual approaches to worship and secular psychology-based counseling programs. While these issues may be worth discussing and debating, this is not the focus of my critique in this book.

Most likely, many of Warren's admirers might feel that what I *am* saying about *America's Pastor* is a sort of misguided heroism and that I am implying that I, and others like me, are more informed and discerning than multitudes of pastors who embrace Warren. Such admirers might see me as one who is giving a black eye to the very Christianity I claim to defend. What do I have to say to these charges? Simply put, my objective is not to attack individuals such as Rick Warren but rather to reveal what certain practices (and the belief system that enfolds them) entail and why Christians should not engage in them. Is this controversial? Yes! However, this is one controversial debate that is vital to the spiritual well-being of millions of people.

I draw your attention now to a section in *The Purpose Driven Life* under Day 11, "Becoming Best Friends with God." In this section, Warren begins by telling readers that more than anything else, God wants to be our friend, that "we were made to live in God's continual presence,"[9] and that "we can now approach God anytime,"[10] but he adds there are "secrets"[11] to having a friendship with God. One of those secrets he refers to is a form of contemplative spirituality called "breath prayers."[12] He says that a relationship with God will never happen by just attending church and having a daily quiet time. He then offers an example of someone who learned this *secret* and had an intimate relationship with God. This person was a Carmelite monk named Brother Lawrence.

The fact that Brother Lawrence was in the Carmelite order means his spiritual practices were derived from or heavily influenced by Teresa of Avila who reformed that order in the previous century. In a book titled *Christian Mystics*, Professor Ursula King makes the startling revelation that:

[G]iven her [Teresa of Avila] partly Jewish background, her thinking was also affected by Jewish Kabbalistic mysticism, elements of which can be detected in her writings.[13]

Brother Lawrence is often quoted by contemplative authors for his habit of what he called "practicing the presence of God."[14] But what was the actual nature of this presence? Was it something that would reflect the true character of God? I find the following account from a devout advocate of Brother Lawrence quite disturbing:

It is said of Brother Lawrence that when something had taken his mind away from love's presence he would receive "a reminder from God" that so moved his soul that he "cried out, singing and dancing violently like a mad man." You will note that the reminders came from God and were not his own doing.[15]

Brother Lawrence says that secret phrases must be "repeat[ed] often in the day,"[16] and "for the right practice of it, the heart must be empty of all other things."[17] He speaks of the trouble of wandering thoughts and says that the habit of practicing the presence of God is the "one remedy"[18] and the "best and easiest method"[19] he knows to dissolve distractions.

Rick Warren has not only favorably introduced this monk to his readers and called his ideas "helpful"[20] but has sandwiched between his comments on Brother Lawrence an unusual rendering of Ephesians 4:6 from the *New Century Version* concerning God that reads, "*He rules everything and is everywhere and is in everything.*"[21] However, Warren neglects to rectify this misleading translation and alert the reader to the fact that Paul is speaking here of the Church body as uniquely united in Christ by one single faith under one single God as is clear by what immediately precedes the verse in question:

There is one body, and one Spirit, even as ye are called in one hope of your calling; One Lord, one faith, one baptism, One God and Father of all. (Ephesians 4:4-6)

And lest anyone should think Paul is speaking in terms of an all-inclusive God-is-in-everybody religion, he only says this after making one of the most concise presentations of the Gospel recorded in Scripture:

> For by grace are ye saved through faith; and that not of yourselves: it is the gift of God: Not of works, lest any man should boast. . . . But now in Christ Jesus ye who sometimes were far off are made nigh by the blood of Christ. (Ephesians 2: 8,9,13)

Without Warren giving any explanation to the verse he quotes, the implication is that God is in all creation, including all persons. Many reading *The Purpose Driven Life* may very well take this to mean that God is in all. Former New Age follower, Warren B. Smith, in his book *Deceived on Purpose: The New Age Implications of the Purpose Driven Church*, expounds:

> Rick Warren's implication . . . that God is "in" every person is at the very heart of all New Age teaching. The Bible does not teach this. The *New Century Version* that Rick Warren quotes is dangerously mistaken in its translation of Ephesians 4:6. . . . New Age teachers with their New Spirituality are trying to co-opt this scripture to make it apply to the whole human race.[22]

Shalem Institute, founded by Tilden Edwards and located in Washington, DC, sees Brother Lawrence as someone whose contemplation includes the belief that God is in everything:

> Christian contemplation means finding God in all things and all things in God. Brother Lawrence, the 17th century Carmelite friar, called it "the loving gaze that finds God everywhere."[23]

Rick Warren has taken Brother Lawrence's advice of repeating "little internal adorations" throughout the day a step further and tells his readers that "practicing the presence of God" can be accomplished through *breath prayers*. Warren states:

The Bible tells us to "pray all the time." How is it possible
to do this? One way is to use "breath prayers" throughout
the day, as many Christians have done for centuries. You
choose a brief sentence or *a simple phrase* that can be
repeated to Jesus in one breath.[24] (emphasis mine)

Warren then advises readers to use visual reminders throughout
the day and gives an example of others who practice breath prayers—
Benedictine monks, known for their contemplative spirituality and
interspirituality. According to Warren, this breath prayer that the
monks practiced (*and now we should practice*) involves taking a
"simple phrase" such as "I belong to you" or "You are my God" and
"Pray it *as often as possible*"[25] (emphasis mine).

British metaphysical author Carolyn Reynolds, in her book
Spiritual Fitness, defines meditation simply as "repeated sounds or
phrases."[26] That is exactly what Warren is promoting. He assures
readers, "Practicing the presence of God is a skill, a habit you can
develop."[27] The key word here is "skill," which reflects Richard Foster's
influence that Christians need to be *trained* in order to interact with
God in any profound way. But it is the nature of this method that
betrays the danger of the contemplative approach.

In Foster's book, *Prayer: Finding the Heart's True Home*, Foster
encourages readers to "bind the mind" with "breath prayers,"[28] quoting Theophane *the Recluse* and making reference to Brother Lawrence,
calling him a practitioner of this type of prayer. Very likely, this is
where Warren picked this up.

I believe this is a question that needs to be asked, "Is breath prayer
a valid practice?" In Sonia Choquette's book on psychic development,
Your Heart's Desire, she says, "All of us need to take the time to expand our mental awareness in order to hear inner guidance."[29] The
way she suggests doing this is through the same principle as breath
prayer. One repeats, "I am calm" over and over again.

When a word or phrase is repeated over and over, after just a few
repetitions, those words lose their meaning and become just sounds.
Have you ever tried repeating a word over and over again? After three

or four times, the word may begin to lose its meaning, and if this repeating of words were continued, normal thought processes could be blocked, making it possible to enter an altered state of consciousness because of a hypnotic effect that begins to take place. It really makes no difference whether the repeated words are "You are my God" or "I am calm," the results are the same. So, if you use Warren's method or the occult method, the use of a mantra will take you to the same place.

What Warren is teaching is a derivative of *The Cloud of Unknowing,* an ancient primer on contemplative prayer, written by an anonymous monk. Contemplative priest, Ken Kaisch, teaches his students this method of prayer found in Brother Lawrence's writings and describes what the term "presence" means:

> You will be gradually able to tune into God's presence . . . you will have a sense of slow, vibrant, deep energy surrounding you . . . Let yourself flow with this energy, it is the Presence of our Lord . . . As you continue to dwell in the Presence, the intensity will grow. It is extremely pleasurable to experience.[30]

Warren not only promotes breath prayers on Day 11 in *The Purpose Driven Life* but also on Day 38, where he tells readers how to become "world-class Christian[s]" through the "practice [of] . . . breath prayers."[31] In addition to these two references, there are four references to using breath prayers on Warren's pastors.com website, which reaches thousands of pastors throughout the world. And on the main Purpose Driven website, Warren again promotes this practice in an article titled "Purpose Driven Life: Worship That Pleases God."[32]

Evidence That Cannot Be Ignored

Skeptics, at this point, may say, "So Rick Warren promotes breath prayers. That hardly qualifies him as a contemplative advocate." Well, let's say for a moment that this is true—that promoting breath prayers is not enough solid evidence. Is there any other indication that Warren aligns with contemplative spirituality? In truth, there *is* ample evidence to prove this vital point.

Through Rick Warren's pastors.com website,* he is able to communicate to over 150,000 pastors and church leaders around the world. In taking a close look at this website, as well as the weekly e-newsletter that goes out via e-mail to these pastors, it doesn't take much effort to find that Warren is promoting Richard Foster, Brennan Manning, Henri Nouwen, and Thomas Merton. These and other contemplatives are favorably endorsed and promoted repeatedly.

While most of the examples I give are directly from Rick Warren himself, my first example is an article written by Saddleback's pastor of spiritual maturity, Lance Witt. In his article (found on Warren's website), titled "Enjoying God's Presence in Solitude," Witt says, "We were created with a need for solitude," and adds:

> Your life is full of pressures, distractions and fast-paced living. According to Thomas Merton, it is reflection and wonder (solitude) that scoops these invaders out of your life. Through solitude, there is finally room in your soul to meet God and for him to do the work in you that He longs to do.[33]

Witt says that "Solitude creates capacity for God," and "The goal of solitude is not so much to unplug from my crazy world, as it is to change frequencies." Witt then quotes Richard Foster as someone who knows how to *change frequencies*:

> Solitude doesn't give us the power to win the rat race, but to ignore it altogether.[34]

On the same website, Rick Warren refers favorably to a book titled *Sacred Pathways* by his "friend" Gary Thomas. Of the book, Warren says:

> Gary has spoken at Saddleback, and I think highly of his work . . . he tells them [readers] how they can make the

---

* The original pastors.com website was revamped after the release of *A Time of Departing*.

most of their spiritual journeys. He places an emphasis on practical spiritual exercises.[35]

What are these "practical spiritual exercises" Warren is speaking of from Thomas' book? In *Sacred Pathways*, Thomas lists different ways people can draw near to God incorporating contemplative prayer. In a section titled "Centering Prayer," he explains:

> It is particularly difficult to describe this type of prayer in writing, as it is best taught in person. In general however, centering prayer works like this: Choose a word (*Jesus* or *Father*, for example) as a focus for contemplative prayer. Repeat the word silently in your mind for a set amount of time (say, twenty minutes) until your heart seems to be repeating the word by itself, just as naturally and involuntarily as breathing.[36]

Does this sound familiar? There's no difference between it and Eastern-style meditation or the experience Thomas Merton taught. In essence, *Sacred Pathways* is a manual for mantra meditation, yet Warren believes we can find ways to "draw near to God" through this book.[37] How many thousands of pastors who read Warren's newsletters might see his avid promotion of *Sacred Pathways* and buy a copy of it? If they do, they will find that Thomas has an affinity for the writings of Annie Dillard, who also promotes contemplative spirituality.

Warren's promotion and endorsement of contemplatives doesn't end with Brother Lawrence, Thomas Merton, Richard Foster, Brennan Manning, and Gary Thomas. In the September 3, 2003 issue of Warren's weekly e-newsletter to pastors, under his "Book Look" section, he listed Tricia Rhodes' book *The Soul at Rest: A Journey into Contemplative Prayer* and said:

> This book is a quiet-time companion for those who hunger for *a greater intimacy with God*. It offers fresh insight into little understood aspects of prayer and introduces a step-by-step journey of learning contemplative prayer.[38] (emphasis mine)

A few months after this endorsement appeared on his website, another mention of Rhodes was made on his weekly communication to pastors around the world, referring to Rhodes as "one of our favorite authors on contemplative prayer."[39]

This "favorite author" of Rick Warren describes a deep-breathing exercise in which the practitioner is to breathe out the bad and breathe in the good, another example of the mantric methods used by mystics in many world religions. Listen to Rhodes give instruction on how to prepare for prayer time:

> Take deep breaths, concentrating on relaxing your body. Establish a slow, rhythmic pattern. Breathe in God's peace, and breathe out your stresses, distractions, and fears. Breathe in God's love, forgiveness, and compassion, and breathe out your sins, failures, and frustrations. Make every effort to "stop the flow of talking going on within you—to slow it down until it comes to a halt."[40]

I don't remember ever reading in Scripture that I could partake of God's love by physically breathing it in or could rid myself of sin by breathing it out. Interestingly, Rhodes also quotes Morton Kelsey in this passage. You will recall Morton Kelsey, whom I discussed in chapter three, said:

> You can find most of the New Age practices in the depth of Christianity . . . I believe that the Holy One lives in every soul.[41]

Rhodes shows her affinity to contemplative prayer when she states:

> Contemplative Prayer penetrates our heart of hearts, probing the deepest rooms of our interior soul. It leaves no stone unturned, no darkness unlit. . . . It is wonderful and painful and through it He changes us into His likeness.[42]

Rhodes encourages readers to use the *Jesus Prayer* in which the name of Jesus is focused on and repeated.* She also says what so many other contemplatives have said in their discontent with simple faith and their disillusionment with the power of the Word of God: "Reading, studying or memorizing God's Word will only take us so far in our quest for spiritual growth."[43] This is my point—contemplatives teach that faith in Christ and dependence on His Word is just not enough—we need a trance-like mystical experience as well.

The pastors.com website is saturated with favorable comments, endorsements, and promotions of many contemplatives. On two separate occasions on the website, Warren makes reference to a book his wife, Kay, recommends:

> My wife, Kay, recommends this book: "It's a short book, but it hits at the heart of the minister. It mentions the struggles common to those of us in ministry: the temptation to be relevant, spectacular and powerful. *I highlighted almost every word!*"[44] (emphasis mine)

The book Kay Warren recommends is *In the Name of Jesus* by Henri Nouwen. Nouwen devotes an entire chapter of that book to contemplative prayer saying:

> Through the discipline of contemplative prayer, Christian leaders have to learn to listen to the voice of love . . . For Christian leadership to be truly fruitful in the future, a movement from the moral to the mystical is required.[45]

Anyone who knows something about the Warrens' background should not be surprised by their promotion of Nouwen. Rick Warren is a graduate of the Robert H. Schuller Institute for Successful Church Leadership. Schuller himself emphasized the impact that Nouwen had on his school:

---

*Technically, the Jesus Prayer is: *Jesus Christ, Son of God, have mercy on me, a sinner,* but it is often shortened to just the word *Jesus.*

All of our students have to watch and listen to Henri Nouwen. I keep interrupting and stopping the video machine, telling them to notice how he uses his hands, to look at the twinkle in his eye, to see how he connects his eye with the eye of the listener, to be aware of the words he uses—all positives, no negatives.[46]

The Warrens took Schuller's word for it with regard to Henri Nouwen. It's no wonder: The Warren's were greatly impacted by Schuller, according to a *Christianity Today* article, which quotes Kay Warren as saying, "He [Schuller] had a profound influence on Rick."[47]

Rick Warren and the Emerging Church

The emerging church movement, which I will discuss further in the next chapter, has gained the support of many Christian leaders. Rick Warren is one of those leaders who has actually helped to launch the movement. In Dan Kimball's popular book, *The Emerging Church*, Rick Warren wrote the foreword and said:

This book is a wonderful, detailed example of what a purpose-driven church can look like in a postmodern world. . . . Dan's book explains how to do it [reach an "emerging generation"] with the cultural-creatives who think and feel in postmodern terms. You need to pay attention to him [Kimball] because times are changing.[48]

Kimball's book describes different methods to reach this generation, including the use of "practicing silence, and lectio divina [a form of contemplative prayer]."[49] Kimball reinforces his promotion of the silence on his "Vintage Faith" website in an article he wrote titled "A-Maze-ing Prayer," which promotes the use of the labyrinth as a way of "Meeting God in the middle."[50]

The labyrinth (discussed more in the next chapter), used in ancient days, is a maze-like structure, which was originally designed to connect with God mystically. As participants walk through the labyrinth (sometimes called a prayer walk or prayer path), chanting words or phrases (centering down), the idea is that by the time they have *centered* their souls, they will reach the center of the labyrinth. Dan Kimball expresses his admiration for the labyrinth, saying:

> Meditative prayer like that we experienced in the labyrinth resonates with hearts of emerging generations. If we had the room, we would set up a permanent labyrinth to promote deeper prayer.[51]

In the back of *The Emerging Church*, under the recommended resources section, Kimball lists several books written by contemplatives. Some of these include *Sacred Pathways* by Gary Thomas, *Renovation of the Heart* by Dallas Willard, *Messy Spirituality* by Mike Yaconelli, *In the Name of Jesus* by Henri Nouwen, *Book of Uncommon Prayer* by Steve Case, and *Four Views of the Church in Postmodern Culture* by Leonard Sweet. All of these authors share one thing in common—the belief that we need the *silence* to draw close to God, and *that* silence is reached through contemplative prayer.

Not only did Rick Warren write the foreword to Kimball's book, but, in random spots throughout the book, he has written side-bar commentaries—seventeen of them to be exact. Of his commentaries, only one was negative and that was over a minor point. Nowhere in the book is there any indication that Warren was not in full support of Kimball's views. Warren made comments such as:

- "This book is a wonderful detailed example."[52]
- "Thank you so much for sharing your background, Dan . . . Go for it."[53]
- "This is so important!"[54]
- "An outstanding chapter, Dan!"[55]

The question must be asked, *is* Rick Warren promoting and endorsing the emerging church movement? This is a valid question considering the fact that the emerging church movement is immersed in contemplative spirituality and other metaphysical practices. Certainly, by writing the foreword to the emerging church signature book, it would be safe to assume the answer is yes!

We can confirm this answer by taking another look at Warren's weekly e-newsletter that goes out to thousands of pastors around the world. In the July 6th, 2005 issue, he devoted the issue to the emerging church movement, including his own feature article titled "Sharing Eternal Truth With an Ever-Emerging Culture." One of the recommended links in that issue was to an organization called, *The Ooze*, where lies a hub of articles, books, and links for emerging and contemplative spirituality. Spencer Burke, the organization's director, features his own book *Making Sense of the Church* on *The Ooze* website. In that book, Burke states:

> I was struck by the incredible wisdom that could be found apart from the "approved" evangelical reading list. A Trappist monk, [Thomas] Merton gave me a new appreciation for the meaning of community. His *New Man and New Seeds of Contemplation* touched my heart in ways other religious books had not. Not long afterward my thinking was stretched again, this time by Thich Nhat Hanh—a Buddhist monk . . . Hanh's *Living Buddha, Living Christ* gave me insight into Jesus from *an Eastern perspective*.[56] (emphasis mine)

This is just one quote that is indicative of the mindset that permeates *The Ooze* website. Why would Warren list that as a recommended site if he were not behind this philosophy? He knows that nearly 150,000 pastors receive his newsletter and that many will share the information with their congregations. It is potentially possible then that millions of people around the world are being influenced by Warren's newsletters each week. In that same issue of his weekly e-newsletter, Warren posted a statement from several of the leading emerging church leaders, including Brian McLaren, Dan Kimball, Tony Jones, Spencer Burke, and Doug Pagitt. Doug Pagitt, pastor of Solomon's Porch in Minneapolis, Minnesota, is an advocate of *Christian* yoga. In his book, *Church Re-Imagined*, Pagitt devotes most of one chapter to the subject, speaking of it in a most favorable manner, giving specific instruction and encouraging the practice.

In essence, Rick Warren has become a conduit for spreading the contemplative message worldwide. He said as much when he avidly endorsed the spiritual formation movement in the *Purpose Driven Church*. Perhaps the most revealing endorsement that illustrates Warren's sympathies toward contemplative spirituality is his promotion and connection to author and futurist Leonard Sweet. Sweet is said to be "one of the church's most important and provocative thinkers."[57] He is a popular lecturer and many of his books are published by Zondervan (Warren's publisher also).

The connections between the two men include a 1994 audio set titled *The Tides of Change*. In the set, Warren and Sweet talk about "new frontiers," "changing times" and a "new spirituality" on the horizon.

Later, in Sweet's 2001 book, *Soul Tsunami*, Warren gives an endorsement that sits on the back as well as on the front cover of the book. Of the book, Warren says:

> Leonard Sweet . . . suggests practical ways to communicate God's unchanging truth to our changing world.[58]

Some of these "practical ways" include using a labyrinth and visiting a meditation center.[59] Sweet also says, "It's time for a Post Modern Reformation,"[60] adding that "The wind of spiritual awakening is blowing across the waters."[61] He says that times are changing and you'd better "Reinvent yourself for the 21st century or die."[62]

To better understand Leonard Sweet's spirituality, I would like to draw your attention to a book he wrote a few years prior to the *Tides of Change* audio set—*Quantum Spirituality*. I highly recommend you take a look at this book yourself—Sweet has now placed the book on his website at www.leonardsweet.com in a format easy to download, which, of course, shows that he still promotes its message.

The acknowledgments section of *Quantum Spirituality* shows very clearly Sweet's spiritual sympathies. In it, Sweet thanks interspiritualists/universalists such as Matthew Fox (author of *The Coming of the Cosmic Christ*), Episcopalian priest/mystic Morton Kelsey, Willis Harman (author of *Global Mind Change*) and Ken Wilber (one of the major intellectuals in the New Age movement) for helping him to find what he calls "New Light."[63] Sweet adds that he trusts "the Spirit that led the author of *The Cloud of Unknowing*."[64]

In the preface of the same book, Sweet disseminates line after line of suggestions that the "old teachings" of Christianity must be replaced with new teachings of "the New Light." And yet these new teachings, he believes, will draw from "ancient teachings" (the Desert Fathers). This "New Light movement," Sweet says, is a "radical faith commitment that is willing to dance to a *new rhythm*."[65]

Throughout the book, Sweet favorably uses terms like *Christ consciousness* and *higher self* and in no uncertain terms promotes New Age ideology:

> [Quantum spirituality is] a structure of human becoming, a channeling of Christ energies through mindbody experience.[66]

The Bible does not describe Jesus Christ as an energy channeling its way in and through us. Without a doubt, this is New Age lingo. The wonderful thing about the Gospel that is presented in Scripture is that Jesus Christ is presented as a personal God who loves us and will have a relationship with anyone who, by faith, comes to the Father through Him. This is where the contemplatives have it wrong. They believe that through this meditative prayer they can reach God.

Sweet also tells his readers that humanity and creation are united as one and we must realize it. Once humanity comes to this realization, Sweet says:

> Then, and only then, will a New Light movement of "world-making" faith have helped to create the world that is to, and may yet, be. Then, and only then, will earthlings have uncovered the meaning . . . of the last words [Thomas Merton] uttered: "We are already one. But we imagine that we are not. And what we have to recover is our original unity."[67]

Leonard Sweet is what could be called an *Alice Bailey Christian* because his views on the role of mysticism in the church are evident. He states:

> Mysticism, once cast to the sidelines of the Christian tradition, is now situated in postmodernist culture near the center. . . . In the words of one of the greatest theologians of the twentieth century, Jesuit philosopher of religion/dogmatist Karl Rahner, "The Christian of tomorrow will be a mystic, one who has experienced something, or he will be nothing." [Mysticism] is metaphysics arrived at through mindbody experiences. Mysticism begins in experience; it ends in theology.[68]

It is this same mysticism (i.e., contemplative prayer) that I believe Rick Warren is also promoting. Warren extends his promotion and endorsement of Sweet to his pastors.com website. Nearly a dozen times Sweet is referred to positively, including an article *featuring* Sweet and another article written *by* him.

You Cannot Serve Both Man and God

While the fact remains that Warren is promoting contemplative prayer through his endorsements and recommendations of numerous contemplative authors and teachers, he takes his sympathies towards this a step further by enlisting contemplatives to teach people who have come under his Purpose Driven wing.

For the past several years, Youth Specialties, a youth-oriented organization, has hosted an annual event called the National Pastor's Convention. Each year the event brings in many contemplative speakers such as Richard Foster, Brennan Manning, Ruth Haley Barton, and others. Available to the convention attendees are an on-site labyrinth, late-night contemplative prayer sessions, and workshops on contemplative prayer, emerging church, and yoga. In 2004, Warren was a featured speaker at this event and in fact spoke right after a yoga workshop.[69]

Some may say that this is hardly enough proof to link someone, that maybe Warren didn't know these activities (yoga, labyrinths, etc.) would be taking place at the conference. Fair enough. However, the following year (2005), Warren invited leaders *from* Youth Specialties to teach at his new Purpose Driven Youth Ministry conference.[70] Surely if he did not agree with Youth Specialties' spiritual persuasions, he would not incorporate its leaders into his own events. Rick Warren's involvement with Youth Specialties is evident. Even Saddleback's youth pastor, Doug Fields, has participated as a speaker at several Youth Specialties events; and in Warren's February 1st, 2006 e-newsletter, Warren promoted Youth Specialties again, linking to it as a place to find resources for youth ministries. "Resources" on the Youth Specialties website that week included books like *The Sacred Way* by emerging church author Tony Jones, *Soul Shaper: Exploring Spirituality and Contemplative Practices in Youth Ministry*, also by Jones, and several *Bible* studies by Youth Specialties president Mark Oestreicher. Recent comments made by Oestreicher on his Internet blog site are disturbing and no doubt confusing to many young people:

"Christianity IS an Eastern religion."[71]

"[Y]oga is really just about stretching and slowing down."[72]

"If a Buddhist is using a breathing exercise to bring some peace to her life, well, bless her. But that should have no bearing on whether or not I choose to focus on my God-created breath."[73]

Youth Specialties also features a book titled *Enjoy the Silence* by Maggie and Duffy Robbins. Maggie Robbins was trained in a five-year course at Kairos School of Spiritual Formation. Kairos trains people in contemplative spirituality and has a course reading list that includes Thomas Keating, Henri Nouwen and Thomas Merton. Duffy Robbins is an associate staff member of Youth Specialties and a speaker at the Purpose Driven Youth Ministry Conference.

Rick Warren says that contemplative prayer is a "hot topic"—in saying that, surely he is aware of the issue. With so many connections to contemplative prayer, it appears that he is not only aware of it, but he is an advocate of it. Because of his level of influence, he will be able to spread contemplative prayer more than Richard Foster or Thomas Merton ever could have hoped for.

In the spring of 2005, someone handed me a book called *A Life with Purpose* by George Mair. The book is written as a positive account of Rick Warren's life. In fact, the subtitle on the front cover reads: *America's Most Inspiring Pastor*. It is clear that the author had a great admiration for Warren. While Mair wrote the book, he spent many Sunday mornings at Saddleback church services, listening to Rick Warren and donating financially. However, after Rick Warren found out about the book, he publicly criticized it. In addition, Saddleback church sent out e-mails to an undisclosed number of people, discrediting Mair's book.[74]

I personally believe Warren's effort to debunk the book was an attempt to conceal some of its observations. What George Mair didn't realize was that in his candid account of Warren, and in his efforts to offer this testament of praise, some things were revealed about the pastor that might have gone undetected by the average person. For instance, Mair explains how New Age prophet Norman Vincent Peale was at the foundation of the church-growth movement and furthermore "many of Peale's uplifting affirmations originated with an 'obscure teacher of occult science' named Florence Scovel Shinn."[75] Referring to many of the methods that Peale taught and his "unification of psychology and religion,"[76] Mair says, "Saddleback distinctly bears the stamp of Reverend Norman Vincent Peale."[77]

It was in Mair's book that I discovered Warren's connections with New Age sympathizer Ken Blanchard. In November of 2003, Rick Warren announced to his Saddleback congregation his global P.E.A.C.E. Plan. In the same sermon, Warren introduced the congregation to Ken Blanchard, playing a video clip of Blanchard's visit to Saddleback a few days earlier. Warren informed his large congregation that Blanchard had:

. . . signed on to help with the P.E.A.C.E. Plan, and he's going to be helping train us in leadership and in how to train others to be leaders all around the world.[78]

So who is Ken Blanchard? Surely, if Rick Warren has enough confidence in Blanchard to have him help train people to become leaders around the world and help with his P.E.A.C.E. Plan, then Warren must trust Blanchard's spirituality.

Blanchard is the author of the bestselling book, *The One Minute Manager*, a highly popular book, known in both the Christian and the secular world. He is also the founder of an organization called *Lead Like Jesus*. Blanchard became a Christian in the mid-eighties, yet he has had an interesting track record of books he has endorsed or written forewords to, comments he has made, and organizations he has been connected with. In a 2001 book titled *What Would Buddha Do at Work?*, Blanchard tells readers in the foreword:

> Buddha points to the path and invites us to begin our journey to enlightenment. I . . . invite you to begin (or continue) your journey to enlightened work.[79]

We also find Blanchard writing the foreword to another book, *Mind Like Water* by Jim Ballard. In the book, Ballard describes methods for practicing Eastern/New Age meditation. Ballard states:

> I signed up for the yoga meditation lessons . . . founded by Paramahansa Yogananda [a Hindu guru]. . . . I had evidently reached a level of consciousness beyond the usual . . . I continue to consider meditation far and away the most important thing I do.[80]

And yet, of the book, Blanchard writes glowing remarks:

> Jim Ballard's wonderful book *Mind Like Water* . . . I hope that you and countless other readers will find in *Mind Like Water* some ways to calm your mind and uplift your consciousness.[81]

Incidentally, Ballard is one of the trainers for the Ken Blanchard Companies. That shouldn't be much of a surprise though—practically all of the endorsements and forewords written by Ken Blanchard are for books written by clairvoyants, mystics, Buddhists, and others with affinities similar to Jim Ballard. It is important to note that Blanchard's endorsements are wholehearted. He never says things like, "While I disagree with the New Age meditation techniques this book promotes, I believe the author has some helpful points on business management (Blanchard's forte)." On the contrary, his endorsements never have any such disclaimers and in fact often recommend meditation techniques and practices.

Some may say that Blanchard wrote these comments when he was a young Christian, but when you look at the history of these endorsements, you see that the longer Blanchard has been a professing Christian, the more blatant the endorsements have become. For example, in the summer of 2005 a book titled *In the Sphere of Silence* was released. The book is a metaphysical manual on meditation (i.e., altered states of consciousness). Author Vijay Eswaran teaches in his book:

> The Sphere of Silence, if it is practiced properly, is a very powerful tool. It is not just oriented to any one religion, it is universally accepted and practiced by almost all faiths on the planet. It is through silence that you find your inner being.[82]

On the author's website, Blanchard gives this glowing endorsement of *In the Sphere of Silence:*

> Effective leadership is more than what we do; it starts on the inside. Great Leaders are able to tap inner wisdom and strength by cultivating the habit of solitude. This book is a wonderful guide on how to enter the realm of silence and draw closer to God.[83]

In early 2006, a book called *The 10-Minute Energy Solution* by Jon Gordon hit the market. The book is filled with suggestions on how to improve energy levels through meditation, yoga, breathing exercises, and other such techniques. Throughout the book, Gordon quotes favorably from the Dalai Lama, meditator Daniel Goleman, Thich Nhat Hanh, New Agers Marilyn Ferguson and Wayne Dyer, and from *A Course in Miracles.** Gordon promotes panentheism (God in all) by saying things such as: "You came from this source [speaking of God] and you are this source."[84]

On the back cover of Gordon's book, Blanchard says:

> Jon Gordon is a master at teaching people the power of positive energy. If you want to increase your joy and effectiveness, as well as your energy level, read this book.[85]

But perhaps Blanchard's most telling involvement with the New Age is his role with an organization called The Hoffman Institute, home of the Hoffman Quadrinity Process. Not only has he given a strong endorsement for the program, saying (after he partook of it) that it "made my spirituality come alive"[86] but is also a current board member of the Hoffman Institute, along with several New Agers. This is an organization that was founded by a psychic and is based on panentheism (i.e., God is in all) and meditation! In the book, *The Hoffman Process,* the institute's mystical perspective is laid out clearly:

> I am you and you are me. We are all parts of the whole.
> . . . You can use a short meditation to remind yourself of this connection to all others in this world of ours. . . .
> As you breathe, feel that breath coming from your core essence . . . When you are open to life, you start noticing the *divine in everything.*[87] (emphasis mine)

Like Leonard Sweet, Ken Blanchard is another Alice Bailey Christian or what some may refer to as a New Age sympathizer. He professes to know Christ, but his connections and affinity to the New Age are unmistakable.

---

*A channeled work.

In view of Blanchard's New Age sympathies and connections, how can he *lead people to be like Jesus*? Not only has Rick Warren allowed Blanchard to "sign on to help" with his global P.E.A.C.E. Plan, but Warren is also a board member of Blanchard's *Lead Like Jesus* organization, along with meditation promoters Laurie Beth Jones and Mark Victor Hansen (*Chicken Soup for the Soul* co-author—see page 93). On the *Lead Like Jesus* website, in an introductory paragraph preceding the list of board members, the following is stated:

> . . . guided by a board of men and women who have discovered the power and potential of leading like Jesus. These board members come from all over the country and from all arenas of life, but they all share a common goal: to see that the Lead Like Jesus Movement be extended across the US and to the farthest reaches of the earth.[88]

There are two questions to be asked here. First, if Rick Warren has been part of a board that is *guiding* Ken Blanchard, how is it possible that Blanchard came to endorse and participate in all those New Age books and activities? With over twenty members on that board, many of them professing Christians, including David McQuiston (representing Focus on the Family)* it would only make sense that someone would have told Blanchard that a book called *What Would Buddha Do At Work?* was not a book that should be endorsed by a Christian. The second question is what "common goal" does Rick Warren have with Ken Blanchard, Mark Victor Hansen, and Laurie Beth Jones? Jones, author of *Jesus CEO*, makes the following comments that clearly expose her beliefs:

> My personal mission and vision is to Recognize, Promote and Inspire Divine Connection in Myself and Others.[89]
> Jesus regularly visualized the success of his efforts.[90]

---

* According to a Focus on the Family phone representative, McQuiston is no longer with Focus on the Family. Their name has since been removed from the Lead Like Jesus list.

Jesus was full of self-knowledge and self-love. His "I am" statements were what he became.[91]

More recently, in another book of Jones, she says that Jesus "wanted everyone to see their connection to each other, and to God,"[92] and admits she has been "challenged by the concept of meditation" leading to her decision to "experience the sheer silence of meditation—undirected prayer."[93] In her book, *The Path*, Jones favorably quotes both a Zen Buddhist teacher (Thich Nhat Hanh) and a Sufi poet. Quoting the poet, Jones says:

> "The universe surrenders to a mind that is still." And in order to truly find The Path, each of us must loosen our minds, and begin from a point of wonder and openness—of being willing to *not* know. We must receive, before we can begin to give.[94]

Rick Warren and Ken Blanchard have also shared speaking platforms together at *Lead Like Jesus* events, at Willow Creek's Leadership Summits, and at other conferences. And in 2004, a seminar took place at Saddleback called the *Preaching and Purpose Driven Life Training Workshop for Chaplains*, a seminar for training Army chaplains. Warren was one of the speakers, and resources used for the seminar included those from Ken Blanchard.

Just prior to the release of this second edition of *A Time of Departing* Blanchard has come out with a book titled *Lead Like Jesus*. The book, which is endorsed by Rick Warren, presents "habits" Blanchard says leaders need to cultivate. One of those is the habit he calls solitude, which is to be practiced, he says, for a forty-five minute time period. Taking into account the endorsements and forewords Blanchard has authored, it is easy to see what he means when he says:

> Before we send people off for their period of solitude, we have them recite with us Psalm 46:10 in this way: Be still and know that I am God. Be still and know. Be still. Be. When people return from their time of solitude, they have big smiles on their faces. While many of them found it difficult to quiet their mind, they say it was a

powerful experience. The reality is most of us spend little
if any time in solitude. Yet if we don't, how can God have
a chance to talk with us?[95]

During Blanchard's instruction on going into solitude, he tells
participants to practice a *palms-down, palms up* exercise, which is
another ritual or practice often used by contemplatives. By Rick
Warren endorsing Blanchard's book, *Lead Like Jesus*, he, in effect,
promotes his spirituality also.

A Slippery Slope

I realize there are serious ramifications regarding the issues discussed
here. What I am saying is that Rick Warren is part of the effort to bring
contemplative prayer into mainstream Christianity. Remember, Warren
makes favorable reference to Dallas Willard and Richard Foster in *The
Purpose Driven Church*. He sees Willard as being on the same level as
Foster in the spiritual formation movement (i.e., contemplative prayer
movement). In Willard's book, *The Spirit of the Disciplines*, the title of
which sounds very close to Foster's book, *Celebration of Discipline*, Willard quotes Merton and Nouwen and extols the practice of the silence:

> In silence we close off our souls from "sounds," whether
> those sounds be noise, music, or words. . . . Many people
> have *never* experienced silence and do not even know that
> they do *not* know what it is.[96]

Like Foster, Willard sees this *spiritual discipline* as the most
powerful way to commune with God. He maintains:

> It is a powerful and essential discipline. *Only silence* will allow us
> life-transforming concentration upon God.[97] (emphasis mine)

Dallas Willard, like Rick Warren, is a Southern Baptist. This
shows the extent to which the mystical paradigm shift is unfolding
within the largest protestant denomination in the nation. The
alignment of the Purpose Driven movement and the spiritual

formation movement has truly monumental ramifications, ones that will, should the Lord tarry, affect generations to come, if successful. If this sounds somewhat dramatic or alarmist, I feel I have justification for it. If you are trying to make up your mind on whether or not Foster, Willard, Warren, et al., are on the right track regarding the *discipline of silence*, please consider this—on the back cover of *The Spirit of the Disciplines* there is a glowing endorsement of the book, which states:

> A profound call to discipleship based on spiritual disciplines [that] awakens us to a forgotten truth, that the transformation to Christ-likeness is realized through taking on the "easy yoke" of the disciplines.[98]

At that time, the person who wrote this endorsement was writing her own books on the value of contemplative spirituality. She was delving into the *Christian* mystical tradition with all of her heart and soul. The person is Sue Monk Kidd!

As you decide for yourself whether Rick Warren's embrace of the contemplative has any consequential significance at all, remember the words of Sue Monk Kidd where she echoes the very essence of Thomas Merton in the conclusions she arrived at:

> I am speaking of recognizing the hidden truth that we are one with *all people*. We are part of them and they are part of us . . . When we encounter another person . . . we should walk as if we were upon *holy ground*. We should respond as if *God* dwells there.[99] (emphasis mine)

These words are alarming when we consider that she started as a Sunday School teacher!

When Rick Warren accepted Ken Blanchard's "sign-on" back in November 2003, Blanchard was sitting on the board of an occult organization. Please reflect on this. He was not just a member of the Hoffman Institute, but on its board! This is the man who would supposedly train Warren's leaders. Over two years later Blanchard is *still* on that board.

Contemplative spirituality, as I have demonstrated time and again, is a slippery slope that leads to interspirituality and the delusion that divinity is within every human being, thereby rendering the message of the Cross unnecessary and the truth of the Gospel void. That is the ultimate tragedy where the hope of the world has been stolen from the hearts of men as they slumbered.

> While the bridegroom tarried, they all slumbered and slept. (Matthew 25:5)

The Christian of the Future?

Within the evangelical world, contemplative prayer is increasingly being promoted and accepted. As a result, it is losing its esoteric aspect and is now seen by many as the wave of the future. One can't help but notice the positive exposure it is getting in the Christian media these days. In *Today's Christian Woman*, a popular and trusted Christian magazine, feature titles make the appeal to *draw closer to God*. The author of one such article says, "Like a growing number of evangelicals, I've turned to spiritual direction because I want to know God better."[1] But without exception, every person she cites is a dedicated contemplative, one being Ruth Haley Barton, author of *Invitation to Solitude and Silence*. Barton was trained at the Shalem Institute (founded by Tilden Edwards), and in fact, that organization was featured in the article as a resource for the reader. However, considering the content of many statements on the Shalem Institute website, how could Shalem even be listed as a resource for Christians? Listen to a few:

> In Christianity and other traditions that understand God to be present everywhere, contemplation includes a reverence for the Divine Mystery, "finding God in all

things," or "being open to God's presence, however it may
appear."[2]

[Thomas] Merton taught that there is only one way to
develop this radical language of prayer: in silence.[3]

The rhythm of the group includes . . . chanting, two
periods of sitting in silence separated by walking
meditation, and a time for optional sharing.[4]

In another magazine article, Ruth Haley Barton, who incidentally
is the former Associate Director of Spiritual Formation at Willow Creek
Community Church, echoes Sue Monk Kidd in many ways, including
the general malaise or condition of the human soul. Barton recounts:

A few years ago, I began to recognize an inner chaos in
my soul . . . No matter how much I prayed, read the
Bible, and listened to good teaching, I could not calm
the internal roar created by questions with no answers.[5]

The following scenario Barton relates could be the wave of the
future for the evangelical church if this movement continues to unfold
in the manner it already has:

I sought out a spiritual director, someone well versed in the
ways of the soul . . . eventually this wise woman said to me
. . . "What you need is stillness and silence so that the sediment
can settle and the water can become clear." . . . I decided to
accept this invitation to move beyond my addiction to words.[6]

By "addiction to words," she means normal ways of praying. She
still uses words, but only three of them, "Here I am." This is nothing
other than the *Cloud of Unknowing* or the *prayer of the heart.*
Like Richard Foster, Barton argues that God cannot be reached
adequately, if at all, without the silence. In referring to 1 Kings 19
when Elijah was hiding in a cave, Barton encourages:

God loves us enough to wait for us to come openly to Him. Elijah's experience shows that God doesn't scream to get our attention. Instead, we learn that our willingness to listen in silence opens up a quiet space in which we can hear His voice, a voice that longs to speak and offer us guidance for our next step.[7]

What Barton fails to mention here is that Elijah was a valiant defender of the belief in the one, unique God—Yahweh (as seen in his encounter with the 450 prophets of Baal), and he never went into an altered state of silence in his personal encounter with God.

Barton is no longer teaching at Willow Creek. She left there to start the Transforming Center and now teaches pastors and other Christian leaders spiritual formation. Hers is just one of many avenues through which contemplative prayer is creating a new kind of Christian, possibly the Christian of the future.

The Emerging Church

The emerging church movement has been on the scene for quite some time now, hovering in the background but is now advancing boldly to the forefront. In fact, Brian McLaren, one of the emerging church leaders, was named by *Time* magazine as one of the 25 most influential evangelical leaders in the country. The emerging (or emergent) church (sometimes called the progressive church), as the term implies, offers the younger generation (known as post-modernists), a completely different approach to living the Christian life. For many *emergents*, even the seeker-friendly method is seen as seriously lacking what is needed to impart a sense of the sacred.

A number of books have come out explaining and promoting the objectives of this supposedly new form of spirituality. As I pointed out in the last chapter, one of the more popular books is Dan Kimball's book *The Emerging Church*. This book explains how post-modernists think and feel very differently from other generations. Kimball says:

The basis of learning has shifted from logic and rational, systematic thought to the realm of experience. People increasingly long for the mystical and the spiritual rather than the evidential and facts-based faith of the modern soil.[8]

What the emergent movement draws upon to accommodate these experience-hungry young Christians is called *vintage Christianity*. The meaning of this term is self-evident. Vintage refers to something good from the past. Therefore, this type of Christianity draws from knowledge or practices from antiquity. As you might have guessed, these are the spiritual disciplines drawn from mysticism. Kimball writes:

> Emerging generations, in their search for proven, ancient, authentic forms of connection with God, are very much attracted to these ancient disciplines and historical spiritual rituals. Their willingness to participate is much stronger than many of us may have realized.[9]

Tony Jones, another major voice within this movement, writes and speaks widely on the subject of the emergent church. In his book, *The Sacred Way*, we again find the theme that continually resurfaces among those who have embraced mystical prayer:

> I was raised in a nice, Midwestern, church-going family. . . . I had more head-knowledge about faith, religion, whatever you want to call it, than a person should, but I really didn't seem to be able to put it into practice. . . . Maybe somewhere along the line some of them [Christians over the last 2,000 years] had come up with ways of connecting with God that could help people like me.[10]

After years of frustration, Jones turned to the contemplative approach in an effort to draw closer to God and listen to His voice. He devotes entire chapters in his book to such subjects as the *Cloud of Unknowing*, centering prayer, and the prayer of the heart. He explains:

> The basic method promoted in *The Cloud* is to move beyond thinking into a place of utter stillness with the Lord . . . the believer must first achieve a state of

silence and contemplation, and then God works in the
believer's heart.[11]

If this sounds a lot like Foster's vision of Christianity, it's because
it is. In a feature article in *Christianity Today* titled "The Emergent
Mystique," Brian McLaren, who is the man referred to as the "de
facto leader" of this movement, named Richard Foster as one of the
"key mentors for the emerging church."[12]

McLaren himself is a prime example of where we are headed
if contemplative prayer continues to become more accepted and
widespread. Episcopalian Bishop Alan Jones, in his book titled *Reimagining Christianity,* insists that it is vital for the church to go in
the direction of mystical prayer. He explains that in the context of:

> . . . the life of contemplative prayer . . . Loved and in
> communion with all things, the soul is born in and out
> of the secret silence of God. This silence at the heart of
> mysticism is not only the meeting point of the great
> traditions but also where all hearts might meet.[13]

The result of this meeting point of silence is, of course,
interspirituality, as Jones states:

> But another ancient strand of Christianity teaches that we
> are all caught up in the Divine Mystery we call God, that the
> *Spirit is in everyone,* and that there are depths of interpretation
> yet to be plumbed. . . . At the cathedral we "break the bread"
> for those who follow the path of the Buddha and walk the
> way of the Hindus.[14] (emphasis mine)

This type of thinking has, in the past, been very much opposed
by those in the Evangelical church. The goal was to evangelize the
Hindus and Buddhists, to bring them into the Body of Christ through
faith in Jesus Christ. But Brian McLaren is more in tune with Jones'
view of an interspiritual Christianity. McLaren has endorsed the back
cover of *Reimagining Christianity* stating:

It used to be that Christian institutions and systems of dogma sustained the spiritual life of Christians. Increasingly, spirituality itself is what sustains everything else. Alan Jones is a pioneer in reimagining a Christian faith that emerges from authentic spirituality. *His work stimulates and encourages me deeply.*[15] (emphasis mine)

This "authentic spirituality" is the same spirituality that drives the emergent church movement. As you can see, the philosophy downplays biblical doctrine and emphasizes the mystical experiential realms.

Mike Perschon, a former free-lance writer for Youth Specialties, wrote of his exploration of the mystical life:

I started using the phrase "listening prayer" when I talked about my own experiences in meditation. I built myself a prayer room—a tiny sanctuary in a basement closet filled with books on spiritual disciplines, contemplative prayer, and Christian mysticism. In that space I lit candles, burned incense, hung rosaries, and listened to tapes of Benedictine monks. I meditated for hours on words, images, and sounds. I reached the point of being able to achieve *alpha brain patterns*, the state in which dreams occur, while still awake and meditating.[16] (emphasis mine)

When I hear a Christian talking like this, it creates a very deep concern within me for that person because I know what is meant by "alpha." In Laurie Cabot's book, *Power of the Witch*, alpha is a term she uses extensively to mean meditation or the silence. In fact, she makes no secret of it but confides:

The science of Witchcraft is based on our ability to enter an altered state of consciousness we call "alpha." In alpha the mind opens up to nonordinary forms of communication, such as telepathy, clairvoyance, and precognition. Here we also may experience out-of-the-body sensations and psychokinesis, or *receive mystical, visionary information* that does not come through the five senses. In alpha the rational filters that process ordinary reality are weakened or removed, and the mind is receptive to nonordinary realities.[17] (emphasis mine)

The importance of this practice is made clear throughout Cabot's book. Without it, there is no "power." She explains:

Alpha is the springboard for all psychic and magical workings. It is the heart of Witchcraft. . . . You must master it first before proceeding to any other spell, ritual, or exercise in this book.[18]

Many of those involved in the emergent movement would cry out in protest, "Now, wait a minute—Perschon is not into witchcraft. He is a devoted Christian trying to walk deeply with the Lord. He hates anything to do with darkness or the occult. How *dare* you compare him with Laurie Cabot!" But Cabot, in one of her statements, makes the very point of my whole book when she says:

Mystics in every religious tradition speak of alpha states of consciousness and the lure of Divine Light, although they do so in their own metaphors and images. In their own ways they have learned how to enter alpha as they pray or worship. They learn how to become enlightened.[19]

For an explanation of Witchcraft or Wicca, please refer back to chapter one of this book. Under the heading, "Why Do They Call It the New Age" is a quote stating, "to see God as 'the All in All.'"[20] This is the occultic view of God found in Wicca.

In a book titled *The Contemplative Experience*, the writer presents the point of view that could be expressed by any of the contemplatives over the past 1,700 years. Speaking of Bernard of Clairvaux:

He realized that God permeates the whole of creation. His experience was that God is the "stone in the stones, the tree in the trees," and in the same way, the center point

of his own soul. *God resides at the heart of all that exists.*[21]
(emphasis mine, see page 14)

The emerging church movement has made wide inroads into the Christian church. And with its emphasis on the metaphysical and its de-emphasis on biblical doctrine, this has had detrimental results in the spiritual lives of countless people. Christian publishers are publishing dozens of books a year that are written by emerging church leaders. Baker Books has released books by contemplative proponents Calvin Miller, James Wakefield (on lectio divina), and the late Robert Webber. In the spring of 2007, Baker released a book titled *Emergent Manifesto*, edited and written by the who's who of emerging church writers. Zondervan is particularly zealous in its release of books that promote the emerging church. Their list of authors includes Henri Nouwen, Tony Jones, Dan Kimball, and a number of others.

Christian colleges, seminaries, and even Christian high schools are increasingly incorporating these books into their course. One emerging church leader who has been especially popular in Christian high schools and youth groups is Rob Bell, former pastor of Mars Hill Bible Church in Michigan and author of *Velvet Elvis*. He is also the creator of the mini-films called *Noomas* (from the Greek word, pneuma; meaning spirit or breath). Bell is very open about his affinities towards the mystical when he states: "We're rediscovering Christianity as an Eastern religion, as a way of life."[22] Bell revealed more about his spiritual foundations when he invited a Dominican sister from the Dominican Center at Marywood in Michigan to speak at a church service at Mars Hill.[23] The Dominican Center has a *Spirituality center*, which offers a wide variety of contemplative opportunities, including Reiki, a Spiritual Formation program, a Spiritual Director program, labyrinths, Celtic Spirituality, and more. Bell stated in this service how much this sister had taught him in his spiritual walk. This is a very sobering revelation when we consider Bell's influence with so many young people.

Labyrinths

As more and more churches are becoming enveloped in contemplative spirituality, many ancient practices are being implemented. One of these is the labyrinth, a maze-like structure that dates back thousands of years. The practice was introduced into modern-day Christianity and made popular largely through the efforts of Dr. Lauren Artress,* author of *Walking a Sacred Path: Rediscovering the Labyrinth as a Spiritual Tool.*

The labyrinth is not actually a true maze in which several different paths exist. The labyrinth has one path to the center and the same one back out. In Buddhism, the labyrinth is called a mandala or sacred design. Those walking the labyrinth will generally engage in centering or contemplative prayer by repeating a chosen word or phrase while they walk, with the hope that when they reach the center of the labyrinth, they will have also *centered down* and reached the *divinity within.* These labyrinths are popping up all over the place including in many evangelical churches.

Drawing of a labyrinth

But is this *divinity* actually God who is being reached? Listen to a woman named Judith (from San Francisco's Grace Cathedral) describe her own labyrinth experience:

> I made my way with ease along the curving path. I remember feeling light, praying prayers of gratefulness to

---

*Dr. Artress is Canon at Grace Cathedral church in San Francisco.

all the spirits that we had called on during our ritual. . .
. First I saw a shimmering, undulating, configuration of
rectangles—vortices of energy above the labyrinth. And
then I saw beings of light-blue in hue, faceless but human
in form in solemn procession as if on their own labyrinth.
. . . I felt wonderful to be sharing the space with these
beings—angels, guardians, of the labyrinth. The labyrinth
was a gateway for me into the unseen world that seems
to accompany us always.[24]

Many proponents of the labyrinth say that anyone can walk the
labyrinth and reach divinity. It doesn't matter what religion one is,
or if he has any religion at all.

But if this were true, it would mean Jesus Christ could be bypassed
in order to reach God. Scripture clearly states Jesus is the only mediator between man and God. And according to Judith's experience, she
came into contact with spirit beings rather than this truth.

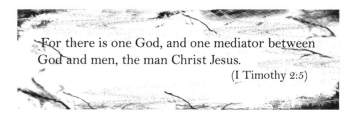

For there is one God, and one mediator between
God and men, the man Christ Jesus.
(I Timothy 2:5)

When one looks around, it is more than just the emerging
church that has grasped onto the labyrinth. At one time, Youth For
Christ offered a Labyrinth Kit on their online store, while numerous Christian colleges and seminaries have added prayer paths (i.e.,
labyrinths) to their campuses, and many different denominations,
including Baptist and Presbyterian, have picked up on the trend. A
simple Google search shows that labyrinth use is increasing steadily.
In March of 2004, there were about 116,000 web pages that listed
the word "labyrinths." Just a decade later, there were over three and
a half million web pages!

Ancient Practices for Youth

The cover of the July/August 1999 issue of *Group Magazine*, a leading resource magazine for Christian youth leaders, featured a teenage girl, eyes shut, doing contemplative prayer. The article, "Ancient-Future Youth Ministry" begins by declaring:

> It's Sunday just after 5 p.m. . . . . Seven adults are sitting around a "Christ-candle" in the youth room. There is no talking, no laughter. For 10 minutes, the only noise is the sound of their breathing . . . now it's 7 p.m.—one hour into the night's youth group gathering. There are 18 senior highers and five adults sitting in a candlelit sanctuary. A gold cross stands on a table. . . . They're chanting the "Jesus Prayer," an ancient meditative practice.[25]

The article discusses two Christian organizations, Youth Specialties and San Francisco Theological Seminary (Presbyterian Church, USA), which teamed together in 1996 to develop an approach to youth ministry that incorporates contemplative practices.[26] Mark Yaconelli, son of the former director of Youth Specialties, the late Mike Yaconelli, was hired to direct the project, which was called the Youth Ministry & Spirituality Project. The article is very open to the fact that sacred word repetition was at the heart of this project. These two organizations sponsored the project in sixteen churches of various denominations. The article reveals that, in all sixteen test congregations, middle school and senior high youth "were eager to learn contemplative spiritual practices."[27] One of the church's associate pastors even went so far as to say, "We shouldn't be surprised it's working so well. It's kind of a no-brainer. If you make the space, the spirit will come."[28] According to the project's mission statement, this model will soon be "made immediately available to youth ministries nationwide."[29]

Just how widespread did this become? In 1997, the Project received a grant from the Lilly Endowment to test a "spiritual formation model." Furthermore:

Youth ministry leaders were trained to meet regularly for faith sharing, contemplative prayer, and communal discernment . . . communities were then encouraged to begin forming young people in contemplative understanding through silence, solitude, and a variety of contemplative exercises. . . .

Spiritual formation tracks, based on the experience of the Project, were implemented at youth ministry conventions and conferences. . . . National news services such as the Wall Street Journal, Knight Rider News Service, CBS radio and ABC World News Tonight all ran stories on various aspects of the Project.[30]

Youth Specialties has been a driving force, having a major impact upon evangelical youth work throughout North America, hosting several annual events including the National Youth Workers Convention, the CORE, and the National Pastors Convention.* Course titles for the conferences include, "Creating Sacred Spaces," "Emerging Worship," and "God Encounters: Spiritual Exercises That Transform Students." In addition, each year Youth Specialties holds conferences and seminars that reach thousands of youth workers worldwide—all with its current teachings on spirituality.

Mike Yaconelli's attraction to and acceptance of contemplative prayer was very similar to the story of Sue Monk Kidd. In his book, *Dangerous Wonder*, Yaconelli relates how lost he had felt after twenty-five years of ministry. In his "desperation," he picked up a book by Henri Nouwen (*In the Name of Jesus*) and said he heard the "voice of Jesus . . . hiding in the pages of Henri's book" and found himself wanting "to start listening again to the voice of Jesus."[31]

In Nouwen's book, we can find the method that led to Yaconelli's claim to a newfound *voice of Jesus*:

---

*Starting with the National Pastors Convention 2006, Zondervan Publishing became the new host.

> Through the discipline of contemplative prayer, Christian
> leaders have to learn to listen again and again to the voice
> of love and to find there the wisdom and courage to address
> whatever issue presents itself to them . . . For Christian
> leadership to be truly fruitful in the future, a movement
> from the moral to the mystical is required.[32]

Nouwen believed that *wisdom and courage* were found in that place of silence, when in reality they are found in God's Word. Yaconelli took Nouwen's admonition to heart and began promoting that prayer method through his own organization.

If this mystical paradigm shift comes to complete fruition, what will the Christian of the future be like? If Christians develop into the spiritual likeness of Henri Nouwen, we will find them meditating with Buddhists as Nouwen did—which he called "dialogue of the heart."[33] We will also find them listening to tapes on the *seven chakras*[34] (which Reiki is based on) as Nouwen did, and above all we will find them wanting to help people "claim his or her own way to God"[35] (universalism; see page 62) as Nouwen did. Nouwen wrote that his solitude and the solitude of his Buddhist friends would "greet each other and support each other."[36] In this one statement lies the fundamental flaw of the contemplative prayer movement—spiritual adultery.

Buddhism proclaims there is nothing outside of yourself needed for salvation. One Buddhist teacher wrote, "The Buddhist approach states that what is ultimately required for human fulfillment is a perfection of being that is found in who we already are."[37] A Christian is one who looks to Jesus Christ as his or her Savior, so to honor the Buddhist approach is to deny the One who gave Himself for us. It is logically impossible to claim Christianity *and* Buddhism as both being true, because each promotes an opposite basis for salvation. Jesus said, "*I am the door: by me if any man enter in, he shall be saved*" (John 10:9). You cannot love and follow the teachings of *both* Buddha and Jesus—for in reality the choice is either trusting in a self-deity or trusting in Jesus Christ as Lord and Savior.

The only way Nouwen's contemplative prayer could support the Buddhist view is if it shares the *same mysticism*, which is the point I am trying to prove in this book. I believe the facts speak for themselves. Once this becomes clear, it is easy to see also that this is the same mysticism many seek to emblazon on the heart of evangelical Christianity.

The question may arise—how can credible Christian organizations justify and condone meditative practices that clearly resemble Eastern meditation? As pointed out earlier in this book, Christian terminology surrounds these practices. It only takes a few popular Christian leaders with national profiles to embrace a teaching that *sounds* Christian to bring about big changes in the church. Moreover, we have many trusting Christians who do not use the Scriptures to test the claims of others. Building an entire prayer method around an out-of-context verse or two is presumptuous, at best. Now more than ever, it is critical that Christians devote themselves to serious Bible study and discernment regarding this issue.

In the spiritual climate of today, a unifying mystical prayer practice fits the paradigm necessary to unite the various world religions—the contemplative prayer movement is such a practice! I believe this movement is taking many on a downward spiral that could lead to the great apostasy. For this to happen, as the Bible says, there will be "seducing spirits" who design a spirituality nearly indistinguishable from the truth. Every Christian must therefore discern whether or not the contemplative prayer movement is a deeper way of walking with God or a deception that undermines the very Gospel itself.

Contemplative prayer stands on the threshold of exploding worldwide; it already has found acceptance in every culture and has even found its way into the writings of prominent, trusted evangelical leaders.

Misguided Shepherds

It has been with great dismay that I have watched one Christian leader after the other succumb to the appeal of contemplative spirituality. I could spend an entire chapter appealing to your spiritual sensibilities in regard to this. Two of these leaders stand out because of their long-time influence in Christianity. There is little doubt in my mind that many others will follow these two in the years to come.

David Jeremiah, pastor of Shadow Mountain Community Church, has enjoyed a wide audience through his *Turning Point* radio program. He has had a reputation of preaching the Gospel, and has certainly been aware of the New Age movement. In 1995, Jeremiah wrote a book titled *Invasion of Other Gods: The Seduction of New Age Spirituality*. His book was an excellent and needed warning to the church about the New Age. And yet, contemplative spirituality seems to have flown right under Jeremiah's radar, to the degree that he too appears to be promoting it. If this is indeed the case, then those who admire and follow him could become open to this dangerous path also.

In 2003, Jeremiah wrote a book called *Life Wide Open*. The subtitle is *Unleashing the Power of a Passionate Life*. In the introduction Jeremiah tells his readers:

> A small handful among us have discovered what the rest of us would pay dearly to know: How can we bring real, living *excitement* into this life?[38]

Jeremiah says that his book is "a map to the life of passion and purpose"[39] and that it will "totally transform the way you see your existence and your purpose."[40] He tells readers that "[God] is in a hurry to help you get to the good things that lie in wait for every human being on this earth."[41] He adds:

> He [God] stands now on the outskirts of your soul, helping you read this page and applying its ideas to your life as He whispers, "Yes! Read it closely! This is where we're going!" Can you hear His voice? Can you feel the changes that are rolling in like a spring rain?[42]

In a book written by a trusted Christian leader, we should be able to assume that David Jeremiah will present to readers a gospel-oriented path to achieve this. And we might also assume that this "small handful" of people who have "discovered what the rest of us would pay dearly to know" will have valuable insights on the truth of the Gospel. However, *Life Wide Open* falls short. In the book, Jeremiah names contemplatives, New Agers, emergents, and mystics including: Sue Monk Kidd (whom I have discussed in earlier chapters), Peter Senge (an advocate of Buddhist-style meditation), Brother Lawrence, Eugene Peterson, Erwin McManus (an emerging church leader), and Calvin Miller.

Jeremiah not only quoted Miller from his book *Into the Depths of God* (a pro-contemplative book), but he favorably quoted him speaking in a derogatory way towards hymns like "A Mighty Fortress is Our God" or "Rock of Ages" as "comfort music for weak-kneed saints."[43] While Jeremiah's comments on beloved hymns don't have anything to do with contemplative prayer, I think it is a perfect illustration of what the Christian of the future could possibly look like. It is perplexing why Jeremiah chose Miller as an example we should follow. In *Into the Depths of God,* Miller encourages readers to engage in centering prayer and explains it as a union between man and God:

> Centering is the merger of two "selves"—ours and his [God's]. Centering is union with Christ. It is not a union that eradicates either self but one that heightens both.[44]

Into the Depths of God is an exhortation in contemplative spirituality and is brimming with quotes by Thomas Merton and other contemplatives. Miller speaks of the "wonderful relationship between ecstasy [mystical state] and transcendence [God]," and says that "Ecstasy is meant to increase our desire for heaven."[45] This state of "Ecstasy" is the same state Thomas Merton likened to an LSD trip and which made him say he wanted to be the best Buddhist he could be.

In *Life Wide Open,* David Jeremiah, under the section subtitled "Excited About the Future," also produces quotes from Buddhist sympathizer Peter Senge. Jeremiah uses Senge to address the issue of getting old and losing vision when he quotes from Senge's book *The Fifth Discipline.* The discipline Senge speaks of in that book is the belief that we can create our own reality, much like the philosophy of the Hoffman Quadrinity Process that Ken Blanchard promotes. Senge says:

Deep down, all of the contemplative traditions of the world, of which there are an extraordinary variety, stem from the same source . . . Before there were all the religions of the last 3,000 years or so, there was a common religion that was shared by indigenous people all around the world.[46]

While it is disconcerting to see David Jeremiah using Peter Senge and Calvin Miller as examples of those who have "secrets" for the rest of us, it is Jeremiah's favorable quoting of Sue Monk Kidd that I find most disturbing of all. As I have shown, Monk Kidd went from being a Southern Baptist Sunday School teacher to a contemplative prayer practitioner. And yet Jeremiah quotes her from *When the Heart Waits* in a manner that would give her credibility with his readers.

In this particular book of Monk Kidd's, she describes her journey to find her *true self* through the writings of Thomas Merton and other mystics. This ultimately led her to embrace the following beliefs in her next book, *The Dance of the Dissident Daughter,* which incidentally was already in print when Jeremiah quoted her in his book. Monk Kidd states:

As I grounded myself in feminine spiritual experience, that fall I was initiated into my body in a deeper way. I came to know myself as an embodiment of Goddess.[47]

Mystical awakening in all the great religious traditions, including Christianity, involves arriving at an experience of unity or nondualism. In Zen it's known as samadhi. . . . Transcendence and immanence are not separate. The Divine is one. The dancer and all the dances are one.[48]

The day of my awakening was the day I saw and knew I saw all things in God, and God in all things.[49]

When the Heart Waits is so filled with contemplative spirituality that it fits right in with more outright New Age books. Recently, I was in a

New Age bookstore in Portland, Oregon where I was doing some research. The store had a "Bestseller" shelf filled with an array of metaphysical and New Age books. On this shelf of bestsellers sat *When the Heart Waits*. I found it ironic to note that on the shelf below Monk Kidd's book sat a channeled book supposedly *written* by a spirit guide named *Abraham*.

How is it that the example David Jeremiah gives for "passion for God" and "something we embrace with heart and soul" is from such a book as *When the Heart Waits?* In *Life Wide Open*, Jeremiah quotes Monk Kidd when she says:

> [A] spiritual journey is a lot like a poem . . . you dance it, sing it, cry it, feel it on your skin and in your bones . . . it lives in the heart and the body as well as the spirit and the head.[50]

But what Monk Kidd feels on her skin and bones and in her heart and body is not the Christian Gospel. How can Jeremiah tell readers to embrace the spirituality and the passion that drive Monk Kidd when her spiritual journey has led her directly into the arms of Thomas Merton who was "impregnated with Sufism" (see page 60)?

In reading Jeremiah's book, *Life Wide Open*, I can only come to one conclusion—Jeremiah has been influenced by the very thing he warned against in 1995 when he wrote about the New Age in his book *Invasion of Other Gods*. In that book, Jeremiah says of the New Age movement:

> This world-view says that God is in everything, so whatever exists, whether it is a person, a pig, or a pickle, is part of God. The problem with this belief is that God's Word teaches that all is *not* God. God stands outside of the creation.[51]

He adds:

> Many people believe that God reveals Himself through some mystical experience . . . The Bible says there is only one way a person can be saved, and that is through Jesus Christ.[52]

And in a chapter he titles, "Invasion from the East," Jeremiah warns:

> Millions of Americans have taken up Hindu practices
> such as yoga, meditation, developing altered states of
> consciousness, seeking Hindu "enlightenment," and
> various occult practices. . . . we need to . . . recognize its
> dangers. . . . the siren song of the New Spirituality may
> be creeping into your home when you thought the doors
> were locked. Will you recognize its stealthy steps?[53]

To Pastor Jeremiah, I ask, "Will *you* recognize the New Spirituality that has even crept into your own recent book?

Right under Jeremiah's nose, contemplatives have slipped into his writings, and now, through his level of influence, may slip into the lives of countless others.

Jeremiah seems to have taken his interest in contemplative spirituality a step further. In 2005, he was scheduled to speak at Ken Blanchard's Lead Like Jesus conference that was to be held in Texas at Max Lucado's church. Laurie Beth Jones (see chapter eight) was also on the ticket. The conference was later cancelled due to Hurricane Katrina; however when my publisher contacted Lead Like Jesus, they were told that David Jeremiah and Ken Blanchard would be working on future projects together. Prior to the cancellation of that conference, Jeremiah wrote to my publisher and said he believed Blanchard to be a committed Christian and added:

> He [Blanchard] told me that his next conference would
> be held in the church of one of my friends, Max Lucado,
> and I was honored to be included as one of the speakers.

I pray that Jeremiah will heed his own 1995 warning and realize that contemplative spirituality and the New Age are one and the same. In the meantime, his own church may be heading in this direction also. On the Shadow Mountain Community Church website, in a 2003 Men's Ministry Newsletter, pastor John Gillette makes mention of the contemplative life and encourages the men of the church in this direction, saying Jesus practiced silence. When my publisher contacted this pastor and asked him which authors he recommended, he named his "favorite" book—*Celebration of Discipline!*

What makes this situation so ironic is that in 1996, while on a trip to Southern California, I attempted to deliver a video tape to Dr. Jeremiah warning him of the dangers of mystical prayer. I myself owned a copy of *Invasion of Other Gods* and saw Jeremiah as a mentor and ally. I gave the tape to his secretary but never heard back from him. You may be wondering what came of that. I suppose the information I have just given you is my answer. But with *When the Heart Waits*, Jeremiah had occultism staring him right in the face.*

I realize that some may see my criticisms as being divisive and overly judgmental. Why have I had to name so many names, some of whom are loved and admired by millions of Christians? I want to point out that I have tried to bring attention only to those who are actually endorsing or promoting contemplative spirituality in a public arena and therefore in a position of misleading many. Furthermore, I have kept my criticisms focused on their teachings, while avoiding commentary or conclusions on their character, personal lives, or motives. I wish to show just how pervasive the contemplative movement has truly become in the Christian church at large.

There is another man I am compelled to mention, for he too is accepted by many as a trusted teacher. Charles (Chuck) Swindoll has a popular radio program called *Insight for Living*. In a September 2005 radio broadcast, Swindoll favorably quoted Henri Nouwen and Richard Foster. But it wasn't until I saw Swindoll's 2005 book *So You Want To Be Like Christ: Eight Essentials to Get You There* that I realized Swindoll had been influenced by contemplative authors. In the book, Swindoll quotes Richard Foster and Henri Nouwen, as well as Eugene Peterson and Dallas Willard. He states that he "sensed a genuine need . . . for the cultivation of intimacy with the Almighty."[54] He says, "[t]here is a deep longing among Christians and non-Christians"[55] for intimacy with God and that intimacy

---

*See Monk Kidd's quote on page 134 of *A Time of Departing*.

with God should be our goal, and "discipline is the means to that end."[56] Chapter three of Swindoll's book is called "Silence and Solitude." In it, he tells readers there are "secrets . . . that will deepen our intimacy with God,"[57] so we can see "what others miss."[58] As he attempts to explain what these secrets are, he refers to the Scripture so often quoted by contemplatives, Psalm 46:10, "Be still, and know that I am God." He goes on to say:

> As we continue our journey toward intimacy with the Almighty, Psalm 46:10 calls us to the discipline of silence. . . . What happens when you and I commit ourselves to periods of absolute, uninterrupted silence?[59]

Swindoll refers to an interview between Mother Teresa (a contemplative and interspiritualist) and former anchorman Dan Rather where she explains to Rather the concept of the silence. Swindoll then exhorts his readers to "discover its secrets for yourself."[60] Yet he avoids describing the actual method of contemplative prayer, saying, "You're on your own with this one," referring to it as "the mystery of godliness"[61] (which actually is a reference in the Bible to the deity of Jesus Christ, not the silence, 1 Timothy 3:16). He brings the proverbial horse right to the water by favorably quoting Foster, Nouwen, and Willard throughout the book.

Swindoll goes so far as to imply that without the silence we cannot *really* know God, adding:

> Sustained periods of quietness are *essential* in order for that [becoming like Christ] to happen . . . I encourage you to experience this for yourself.[62] (emphasis mine)

He finally quotes from Henri Nouwen's, *The Way of the Heart* and then reflects, "I do not believe anyone can ever become a deep person [intimate with God] without stillness and silence."[63]

This is really quite a misleading statement. It is not the silence that draws us closer to God and allows us to become a "deep person" as Swindoll and the contemplatives insist. Scripture clearly teaches that it is only through the blood atonement of Jesus Christ that we can gain access to Him. We cannot add or take away from that. When we are born again, we are as united to Him as we will ever be. Atonement by the blood is the only direct and truly genuine means of meeting with God. The Old Testament speaks of the "mercy seat" wherein the Lord says "there I will meet with thee" (Exodus 25:22). How awesome! A Holy God meets with man, but only when there is blood to atone for man. Hebrews 10:19-22, a clear reference to the Old Testament passage says that Jesus, the sacrificial Lamb, is the fulfillment. When Jesus died, the curtain was torn apart, signifying that now in Christ (the new covenant), the Holy Place, God's presence is open to ALL who believe. We do not need to go into a meditative, self-induced state to be in God's presence.

Some may say that Swindoll is only referring to a quiet time away from the hustle and bustle of life when he speaks of silence. If that were the case, then why does he differentiate between silence and solitude? He refers to solitude as getting away from it all, an external quietness, and makes it clear that silence is an internal stillness like Henri Nouwen described in *The Way of the Heart*.

While at this point, Swindoll does not actually teach mantras or altered states, his promotion and extensive quoting of contemplatives gives every indication that he is moving toward the contemplative camp. Typically, those who begin following the teachings of the authors I have warned about in my book, and begin promoting the silence, continue steadily on a downward spiral into outright mysticism and deception. It is vital to understand that Nouwen's book *The Way of the Heart* is a virtual primer on the practice of contemplative prayer. For instance, in the 2005 radio broadcast, Swindoll read a portion of *The Way of the Heart* where Nouwen makes reference to the silence of the mind contrasting it with regular silence as in not speaking.

Be Still and Know . . .

Evidence of the growing popularity of contemplative spirituality within today's Christianity is everywhere. In April of 2006, Fox Home Entertainment released a DVD called *Be Still*. Fox describes the film as:

... an extraordinary film that demonstrates contemplative reflection as a vital part of our everyday lives . . . features a useful "how to" section that shows how contemplative prayer can be used by anyone at anytime to better one's life. (from Fox's website)

The film features such prominent contemplative proponents as Richard Foster, Calvin Miller, Jan Johnson* and Dallas Willard, which would be expected from a film of this nature. But what was very surprising to see were two other well-known Christian leaders that participated in the project, Beth Moore and Max Lucado.

Moore's Bible studies are used extensively by Christian women, and her books are found in most Christian bookstores. She is vibrant, articulate, and her materials are considered trustworthy and helpful. What would she be doing on an infomercial for contemplative prayer in which Richard Foster says:

The wonderful thing about contemplative prayer is that it can be found everywhere, anywhere, anytime for anyone. We become a portable sanctuary, so that we are living our life, wherever it is, aware of the goodness of God, the presence of God.[64]

If what Foster is saying is true, that anyone can practice contemplative prayer and become a portable sanctuary (a house for God to dwell), then the Bible is wrong when it states that God will dwell only in the person who is born-again through Jesus Christ. Remember what Jesus told Nicodemus, "Except a man be born again, he cannot see the kingdom of God" (John 3:3).

Skeptics might say, *Well, Foster doesn't mean everyone—he's not talking about unbelievers being able to practice contemplative prayer.* But he is! Listen to what he says in his well-known book, *Celebration of Discipline*:

---

*See page 82 for Jan Johnson's view of contemplative.

We need not be well advanced in matters of theology to practice the Disciplines. Recent converts—for that matter people who have yet to turn their lives over to Jesus Christ—can and should practice them.*

Thus, when Foster says in the *Be Still* DVD, "anyone," he means anyone. In the DVD, Foster also quotes 18th-century Jesuit priest, Jean Nicholas Grou as saying: "O Divine Master, teach me this mute language which says so much."[65] This "mute language" is that language of Thomas Merton, Henri Nouwen and so many others that I have referred to in this book.

So the question must be asked, is Beth Moore a proponent of this prayer language of the mystics? I think that is a fair question to ask in light of her involvement on the DVD. After the release of the *Be Still* DVD, some people were concerned about Moore being in the film. E-mails and calls to her ministry, Living Proof Ministries, resulted in a statement issued by Moore, in which she responded:

> Since its [*Be Still* DVD] release, I've been baffled by some inquiries into whether or not I am a proponent of approaches to prayer with overtones of Eastern meditation. Not only is my answer no, the thought never even occurred to me. . . . I am not involved in any kind of emergent church movement or any kind of mystical prayer movement.[66]

A few weeks after Moore's initial statement, her ministry issued a second response, which affirmed her support for the DVD: "[W]e believe that once you view the *Be Still* video you will agree that there is no problem with its expression of Truth." The e-mail offered to send anyone a loan copy of the DVD to "assure . . . that there is no problem with Beth's participation in the *Be Still* video."[67] Living Proof sent this e-mail out weeks subsequent to my publisher contacting their office and sending a copy of *A Time of Departing*

---

*Celebration of Discipline, 1988 Revised Edition, p. 2

to underscore our concerns. To my knowledge, there was never any response from Beth Moore or her ministry regarding my book and the warning it gives on contemplative prayer.

The answer to where Moore stands on this issue may be found in her book *When Godly People Do Ungodly Things*. In that book, Moore reveals her glowing affinity for Brennan Manning when she favorably quotes him throughout the book and states: "What God has used Manning to bring to the mixed bag of our generation of believers may be a gift without parallel."[68] Of Manning's book, *Ragamuffin Gospel*, Moore says it is "one of the most remarkable books"[69] she has ever read. But in his book, Manning pays homage to Basil Pennington* (for introducing him to centering prayer) and numerous other contemplatives, including Sue Monk Kidd!

In a section of Moore's book about unceasing prayer, Moore states:

> I have picked up on the terminology of Brother Lawrence, who called praying unceasingly practicing God's presence. In fact, practicing God's presence has been my number one goal for the last year.[70]

Moore chose as an example for unceasing prayer someone who is considered by contemplatives to be a model of mystical prayer. In the DVD, she states:

> [I]f we are not still before Him [God], we will never truly know to the depths of the marrow in our bones that He is God. There's got to be a stillness.[71]

If what she means by stillness is simply a quiet time to reflect or ponder then there would be no controversy. But that is not what the contemplative prayer movement espouses. What it promotes is quite the opposite. Stillness, in this context, is an altered state of consciousness, one brought on through repetition of words or

---

*See page 64 of *A Time of Departing*.

phrases. After having read the documentation that I have presented in this book, I believe it is irrefutable that this is the common view of what the stillness entails.

While the *Be Still* DVD never comes right out and teaches mantra-like techniques, it whets people's appetite and makes them more open to the overtures of the thousands of spiritual directors who will teach them these techniques.

My intent here is not to malign Beth Moore but rather to point out that a major conservative Christian leader is promoting contemplative prayer.

Living in a Time of Departing

Contemplative advocates propose that there has been something vital and important missing from the church for centuries. The insinuation is that Christians have been lacking something necessary for their spiritual vitality; but that would mean the Holy Spirit has not been fully effective for hundreds of years and only now the secret key has been found that unlocks God's full power to know Him. These proponents believe that Christianity has been seriously crippled without this extra ingredient. This kind of thinking leads one to believe that traditional, biblical Christianity is merely a philosophy without the contemplative prayer element. Contemplatives are making a distinction between studying and meditating on the Word of God versus experiencing Him, suggesting that we cannot hear Him or really know Him simply by studying His Word or even through normal prayer—we must be contemplative to accomplish this. But the Bible makes it clear that the Word of God is living and active, and has always been that way, and it is in filling our minds with it that we come to love Him, not through a mystical practice of *stopping the flow of thought* (the stillness) that is never once mentioned in the Bible, except in warnings against vain repetitions.

In chapter three I quoted Thomas Merton's statement that he saw various Eastern religions "come together in his life" (as a Christian mystic). On a rational, practical level Christianity and Eastern religions will not mix; but add the mystical element and they do blend together like adding soap to oil and water. I must clarify what I mean: Mysticism *neutralizes* doctrinal differences by sacrificing the truth of Scripture for a mystical experience. Mysticism offers a common ground, and supposedly that commonality is *divinity in all*. But we know from Scripture "there is one God; and there is none other but he" (Mark 12:32).

In a booklet put out by Saddleback Church on spiritual maturity, the following quote by Henri Nouwen is listed:

> Solitude begins with a time and place for God, and Him alone. If we really believe not only that God exists, but that He is actively present in our lives—healing, teaching, and guiding—we need to set aside *a time and space* to give Him our undivided attention.[72] (emphasis mine)

When we understand what Nouwen really means by "time and space" given to God we can also see the emptiness and deception of his spirituality. In his recent biography of Nouwen, *God's Beloved*, Michael O' Laughlin says:

> Some new elements began to emerge in Nouwen's thinking when he discovered Thomas Merton. Merton opened up for Henri an enticing vista of the world of contemplation and a way of seeing not only God but also the world through new eyes. . . . If ever there was a time when Henri Nouwen wished to enter the realm of the spiritual masters or dedicate himself to a *higher spiritual path*, it was when he fell under the spell of Cistercian monasticism and the *writings of Thomas Merton*.[73] (emphasis mine)

In his book, *Thomas Merton: Contemplative Critic*, Nouwen talks about these "new eyes" that Merton helped to formulate and said that Merton and his work "had such an impact" on his life and that he was the man who had "inspired" him greatly.[74] But when we read Nouwen's very revealing account, something disturbing is unveiled. Nouwen lays out the path of Merton's spiritual pilgrimage into contemplative spirituality. Those who have studied Merton from a critical point of view, such as myself, have tried to understand what are the roots behind Merton's spiritual affinities. Nouwen explains that Merton was influenced by LSD mystic Aldous Huxley who "brought him to a deeper level of knowledge" and "was one of Merton's favorite novelists."[75] It was through Huxley's book, *Ends and Means*, that first brought Merton "into contact with mysticism."[76] Merton states:

> He [Huxley] had read widely and deeply and intelligently in all kinds of Christian and Oriental mystical literature, and had come out with the *astonishing truth* that all this, far from being a mixture of dreams and magic and charlatanism, was *very real and very serious*.[77] (emphasis mine)

This is why, Nouwen revealed, Merton's mystical journey took him right into the arms of Buddhism:

> Merton learned from him [Chuang Tzu—a Taoist] what Suzuki [a Zen master] had said about Zen: "Zen teaches nothing; it merely enables us to wake and become aware."[78]

Become aware of what? The Buddha nature. Divinity within all. That is why Merton said if we knew what was in each one of us, we would bow down and worship one another. Merton's descent into contemplative led him to the belief that God is in all things and that God *is* all things. This is made clear by Merton when he said:

> True solitude is a participation in the solitariness of God—Who is in all things.[79]

Nouwen adds:

> [Chuang Tzu] awakened and led him [Merton] . . . to the deeper ground of his consciousness.[80]

This has been the ploy of Satan since the Garden of Eden when the serpent said to Eve, "ye shall be as gods" (Genesis 3:4). It is this very essence that is the foundation of contemplative prayer.

In Merton's efforts to become a mystic, he found guidance from a Hindu swami, whom Merton referred to as Dr. Bramachari. Bramachari played a pivotal role in Merton's future spiritual outlook. Nouwen divulged this when he said:

> Thus he [Merton] was more impressed when this Hindu monk pointed him to the Christian mystical tradition. . . . It seems providential indeed that this Hindu monk relativized [sic] Merton's youthful curiosity for the East and made him sensitive to the richness of Western mysticism.[81]

Why would a Hindu monk advocate the *Christian* mystical tradition? The answer is simple: they are one in the same. Even though the repetitive words used may differ (e.g. Christian words: Abba, Father, etc. rather than Hindu words), the end result is the same. And the Hindu monk knew this to be true. Bramachari understood that Merton didn't need to switch to Hinduism to get the same *enlightenment* that he himself experienced through the Hindu mystical tradition. In essence, Bramachari backed up what I am trying to get across in *A Time of Departing*, that all the world's *mystical* traditions basically come from the same source and teach the same precepts . . . and that source is not the God of the Old and New Testaments. The biblical God is not interspiritual!

Evangelical Christianity is now being invited, perhaps even catapulted into seeing God with these *new eyes* of contemplative prayer. And so the question must be asked, is Thomas Merton's silence, Henri Nouwen's space, and Richard Foster's contemplative prayer the way in which we can know and be close to God? Or is this actually a spiritual belief system that is contrary to the true message that the Bible so absolutely defines—that there is only one way to God and that is through His only begotten Son, Jesus Christ, whose sacrifice on the Cross obtained our full salvation? In this book, I have endeavored to answer these questions with extensive evidence and documentation showing the dangers of contemplative prayer.

If indeed my concerns for the future actually come to fruition, then we will truly enter a time of departing. My prayer is that you will not turn away from the faith to follow a different gospel and a different Jesus but will rather stay the course and finish the race, so that after having done all you can, you will stand.

> Wherefore take unto you the whole armour of God, that ye may be able to withstand in the evil day, and having done all, to stand. (Ephesians 6:13).

There *is* hope for the Christian of the future. In Christ, we do have a sure hope, and we have His promise in Matthew 16:18 that the gates of hell will not prevail against us. Yes, there will be a time of departing as the Bible predicts, and we can be sure an apostate church will help usher in the "man of sin" at the appointed time, but there will also be the Bride who makes herself ready for the Lord's return. And with that, my friend, I bid you godly discernment and a safe passage!

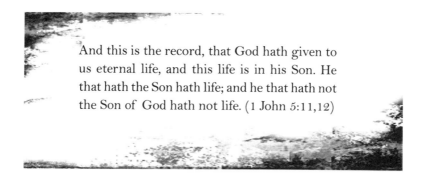

> And this is the record, that God hath given to us eternal life, and this life is in his Son. He that hath the Son hath life; and he that hath not the Son of God hath not life. (1 John 5:11,12)

SPECIAL NOTE FROM RAY YUNGEN

If after having read this book, you are left wondering about your relationship with God, remember that knowing Jesus Christ is not merely religion or spirituality but is rather a personal relationship with Him.

Romans 10:2 speaks of those who have a "zeal for God but not according to knowledge." Many contemplative writers describe a spiritual despondency they suffer before turning to mystical prayer as a remedy, and consequently they have an acute sense of spiritual failure that propels them into the waiting arms of *the silence.* In contrast, the Gospel presents a plan that is uniquely initiated by God.

Scripture clearly states that salvation depends entirely on the grace of God: "For by grace are ye saved through faith; and that not of yourselves: it is the gift of God: Not of works, lest any man should boast" (Ephesians 2: 8, 9). Furthermore, Christ's death on the Cross for our sins, fully solidifies in our minds a tangible expression of the unearned and undeserved nature of our salvation. When Jesus said, "It is finished." (John 19:30), He proclaimed in three words that our salvation depends entirely on the finished work of Christ on the Cross.

Let me therefore caution you in following any teaching that suggests that Christ's work was incomplete or unnecessary, or that there are other paths to God. Jesus said, "I am the way, the truth, and the life: no man cometh unto the Father, but by me" (John 14:6).

Christianity is uniquely different from all religions in that it does not contain the erroneous premise that man is basically good (or divine) and consequently can earn his way to Heaven.

If you have never found the peace of knowing Christ, I urge you to read the first five chapters of the book of Romans and allow the Holy Spirit to draw you to what is being said and offered. The only prerequisite is to recognize your inability as a sinner to save yourself. Then, in simple faith, tell God you are now trusting Christ, and Him alone, to be your Lord and Savior.

> Therefore being justified by faith, we have peace with God through our Lord Jesus Christ: By whom also we have access by faith into this grace wherein we stand, and rejoice in hope of the glory of God. (Romans 5:1-2)

Glossary of Terms

Altered State of Consciousness

A meditative or drug induced non-ordinary state of mind.

Ancient Wisdom

The supposed laws of the Universe that, when mastered, enable one to see one's own divinity—another word for metaphysics or occultism.

Aquarius/Aquarian Age

Sign of the Zodiac represented by the water carrier, Earth Age, associated with this astrological sign. The term New Age refers to the coming Aquarian age which is in the process of replacing the Pisces age. According to astrologers, every 2,000 years constitutes an age. New Agers predict this Aquarian age will be a time of utopia.

Biblical *Meditation* or Contemplation

A normal thinking process of reflecting on the things of God and biblical precepts.

Centering/Centering Prayer

Another term for contemplative meditation (going deep within your center). A type of meditation being promoted in many mainline churches under the guise of prayer.

Chakras

Believed by New Agers to be the seven energy centers in man which open up during the kundalini effect in meditation.

Christ Consciousness

Taught by New Agers to be the state of awareness, reached in meditation, in which one realizes that one is divine and one with God and thereby becoming a Christ or an enlightened being.

Contemplative Prayer

Going beyond thought by the use of repeated words or phrases.

Creative Visualization

Imaging in the mind, during meditation, what you want to occur and then expecting it to happen. In simple terms, you are creating your own reality.

Desert Fathers

Monks who lived as hermits beginning around the third century who first taught the practice of contemplative prayer.

False Self

The *false self* is the ego or personality that is observable by others. One rids oneself of the false self to find the *true self* through mantra-meditation. New Agers would consider people like Buddha, Ghandi, and even Jesus Christ as examples of people who found their true self.

Higher Self

Supposed God-self within that New Agers seek to connect with through meditation. Also called the Christ-self or True-self.

Interspirituality

The view that all the world's religions are identical at the mystical level and therefore there should be solidarity among them.

Jesus Prayer

A popular version of this prayer is *Lord Jesus Christ, Son of God, have mercy on me, a sinner,* often abbreviated to *Jesus.*

Kundalini

Powerful energy that is brought on through meditation, associated with the Chakras.

Lectio Divina

Means sacred reading. In today's contemplative movement, it often involves taking a single word or small phrase from Scripture and repeating the words over and over again.

Mantra

Word or words repeated either silently or verbally to induce an altered state of consciousness.

Meditation

Meditation is practiced by all major world religions and is often described as an essential discipline for spiritual growth. Yet, like mysticism, there is great diversity in the practice of meditation. While some see mediation as simply spending time thinking quietly about life or about God, others use meditation techniques to experience altered states of consciousness that allow them to have esoteric experiences. In addition, meditation is promoted in secular society for the personal benefits of health, relaxation, and improved productivity.

Metaphysical

Beyond the physical realm or pertaining to the supernatural.

Mysticism

A direct experience of the supernatural realm.

New Age

The Age of Aquarius, supposedly the Golden Age, when man becomes aware of his power and divinity.

New Thought

A movement that tries to merge classic occult concepts with Christian terminology.

Occult/Occultism
Kept secret or hidden; the practice of metaphysics throughout history.

Pantheism
God *is* all things. The universe and all life are connected in a sum. This sum is the total reality of God. Thus, man, animals, plants, and all physical matter are seen as equal. The assumption—all is one, therefore all is deity.

Panentheism
God is *in* all things. In panentheism God is both personal and is also in all of creation. It is a universal view that believes God is in all people and that someday all of God's creation will be saved and be one with Him.

Reiki
Spiritual energy that is channeled by one attuned to the Reiki power. Literally translated God energy.

Sacred Space
Either a physical spot where one goes to engage in a mystical practice or the actual silence or the state of being during the mystical experience.

Spiritual Formation
The teaching and application of the *spiritual disciplines.*

The Silence
Absence of normal thought.

Spiritual Director
One who promotes or trains people in the spiritual disciplines including the silence.

Universalism
The belief that all humanity has or will ultimately have a positive connection and relationship with God.

A Few Commonly Asked Questions

Question: What is wrong with spiritual disciplines?

Answer: While there is nothing "wrong" with fasting, praying, and performing good service for others, it is rare if ever that when the "spiritual disciplines" are taught they do not include the discipline of the silence. Therefore, when the term spiritual disciplines is used, it is almost always incorporating contemplative spirituality.

Question: Isn't I Kings 19:12 an example of when contemplative prayer is condoned in Scripture? Elijah heard a "still, small voice." Isn't that referring to the silence?

Answer: This passage in no way indicates that Elijah was practicing a mantra exercise. On the contrary, it was the prophets of Baal who "called on the name of Baal from morning even till noon, saying, 'O Baal, hear us!" (I Kings 18:26). Now Elijah was in a cave, not to practice contemplative prayer, but to hide from Jezebel's threat to take his life. Also, his encounter with God was something he did not initiate but God initiated Himself, thereby emphasizing that Elijah was not practicing a mantra. If anything, from his conversation with God, we might conclude that he was also hiding from his ministry and God Himself, as he was feeling hopeless.

Question: What is the difference between Eastern meditation and Christian meditation?

Answer: Any kind of repetition that disrupts natural thought is the same dynamic or principle as Eastern mysticism. Only the context has changed (i.e., Christian mantras). But in essence the actual results are the same. This is why one finds such a strong correlation between Eastern mystics and Western mystics. This is why Thomas Merton said he was deeply "impregnated with Sufism." He wasn't a Sufi, but he experienced their precepts through "Christian contemplative prayer." When Christian contemplatives say they are not emptying the mind like one does in Eastern meditation, but are rather filling it, they are inaccurate. No mystical tradition empties the mind just to have it empty. It is always a prerequistite to having it filled with what is perceived to be the "divine." You can't be a mystic without doing the mantra. Also see page 81.

Christian Mystics of the Past

Hildegard of Bingen (1098-1179)

St. Catherine of Siena (1347-1380)

Meister Eckhart (1260-1327)

The Cloud of Unknowing (anonymous monk)

Richard Rolle (c. 1300-1349)

Julian of Norwich (1342-1423)

St. Ignatius Loyola (1491-1556)

St. Teresa of Avila (1515-1582)

St. John of the Cross (1542-1591)

Brother Lawrence (1611- 1691)

George Fox (1624-1691)

Madam Guyon (1647-1717)

William Law (1686-1761)

Evelyn Underhill (1875-1941)

Pierre Teilhard de Chardin (1881- 1955)

Thomas Merton (1915-1968)

Endnotes
1/The Invisible Denomination

1. M. Scott Peck, *Further Along the Road Less Traveled* (Simon & Schuster Audioworks, 1992).

2. Jack Canfield, "Choosing to Be Happy" (*India Today Plus*, Third Quarter, 1997).

3. John Michael Talbot, *Come to the Quiet* (New York, NY: Tarcher, 2002), front matter, Introduction, p. 8.

4. Ken Blanchard, *What Would Buddha Do At Work?* (Berkeley, CA: Seastonre, an imprint of Ulysses Press, 2001), Foreword.

5. Brian McLaren, *A Generous Orthodoxy* (Grand Rapids, MI: Zondervan, 2004), p. 260.

6. Steve Turner interviewing Matthew Fox, "Natural Mystic?" (Nine O Clock Service, March 1995, http://members.tripod.com/nineoclockservice/mattiefx.htm).

7. David Spangler, *Emergence, the Rebirth of the Sacred* (New York, NY: Dell Publishing Co., New York, NY, 1984), p. 26.

8. Michael D. Antonio, *Heaven on Earth* (New York, NY: Crown Publishing, 1992), p. 13.

9. Robert C. Fuller, *Spiritual But Not Religious* (New York, NY: Oxford University Press Inc., 2001), p. 99.

10. William Lee Rand, "Keeping Reiki Free" (*Reiki News Magazine*, Spring 2005), p. 37.

11. Marion Weinstein, *Positive Magic: Occult Self-Help* (Custer, WA: Phoenix Publishing, 1978), p. 19.

12. Ibid., p. 25.

13. Mark B. Woodhouse, *Paradigm Wars, World Views for a New Age* (Frog Ltd. Publishing, 1996), p. 47.

14. Richard Kirby, *The Mission of Mysticism* (London, UK: SPCK, 1979), p. 6.

15. Ann Wise, *The High Performance Mind* (Los Angeles, CA: Tarcher/Putnam,1995), p. 57.

16. Barry Long, *Meditation, a Foundation Course* (Barry Long Books, 1995), p. 13.

Note: At the time this edition was prepared, the website addresses listed in the Endnotes section were active links; however, due to the ever-changing nature of the Internet, some website addresses may no longer be active.

17. Swami Rama, *Freedom From the Bondage of Karma* (Himalayan Institute, 1977), p. 66.

18. Mary Ellen Lafferty, "The Joys and Frustrations of Being a Healer" (*Life Times*, Issue Number 3), p. 59.

19. W.E. Butler, *Lords of Light* (Rochester, VT: Destiny Books, 1990), p. 74.

20. David L. Smith, *A Handbook of Contemporary Theology* (Victor Books, 1992), p. 273.

21. Brian Tracy, *Maximum Achievement* (New York, NY: Simon and Schuster, 1993), pp. 179, 17.

22. "Change of Heart," (*The Sunday Oregonian*, September 19, 1993), p. L1.

23. *AM Northwest Morning Talk Show*, KATU Channel 2, Portland, OR, Interview with Wayne Dyer, March 27, 1997.

24. Jeremy Tarcher, "Living with Vision" (*Science of Mind*, April 1, 1992), p. 44.

25. Shakti Gawain, *Creative Visualization* (Novato, CA: Nataraj Publishing, 2002), back cover.

26. Ibid., 1983, 9th Printing, p. 57.

27. Julia Cameron, *The Artist's Way* (New York, NY: William Morrow Co., 10th Anniversary Edition), front & back covers.

28. *What's New at Stiles* newsletter, 1985.

29. Terry Mattingly, "Marketplace of the Gods" (*Christian Research Journal*, May/June 1986), p. 6.

30. Ross Robertson, "Synchronicity Goes to Hollywood" (*What is Enlightenment?* magazine, November 2004/February 2005), p. 65.

31. W.E. Butler, *Lords of Light*, op. cit., p. 164.

32. Storma Swanson, *Attuning to Inner Guidance* (Beaverton, OR: Seabreeze Press, 1982).

33. Jacqueline Small, *Embodying Spirit* (New York, NY: Harper Collins Publishing, 1994), p. 97.

34. Geoffrey Parrinder, *World Religions from Ancient History to the Present* (*Facts on File Publications*, New York, N.Y., 1971), p. 155.

35. Peter Caddy at the "Whole Life Expo" in California in the 1980s, a conference which Ray Yungen attended.

36. Rev. Leddy Hammock, *Questions, Answers, and Ultimate Answers* pamphlet (Unity-Clearwater Church, Clearwater, FL).

37. David Eastman, "Kundalini Demystified" (*Yoga Journal*, Issue 64, September/October 1985), p. 43.

38. "Baba Beleaguered" (*Yoga Journal*, Issue 63, July/August 1985), p. 30, reprinted from Co-Evolution Quarterly.

39. Ibid., p. 30.

2/The Yoga of the West

1. William Johnston, *Letters to Contemplatives* (Orbus Books, 1992), p. 1.

2. Alice Bailey, *From Intellect to Intuition* (New York, NY: Lucis Publishing Co., 1987, 13th printing), p. 193.

3. William Johnston, *Lord, Teach Us to Pray* (New York, NY: Harper Collins Publishers, 1991), p. 54.

4. Ibid., p. 58.

5. Walter A. Elwel, *Evangelical Dictionary of Theology* (Grand Rapids, MI: Baker Book House, 1984), p. 818.

6. Ken Kaisch, *Finding God: A Handbook of Christian Meditation* (New York, NY: Paulist Press, 1994), p. 283.

7. William Johnson, *The Mystical Way* (New York, NY: Harper Collins, 1993), p. 224.

8. William Shannon, *Silence on Fire* (New York, NY: The Crossroad Publishing Company, 1991), p. 99.

9. Willigis Jager, *Contemplation: A Christian Path* (Ligouri, MO: Triumph Books, 1994), p. 93.

10. Richard Kirby, *The Mission of Mysticism*, op. cit., p. 7.

11. William Johnston, *Letters to Contemplatives*, op. cit., p. 13.

12. Willigis Jager, *Contemplation: A Christian Path* (Triumph Books, 1994), p. 31.

13. Ken Kaisch, *Finding God*, op. cit., cited from *The Cloud of Unknowing*, p. 223.

14. Kenneth L. Woodward, "Talking to God" (*Newsweek*, January 6, 1992), p. 44.

15. Jerry Alder, "In Search of the Spiritual" (*Newsweek*, August/September 2005, Special Report: "Spirituality in America"), p. 48.

16. Michael Leach (*America*, May 2, 1992), p. 384.

17. M. Basil Pennington, *Centered Living: The Way of Centering Prayer* (New York, NY: Doubleday Publishing, Image Book edition, September 1988), p. 10.

18. Sheed & Ward Catalog, Winter/Lent, 1978, p. 12.

19. William Shannon, *Seeds of Peace* (New York, NY: Crossroad

Publishing, 1996), p. 25.

20. Anne A. Simpson, "Resting in God" (*Common Boundary* magazine, Sept./Oct. 1997, http://web.archive.org/web/20150415153649/http://www.livingrosaries.org/interview.htm), p. 25.

21. *Catechism of the Catholic Church* (Urbi et Orbi Communications, 1994), p. 652.

22. Randy England, *The Unicorn in the Sanctuary* (Trinity Communications, 1990), p. 159.

23. Marcus Borg, *The Heart of Christianity* (San Francisco, CA: Harper, 2004), p. 7.

24. Kimberly Winston, "Get Thee to a Monastery" (*Publisher's Weekly,* April 10, 2000), p. 39.

25. Bruce Epperly, *Crystal & Cross* (Mystic, CT: Twenty-third Publishers, 1996), p. 14.

26. Spiritual Directors International, Conference Workshops: "Exile or Return? Accompanying the Journey into Contemplative Prayer" (http://web.archive.org/web/20110106132115/http://sdiworld.org/conference_workshops.html).

27. William Shannon, *Seeds of Peace,* op. cit., p. 66.

28. Daniel Goleman, *The Meditative Mind* (Los Angeles, CA: Tarcher/Putnam Inc., 1988), p.53.

29. Ken Kaisch, *Finding God,* op. cit., p.191.

30. Father William Teska, *Meditation in Christianity* (Himalayan Institute., 1973), p.65.

31. Tilden Edwards, *Living in the Presence* (San Francisco, CA: Harper & Row, 1987), Acknowledgement page.

32. Jacquelyn Small, *Awakening in Time* (New York, NY: Bantam Books, 1991), p. 261.

33. Ronald S. Miller, Editor of *New Age Journal, As Above So Below* (Los Angeles, CA: Tarcher/Putnam, 1992), p. 52.

34. Tav Sparks, *The Wide Open Door* (Center City, MN: Hazelden Educational Material, 1993), p. 89.

35. Tilden Edwards, *Spiritual Friend* (New York, NY: Paulist Press,1980), pp. 162-163.

36. Ibid., p. 18.

37. Charles Spurgeon, *Morning and Evening* (Hendrickson Publishers, 1991), p. 392.

38. Philip St. Romain, *Kundalini Energy and Christian Spirituality*

(New York, NY: Crossroad Publishing Company, 1995), p. 24.

39. Ibid., pp. 20-21.

40. Ibid., pp. 22-23.

41. Ibid., pp. 28-29.

42. Ibid., p. 107.

43. Ibid., pp. 48-49.

44. Ibid., p. 39.

45. Ibid., pp. 75-76.

46. Deborah Hughes and Jane Robertson-Boudreaux, *Metaphysical Primer: A Guide to Understanding Metaphysics* (Estes Park, CO: Metagnosis Pub., 1991), p. 27.

47. St. Romain, *Kundalini Energy and Christian Spirituality*, op. cit., p. 107.

48. Willigis Jager, *Contemplation: A Christian Path*, op. cit., p. 72.

49. Michael J. Gelb, *The How to Think Like Leonardo da Vinci Workbook* (New York, NY: Dell Publishing, 1999), p. 142.

50. Wayne Teasdale, "Mysticism as the Crossing of Ultimate Boundaries: A Theological Reflection" (*The Golden String* newsletter, http://clarusbooks.com/Teasdale.html, accessed 10/2009).

51. Wayne Teasdale, *A Monk in the World* (Novato, CA: New World Library, 2002), p. 64.

52. Jan Alsever quoted in Statesman Journal, January 27th, 1996, Religion Section.

53. Katherine Kurs, "Are You Religious or Are You Spiritual?" (*Spirituality & Health Magazine,* Spring 2001), p. 28.

3/Proponents and Visionaries

1. Michael Tobias, *A Parliament of Souls in Search of a Global Spirituality* (KQED Inc., San Francisco, CA, 1995), p. 148.

2. Marilyn Ferguson, *The Aquarian Conspiracy* (Los Angeles, CA: J.P. Tarcher Inc.,1980), p. 419.

3. *Life magazine,* December 1992, p. 73.

4. *Wall Street Journal,* as quoted in *The Road Less Traveled Seminar,* brochure presented by Career Track, 1992, p. 7.

5. M. Scott Peck, *The Road Less Traveled* (New York, NY: Simon & Schuster, 1978), p. 283.

6. Ibid., p. 309.

7. *New Age Journal,* December 1985, pp. 28-30.

8. M. Scott Peck, *A World Waiting to be Born* (New York, NY:

Bantam Books, 1993), p. 88.

9. Ibid., p. 21.

10. Ibid., p. 21.

11. Ibid., p. 83.

12. Ibid., back cover.

13. Matthew Fox, *The Coming of the Cosmic Christ* (San Francisco, CA: Harper & Row, 1988), pp. 154, 232.

14. Ibid., back cover.

15. Ibid.

16. M. Scott Peck, *Further Along the Road Less Traveled*, op. cit.

17. Ibid.

18. Ibid.

19. Ibid.

20. Ibid.

21. Ibid.

22. Ibid.

23. Michael D. Antonio, *Heaven on Earth* (New York, NY: Crown Publishing, 1992), p.342, 352.

24. Thomas Merton, *Conjectures of a Guilty Bystander* (Garden City, NY: Doubleday Publishers, 1989), pp. 157-158.

25. *Credence Cassettes* magazine, Winter/Lent, 1998, p. 24.

26. M. Basil Pennington, *Thomas Merton, My Brother* (Hyde Park, NY: New City Press, 1996), p. 115, citing from *The Hidden Ground of Love)*, pp. 63-64.

27. Nevill Drury, *The Dictionary of Mysticism and the Occult* (San Francisco, CA: Harper & Row, 1985), p. 85.

28. Rob Baker and Gray Henry, Editors, *Merton and Sufism* (Louisville, KY: Fons Vitae, 1999), p. 109.

29. Ibid., p. 110.

30. Ibid., p. 69.

31. Ibid., p. 41.

32. William Shannon, *Silent Lamp, The Thomas Merton Story* (New York, NY: Crossroad Publishing Company, 1992), p. 276.

33. Ibid., p. 281.

34. Ibid., p. 273.

35. Deba P. Patnaik, *The Message of Thomas Merton*, editor Brother Patrick Hart (Kalamazoo, MI: Cistercian Publishing, 1981), p. 87.

36. Michael Ford, *Wounded Prophet: A Portrait of Henri J. M. Nouwen* (New York, NY: Doubleday, 1999), p. 35.

37. Henri Nouwen, *Sabbatical Journey* (New York, NY: Crossroad Publishing, 1998), p. 51.

38. Eknath Easwaran, *Meditation* (Tomoles, CA: Nilgiri Press, 1991 edition), back cover.

39. Thomas Ryan, *Disciplines for Christian Living* (Mawah, NJ: Paulist Press, 1993), pp. 2-3.

40. Henri Nouwen, *The Way of the Heart* (San Francisco, CA: Harper, 1991), p. 81.

41. Henri Nouwen, *Bread for the Journey* (San Francisco, CA: Harper, 1997), Jan. 15 and Nov. 16 daily readings.

42. Henri Nouwen, *The Way of the Heart*, op. cit., p. 66.

43. Henri Nouwen, *Sabbatical Journey*, op. cit., p. 149.

44. Andrew Harvey, *The Direct Path* (New York, NY: Broadway Books, 2000), p. 34.

45. Henri Nouwen, *Sabbatical Journey*, op. cit. p. 149.

46. M. Basil Pennington, Thomas Keating, Thomas E. Clarke, *Finding Grace at the Center* (Petersham, MA: St. Bede's Pub., 1978), pp. 5-6.

47. Thomas Keating, *Intimacy with God* (New York, NY: Crossroad, 1994), p. 153.

48. Kenneth L. Woodward, "Talking to God," op. cit., p. 44.

49. Jerry Alder, "In Search of the Spiritual," op. cit., p. 48.

50. Tilden Edwards, "The Center for Spiritual Development" (Trinity Episcopal Cathedral, Fall 2004 - Spring 2005), p. 4.

51. Gerald May, *Simply Sane* (Ramsey, NJ: Paulist Press,1977), "In Appreciation" section.

52. Gerald May, *Addiction and Grace* (San Francisco, CA: Harper, Paperback edition), p. 102.

53. Ibid., p. 166.

54. Gerald May, *The Awakened Heart* (San Francisco, CA: Harper, 1991), p. 179.

55. Ibid., pp. 179-180.

56. Gerald May cited in Kim Boykin's *Zen for Christians* (San Francisco, CA: Joesy-Bass, 2003), Foreword.

57. Charles H. Simpkinson, "In the Spirit of the Early Christians" (*Common Boundary* magazine, Jan./Feb. 1992), p. 19.

58. Morton Kelsey cited in Charles H. Simpkinson, "In the Spirit of the Early Christians," op. cit.

59. Morton Kelsey, *New Age Spirituality* (Louisville, KY: Westminster John Knox Press, 1st edition,1992, edited by Duncan S. Ferguson), pp. 56-58.

60. Matthew Fox, *The Coming of the Cosmic Christ* (New York, NY: HarperCollins Publishers, 1980), p. 154.

61. Ibid., p. 65.

62. Robert Aitken & David Steindl Rast, *The Ground We Share* (Boston, MA: Shambhala Publications, Inc., 1994), p. 45.

63. Frank X. Tuoti, *The Dawn of the Mystical Age* (New York, NY: Crossroad Publishing, 1997), p. 86.

64. Michael Ingham, *Mansions of the Spirit* (Toronto, ON: Anglican Book Centre, 1997), p. 61.

4/Evangelical Hybrids

1. Richard Foster, *Celebration of Discipline* (San Francisco, CA: Harper & Row, 1978 edition), p. 13.

2. *Renovare Conference* brochure, Oct. 15-16, 1999, Lynden, WA.

3. *Renovare Conference* brochure, Sept. 13-14, 1996, Fuller Theological Seminary.

4. Richard Foster, *Prayer: Finding the Heart's True Home* (San Francisco, CA: Harper, 1992), p. 160.

5. M. Basil Pennington, *Centered Living, The Way of Centering Prayer* (New York, NY: Doubleday, 1986 and 1988 editions), p. 104.

6. Matthew Fox, *The Coming of the Cosmic Christ* (San Francisco, CA: Harper & Row, 1988), p. 123.

7. Timothy Freke, *The Spiritual Canticle, the Wisdom of the Christian Mystics* (Godsfield Press, 1998), p. 60.

8. Willigis Jager, *The Search for the Meaning of Life* (Ligouri, MO, Liguori/Triumph, 1995), p. 125.

9. Richard Foster, *Prayer: Finding the Heart's True Home*, op. cit. p. 122.

10. Richard Foster, *Celebration of Discipline*, 1978 Edition, op. cit. p. 15.

11. Richard Foster, *Prayer: Finding the Heart's True Home*, op. cit., p. 124.

12. Anthony de Mello, *Sadhana: A Way to God* (St. Louis, the Institute of Jesuit Resources, 1978), p. 28.

13. Richard Foster, *Renovare Conference*, Salem, OR, Nov. 1994.

14. Ibid.

15. David Steindl-Rast, "Recollection of Thomas Merton's Last Days in the West" (Monastic Studies, 7:10, 1969).

16. Raymond Bailey, *Thomas Merton on Mysticism* (Image Books, 1987), p. 191.

17. Richard Foster and Emilie Griffin, *Spiritual Classics* (San Francisco,

CA: Harper, 2000), p. 17.

18. Richard Foster, *Meditative Prayer* (Downers Grove, IL: InterVarsity Christian Fellowship, 1983).

19. Richard Foster and James Bryan Smith, *Devotional Classics* (San Francisco, CA: Harper, 1990, 1991, 1993), p. 61.

20. Ibid.

21. Brother Patrick Hart-Editor, *The Message of Thomas Merton* (Kalamazoo, MI: Cistercian Publications, 1981), p. 63.

22. Rosemary Ellen Guiley, *The Miracle of Prayer* (Simon & Schuster, Pocket Books, 1995), p. 227.

23. Richard Foster, *Celebration of Discipline*, op., cit., Revised Edition 1988, p. 103.

24. Ibid., p. 7.

25. "Book of the Year Reader's Poll" (*Christianity Today*, April 5, 1993), p. 26.

26. Ibid., p. 27.

27. William Shannon, *The Silent Lamp* (New York, NY: Crossroad, 1991), p. 281.

28. Jan Johnson, *When the Soul Listens* (Colorado Springs, CO: NavPress, 1999), p. 16.

29. Ibid., p. 120.

30. Brennan Manning, *The Signature of Jesus*, (Sisters, OR: Multnomah, 1996, Revised Edition), p. 212.

31. Brennan Manning, *The Ragamuffin Gospel*, (Sisters, OR: Multnomah, 2000 Edition), p. 212.

32. Brennan Manning, *Reflections for Ragamuffins*, (San Francisco, CA: Harper, 1998), back cover.

33. Brennan Manning, *The Signature of Jesus*, op. cit., p. 211.

34. *Credence Cassettes*, Winter/Lent 1985 Catalog, p. 14.

35. Ibid.

36. Agnieszka Tennant, "Ragamuffin" (*Christianity Today*, June 2004), pp. 44-45.

37. Tilden Edwards, *Spiritual Friend* (New York, NY: Paulist Press, 1980), p. 18.

38. Interview with Brennan Manning by Paul Rinehart, "Living as God's Beloved" (*Discipleship Journal*, Issue 100, July/Aug. 1997), p. 78.

39. William Shannon, *Silence on Fire*, op. cit., p. 160.

40. Rodney R. Romney, *Journey to Inner Space* (New York, NY: Riverview Press., 1986), p. 132.

41. Ibid., p. 138.

42. Ken Carey, *The Starseed Transmissions* (A Uni-Sun Book, 1985 4th printing), p. 33.

43. Brennan Manning, *The Signature of Jesus*, op. cit., p. 212.

44. Ibid., p. 216.

45. Ibid., p. 218.

46. Ibid., p. 215.

47. Brother Patrick Hart-Editor, *The Message of Thomas Merton*, op. cit., p. 200.

48. Thomas Keating, *Kundalini Energy and Christian Spirituality* by Philip St. Romain (New York, NY: The Crossroad Publishing Company, 1991), Foreword.

5/Discernment

1. Jack Canfield, Mark Victor Hansen, *Dare to Win* (New York, NY: Berkeley Books, 1994), p. 195.

2. Arielle Ford, *Hot Chocolate for the Mystical Soul* (New York, NY: Penguin Putnam, 1998), pp. 244-247, 361.

3. Ibid., p. 36-39.

4. Ibid., p. 15.

5. Ibid., pp. xiii-xiv.

6. Ibid., back cover.

7. Jack Canfield, *The Success Principles* (New York, NY: HarperCollins, 2005), p. 316.

8. Ibid., p. 317.

9. Sara Ban Breathnach, *Simple Abundance: A Daybook of Comfort and Joy* (New York, NY: Warner Books, 1995, October 31).

10. "Healing Hands" (*New Woman Magazine,* March, 1986), p. 78.

11. William Rand, *Reiki: The Healing Touch* (Southfield, MI: Vision Pub.,1991), p. 48.

12. Diane Stein, *Essential Reiki* (Berkley, CA: Crossing Press, 1995), p. 107.

13. William Lee Rand, "Reiki, A New Direction" (*Reiki News*, Spring 1998, http://web.archive.org/web/20160310205151/http://www.rciki. org/reikinews/reikinewdir.html), p. 4.

14. *Reiki News*, Winter, 1998, p. 5.

15. Phylameana lila Desy, *The Everything Reiki Book* (Avon, MA: Adams Media, 2004), p. 144.

16. Ibid., p. 270.

17. Janeanne Narrin, *One Degree Beyond: A Reiki Journey into Energy Medicine* (Seattle, WA: Little White Buffalo, 1998), p. xviii.

18. Brian C. Taylor, *Setting the Gospel Free* (New York, NY: Continuum Publishing , 1996), p. 76.

19. *USA Weekend* Sunday Supplement, July 24-26, 1987, p. 12.

20. Interview with John Randolph Price (*Science of Mind* magazine, August 1989), p. 24.

21. Mindy Ribner cited by Rabbi Rifat Sonsino, *Six Jewish Spiritual Paths* (Woodstock, VT: Jewish Light Publishing, 2000), p. 101.

22. Joan Borysenko, *Fire in the Soul* (New York, NY: Warner Books, 1993), p. 165.

23. Ann Wise, *The High Performance Mind* (Los Angeles, CA: J. Tarcher Pub., 1995), pp. 185-186.

24. Joel Stein, "Just Say Om" (*Time* magazine, August 4, 2003), p. 50.

25. Ibid., p. 51.

26. Mary Talbot, "OM is Where the Heart Is" (*Newsweek* magazine, Feb. 3, 1992), p. 71.

27. "Yoga's Wider Reach," (*USA Weekend* supplement, March 27-29, 1998), p. 12.

28. Linda Johnsen, "Hatha Traditions" (Yoga Internationals 1999 Guide to Yoga Teachers & Classes), p. 43.

29. Lisa Takeuchi Cullen Mahtomedi, "Stretching for Jesus" (*Time* magazine, September 5, 2005), p. 75.

30. "World of Yoga" (*Yoga Journal,* September/October 1994), p. 49.

31. Ibid.

32. Ibid.

33. Oprah Winfrey cited in Eric Butterworth's, *Discover The Power Within You* (San Francisco, CA: Harper Row), front cover.

34. Gary Zukav, *The Seat of the Soul* (New York, NY: Simon & Schuster, 1990, Fireside Edition), p. 239.

35. Oprah Winfrey, *Live Your Best Life* (Des Moines, IA: Oxmoor House, first edition, September, 2005), p. 105.

36. Wayne Muller, *Sabbath* (New York, NY: Bantam, 2000), p. 84.

37. Mr. Fred Rogers cited in *Sabbath* by Wayne Muller, op. cit., front matter.

38. David Spangler, "The New Age is Here" (*New Thought* magazine, Spring 1989), p. 6.

39. A personal e-mail sent to Ray Yungen in 2005.

40. Joy Gardner-Gordon, *Pocket Guide to the Chakras* (Berkley, CA: Crossing Press, 1998), p. 31.

41. Glenn Derrick, "Reiki and Chi Kung" (*Reiki News,* Winter 1994, http://www.reiki.org//reikinews/reikin 19.html, p. 12.

42. Neil T. Anderson, Terry E. Zuehlke, Julianne S. Zuehlke, *Christ Centered Therapy: The Practical Integration of Theology and Psychology* (Grand Rapids, MI: Zondervan Publishing House, 2000), p. 61.

6/Could This Really Be the End of the Age?

1. Harold Belyoz, *Three Remarkable Women* (Flagstaff, AZ: Altai Pub., 1986), p. 207.
2. Ibid., p. 210.
3. Ibid., p. 217.
4. Simons Roof, *About the Aquarian Age* (The Mountain School for Esoteric Studies, 1971), p. 7.
5. John Davis and Naomi Rice, *Messiah and the Second Coming* (Wyoming, MI: Coptic Press, 1982), p. 150.
6. James S. Gordon, *The Golden Guru: The Strange Journey of Bhagwan Shree Rajneesh* (Lexington, MA: The Stephen Green Press, 1987), p. 236.
7. Alice Bailey, *The Reappearance of the Christ* (New York, NY: Lucis Pub. Co., 4th Printing, 1962), p. 124.
8. "Sri Chinmoy Lifts Over 7,000 lbs. with One Arm" (*Life Times* magazine, Vol. 1, Number 3), p. 45.
9. Marjorie L. Rand, "Healing: A Gift That Awakens" (*The Whole Person* magazine, June 1988), p. 40.
10. Davis and Rice, *Messiah and the Second Coming*, op. cit., p. 49.
11. John White, "Jesus, Evolution and the Future of Humanity" (*Science of Mind* magazine, Oct. 1981), pp. 40-42.
12. Donald H. Yott, *Man and Metaphysics* (New York, NY: Samuel Weiser, 1980), p. 74.
13. Armand Biteaux, *The New Consciousness* (Willits, CA: Oliver Press, 1975), p. 128.
14. John Randolph Price, *The Planetary Commission* (Austin, TX: Quartus Books, 1984), pp. 143, 145.
15. John R. Yungblut, *Rediscovering the Christ* (Rockport, MA: Element Inc., 1991), p. 164.
16. Willigis Jager, *Contemplation: A Christian Path* (Liguori, MO: Triumph Books, 1994), pp. 93-94.
17. Melinda Ribner, *New Age Judaism* (Deerfield Beach, FL: Simcha

Press, 2000), p. xv, "Author to Reader" section.

18. Ibid., pp. 196-197.

19. William Rand, "Reiki in the Holy Land" (*Reiki News*, Winter 2003), p. 20.

20. Rabbi David Cooper, *God is a Verb* (New York, NY: Riverhead Books, 1997), p. 58.

21. Alice Bailey, *Problems of Humanity* (New York, NY: Lucis Publishing, 1993), p. 152.

22. Alice Bailey, *The Externalization of the Hierarchy* (New York, NY: Lucis Publishing, 1976), p. 510.

23. Alice Bailey, *Problems of Humanity* (New York, NY: Lucis Publishing, 1993), p. 152.

24. Joel Beversluis, Project Editor, *A Source Book for Earth's Community of Religions* (Grand Rapids, MI: CoNexus Press, 1995, Revised Edition), p. 151.

25. Swami Vivekananda's "Addresses at the Parliament of Religions" (Chicago, September 27, 1893, http://web.archive.org/web/20081203204726/http://www.interfaithstudies.org/interfaith/vivekparladdresses.html).

26. M. Basil Pennington, *Centered Living* (New York, NY: Image Books, 1988), p. 192.

27. Tilden Edwards, *Spiritual Friend* (New York, NY: Paulist Press, 1980), p. 172.

28. "Catholics Urged To Appreciate Other Faiths" (*The Catholic Sentinel*, May 24, 2002), p. 3.

29. Richard Kirby, *The Mission of Mysticism*, op, cit., p. 85.

30. Reynolds R. Ekstrom, *New Concise Catholic Dictionary* (Mystic, CT: Twenty-third Publications/Bayard, 1995).

31. Janina Gomes "Rethinking Mission in India" (*America*, Nov. 12, 2001), p. 12.

32. Ibid., p. 13.

33. Ibid., p. 12.

34. Anchorman Bob Abernethy, "Exploring Religious America" (*Religion & Ethics NewsWeekly*, April 26, 2002, Episode #534).

35. John Gray, *How to Get What You Want and Want What You Have* (New York, NY: HarperCollins, 1999), pp. 97-98.

7/Seducing Spirits

1. Interview with Richard Foster, *Lou Davies Radio Program* (Nov. 24, 1998, KPAM radio, Portland, Oregon).

2. Thomas Merton, *Contemplative Prayer* (New York, NY: Image Books, Doubleday Pub., 1989), pp. 115-116.

3. Henri Nouwen, *Bread for the Journey*, op. cit.

4. Dr. Paul Bubna, President Briefings, C&MA, "Purveyors of Grace or Ungrace," March 1978.

5. Richard Foster, *Celebration of Discipline* (San Francisco, CA: Harper, 1988), p. 19.

6. John R. Yungblut, *Rediscovering the Christ* (Rockport, MA: Element Books, 1991), p. 142.

7. Richard Foster, *Celebration of Discipline* (San Francisco, CA: Harper, 1988), p. 20.

8. Sue Monk Kidd, *When the Heart Waits* (San Francisco, CA: Harper, 1990), pp. 47-48.

9. Sue Monk Kidd, *God's Joyful Surprise* (San Francisco, CA: Harper, 1987), p. 55.

10. Ibid., p. 56.

11. Ibid., p. 198.

12. Ibid., pp. 233, 228.

13. Ibid., pp. 228-229.

14. Sue Monk Kidd, *The Dance of the Dissident Daughter* (San Francisco, CA: HarperCollins, 1996), pp. 162-163.

15. Ibid., p. 76.

16. The Ganges is a famous river in India, thought to have holy powers but is actually very polluted.

17. Ursula Burton and Janlee Dolley, *Christian Evolution* (Wellingborough, Northamptonshire, GB: Turnstone Press, 1984), p. 101.

18. M. Basil Pennington, *Thomas Merton, My Brother* (Hyde Park, NY: New City Press, 1996), pp. 199-200.

19. Lewis Sperry Chafer, *Grace, the Glorious Theme* (Grand Rapids, MI: Zondervan Publishing, 1977 Edition), pp. 313-314.

20. Richard Foster, *Streams of Living Water* (San Francisco, CA: Harper, 1998), p. 273.

21. Ibid., p. 274.

22. *Credence Communications Catalog*, Gift Ideas Edition.

23. Ibid.

24. Ibid.

25. Frank X. Tuoti, *The Dawn of the Mystical Age* (New York, NY: Crossroad Publishing, 1997), p. 127.

26. Brennan Manning, *Abba's Child* (Colorado Springs, CO: NavPress, 1994), p. 180.

27. Virginia Manss and Mary Frohlich, Editors, *The Lay Contemplative* (Cincinnati, OH: St. Anthony Messenger Press, 2000), p. 180.

8/"America's Pastor"

1. Adrian Rogers, *Purpose Driven Church* (Grand Rapids, MI: Zondervan, 1995), front matter.

2. Timothy C. Morgan citing Rick Warren, "Purpose Driven in Rwanda"(*Christianity Today*, October 2005).

3. Staff Article, "Rick Warren tour to mark 2-year point for *Purpose-Driven Life*"citing Rick Warren, (Baptist Press, September 14, 2004).

4. Rick Warren, Beliefnet Editor David Kuo Interviews Rick Warren, http://web.archive.org/web/20130709091733/http://www.beliefnet.com/Faiths/Christianity/2005/10/Rick-Warren-God-Didnt-Need-Us-He-Wanted-Us.aspx.

5. Rick Warren, *Purpose Driven Church*, op.cit., p. 126.

6. Ibid., p. 127.

7. Ibid.

8. Rick Warren, *Purpose Driven Life* (Grand Rapids, MI: Zondervan, 2002), p. 118.

9. Ibid., p. 85.

10. Ibid., p. 86.

11. Ibid., p. 87.

12. Ibid., p. 89.

13. Ursula King, *Christian Mystics* (New York, NY: Simon & Schuster, 1998), p. 138.

14. Brother Lawrence, *The Practice of the Presence of God*, (Grand Rapids, MI: Christian Classics Ethereal Library, online version at http://www.ccel.org/ccel/lawrence/practice.html).

15. Gerald May, *The Awakened Heart* (New York, NY: HarperCollins, First HarperCollins Paperback Edition, 1993) p. 87, citing from *The Practice*

of the Presence of God by Brother Lawrence, translated by John Delaney, Image Books, 1977, p. 34.

16. Brother Lawrence, *The Practice of the Presence of God*, Christian Classics Ethereal Library, online version, op, cit.

17. Ibid.

18. Ibid.

19. Ibid.

20. Rick Warren, *The Purpose Driven Life*, op. cit., p. 88.

21. Ibid.

22. Warren Smith, *Deceived on Purpose* (Magalia, CA: Mountain Stream Press, 2004), pp. 81, 83.

23. A Shalem Senior Staff, "Contemplative Spirituality" (ShalemInstitute, http://web.archive.org/web/20060519165454/http://www.shalem.org/publication/articles/contemplativespirituality.html).

24. Rick Warren, *Purpose Driven Life*, op. cit., p. 89.

25. Ibid.

26. Carolyn Reynolds, *Spiritual Fitness* (Camarillo, CA: DeVorss & Company, 2005), p. 105.

27. Rick Warren, *Purpose Driven Life*, op. cit., p. 89.

28. Richard Foster, *Prayer: Finding the Heart's True Home*, op. cit., p. 124.

29. Sonia Choquette, *Your Heart's Desire* (New York, NY: Three Rivers Press, 1997), p. 107.

30. Ken Kaisch, *Finding God: A Handbook of Christian Meditation* (Mahwah, NJ: Paulist Press, 1994), pp. 63, 64.

31. Rick Warren, *Purpose Driven Life*, op. cit., p. 299.

32. Rick Warren, "Purpose Driven Life: Worship That Pleases God" (http://web.archive.org/web/20081227043413/http://legacy.pastors.com/RWMT/?ID=71).

33. Pastor Lance Witt, "Enjoying God's Presence in Solitude" (http://web.archive.org/web/20081227044901/http://legacy.pastors.com/RWMT/?ID=59).

34. Ibid., citing Richard Foster.

35. Rick Warren's Ministry Toolbox, "Book Look" section (Issue #40, 2/20/2002, http://web.archive.org/web/20081227043345/http://legacy.pastors.com/RWMT/?ID=40).

36. Gary Thomas, *Sacred Pathways* (Grand Rapids, MI: Zondervan, 2000, First Zondervan Edition), p. 185.

37. Rick Warren, "Purpose Driven Life: Worship That Pleases God" op. cit.

38. Rick Warren's Ministry Toolbox, (September 3, 2003, http://web.archive.org/web/20081227031846/http://legacy.pastors.com/RWMT/?ID=118).

39. Rick Warren's Ministry Toolbox (February 18, 2004, http://web.archive.org/web/20081227044251/http://legacy.pastors.com/RWMT/?ID=142).

40. Tricia Rhodes, *The Soul at Rest* (Minneapolis, MN: Bethany House Publishers, 1996), p. 28.

41. Morton Kelsey cited in Charles H. Simpkinson, "In the Spirit of the Early Christians," op. cit.

42. Tricia Rhodes, *The Soul at Rest*, op. cit., p. 199.

43. Ibid., p. 55.

44. Rick Warren quoting Kay Warren on the Ministry Toolbox (Issue #54, 6/5/2002, http://web.archive.org/web/20081227044856/http://legacy.pastors.com/RWMT/?ID=54).

45. Henri Nouwen, *In the Name of Jesus* (New York, NY: Crossroad Publishing, 2000), pp. 6, 31-32.

46. Robert Schuller cited in *Wounded Prophet* by Michael Ford (New York, NY: Doubleday, 1999), p. 35.

47. Tim Stafford, "A Regular Purpose-Driven Guy" (*Christianity Today*, November 18, 2002).

48. Rick Warren, *The Emerging Church* by Dan Kimball (Grand Rapids, MI: Zondervan, 2003), Foreword.

49. Dan Kimball, *The Emerging Church*, op. cit., p. 223.

50. Dan Kimball, "A-Maze-ing Prayer" (http://web.archive.org/web/20041019214503/www.vintagefaith.com/artilces/labyrinth.html).

51. Ibid.

52. Rick Warren, *The Emerging Church*, op. cit., p. 7.

53. Ibid., p. 147.

54. Ibid., 154.

55. Ibid., p. 210.

56. Spencer Burke, *Making Sense of the Church* (Grand Rapids, MI: Zondervan, 2003), pp. 136, 137.

57. Robert A. Schuller introducing Leonard Sweet at the 34th Institute of Church Leadership, "The Whole Shebang! . . . In Six Words" (Hour of Power Website, 2/02/03, http://web.archive.org/web/20030203222919/http://www.hourofpower.com/).

58. Rick Warren, *Soul Tsunami* by Leonard Sweet (Grand Rapids, MI: Zondervan, 1999), cover.

59. Ibid., Leonard Sweet, *Soul Tsunami*, op. cit., pp. 431, 432.

60. Ibid., p. 17.

61. Ibid., p. 408.

62. Ibid., p. 75.

63. Leonard Sweet, *Quantum Spirituality* (Dayton, OH: Whaleprints, 1991), Acknowledgments, viii-ix.

64. Ibid., xi.

65. Ibid., Preface, p. 7.

66. Ibid., p. 70.

67. Ibid., p. 13 in Preface.

68. Ibid., p. 76.

69. Taken from the a daily schedule for the 2004 National Pastor's Convention.

70. Speakers for the 2005 *Purpose Driven Youth Ministry Conference* (http://tinyurl.com/9rbea).

71. Mark Oestreicher, former president of Youth Specialties, (October 27, 2005, http://web.archive.org/web/20060629014059/http://www.ysmarko.com/?p=232).

72. Ibid.

73. Ibid.

74. For more information about this, including copies of letters and e-mails sent from Rick Warren and/or Saddleback regarding George Mair, see http:/www.lighthousetrailsresearch .com/furtherinformation.htm. Also see chapter 5 of A "Wonderful" Deception by Warren B. Smith.

75. George Mair, *A Life With Purpose* (Berkeley, CA: Penguin, 2005), pp. 98-99.

76. Ibid., p. 100.

77. Ibid.

78. Rick Warren, sermon at Saddleback, November 2003.

79. Ken Blanchard, *What Would Buddha Do At Work?* by Frank Metcalf

(Berkeley, CA: Ulysses Press, 2001), Foreword, p. xii.

80. Jim Ballard, *Mind Like Water* (Hoboken, NJ: John Wiley & Sons, 2002), pp. 77-78.

81. Ken Blanchard, *Mind Like Water* by Jim Ballard, op. cit., Foreword, pp. vii-viii.

82. Vijay Eswaran, *In the Sphere of Silence* "Authors Message" on his website (RYTHM House, 2005, no longer online).

83. Ken Blanchard endorsement of *In the Sphere of Silence*, on the author's website, http://www.inthesphereofsilence.com (no longer online—on file at LT).

84. Jon Gordon, *The 10-Minute Energy Solution* (New York, NY: G. P. Putnam's Sons, 2006), p. 207.

85. Ibid., Ken Blanchard's endorsement on back cover.

86. Ken Blanchard endorsement of the *Hoffman Quadrinity Process* on the Hoffman Institute website (http://web.archive.org/web/20100315031531/http://hoffmaninstitute.org/about/directors-advisors/advisors.html) and in the book, *The Hoffman Process* by Tim Laurence (New York, NY: Bantam Dell, 2003), front matter.

87. Tim Laurence, *The Hoffman Process* (New York, NY: Bantam Dell, 2003), pp. 206, 207, 209.

88. Lead Like Jesus website, http://www.leadlikejesus.net/templates/cus-leadlikejesus/details.asp?id=21633&PID=88945 (no longer online—on file at LT).

89. Laurie Beth Jones "Mission" statement on her website, http://web.archive.org/web/20051224202543/http://www.lauriebethjones.com/main/content/blogcategory/71/133.

90. Laurie Beth Jones, *Jesus CEO* (New York, NY: Hyperion, 1995), p. 7.

91. Ibid., p. 8.

92. Laurie Beth Jones, *Teach Your Team to Fish* (New York, NY: Three Rivers Press, 2002), p. 7.

93. Ibid., p. 142.

94. Laurie Beth Jones, *The Path* (New York, NY: Hyperion, 1996), p. 24.

95. Blanchard, *Lead Like Jesus* (Nashville, TN: W. Publishing Group of Thomas Nelson, December 2005), pp. 158, 159.

96. Dallas Willard, *The Spirit of the Disciplines* (New York, NY: HarperCollins, 1991, First HarperCollins Paperback Edition), p. 163.

97. Ibid., p. 164.

98. Ibid., back cover, endorsement by Sue Monk Kidd.

99. Sue Monk Kidd, *God's Joyful Surprise* (New York, NY: HarperCollins, First Harper & Row Paperback Edition, 1989), pp. 233, 228.

9/The Christian of the Future?

1. Agnieszka Tennant, "Drawing Closer to God"(*Today's Christian Woman*, September/October 2004, Vol. 26, No. 5), p. 14. Published by *Christianity Today International*, Carol Stream, Illinois.

2. Shalem Institute, "What Does Contemplative Mean?" (Shalem Institute About Shalem page, http://web.archive.org/web/20050204190729/http://shalem.org/about.html#contemplative).

3. Ann Kline, "A New Language of Prayer" (Shalem Institute newsletter, Vol. 29, No. 1, Winter 2005, http://web.archive.org/web/20060930230219/http://www.shalem.org/publication/newsletter/archives/2005/2005_winter/article_04).

4. Shalem Institute website, General Events, "Radical Prayer: A Simple Loving Presence Group" (http://www.shalem.org/programs/generalprograms/groupsevents_folder; no longer online—on file at LT).

5. Ruth Haley Barton, "Beyond Words"(*Discipleship Journal*, Issue #113, September/October, 1999, http://web.archive.org/web/20060628075740/http://www.navpress.com/EPubs/DisplayArticle/1/1.113.13.html), p. 35.

6. Ibid.

7. Ibid., pp. 37-38.

8. Dan Kimball, *The Emerging Church* (Grand Rapids, MI: Zondervan, 2003), p. 60.

9. Ibid., p. 223.

10. Tony Jones, *The Sacred Way* (Grand Rapids, MI: Zondervan, 2004), p. 15.

11. Ibid., pp. 71-72.

12. Andy Crouch, "The Emergent Mystique" (*Christianity Today*, October 22, 2004).

13. Alan Jones, *Reimagining Christianity* (Hoboken, NJ: John Wiley & Sons, 2005), p. 174.

14. Ibid., p. 89.

15. Ibid., Brian McLaren's endorsement on back cover.

16. Mike Perschon, "Desert Youth Worker: Disciplines, Mystics, and

the Contemplative Life" (*Youthworker* magazine, November/December 2004, http://web.archive.org/web/20050309052749/http://youthspecialties.com/articles/topics/spirituality/desert.php).

17. Laurie Cabot, *Power of the Witch* (New York, NY: Bantam Doubleday Dell Publishing, 1989), p. 173.

18. Ibid., p. 183.

19. Ibid., p. 200.

20. Richard Kirby, *The Mission of Mysticism*, op. cit., p. 6.

21. Joseph Chu-Cong, *The Contemplative Experience* (New York, NY: Crossroad Publishing Company, 1999), p. 3.

22. Andy Crouch, "The Emergent Mystique," op. cit.

23. Mars Hill Bible Church service, March 19, 2006 (http://web.archive.org/web/20060410083942/http://www.mhbcmi.org/listen/).

24. Lauren Artress, *Walking a Sacred Path* (New York, NY: Riverhead Books, 1995), pp. 95-96.

25. Mark Yaconelli, "Ancient Future Youth Ministry" (*Group Magazine*, July/August 1999, http://web.archive.org/web/20050413072147/http://www.ymsp.org/resources/ancient_future_article.html), pp. 33-34.

26. The Youth Ministry & Spirituality Project (history page, http://web.archive.org/web/20050404061755/http://www.ymsp.org/about/history.html).

27. Mark Yaconelli, "Ancient Future Youth Ministry," op. cit., p. 39.

28. Ibid., p. 39

29. Ibid.

30. The Youth Ministry & Spirituality Project, op. cit.

31. Michael Yaconelli, *Dangerous Wonder* (Colorado Springs, CO: NavPress, 2003, revised edition), p. 16.

32. Henri Nouwen, *In the Name of Jesus*, op. cit.

33. Henri Nouwen, *Sabbatical Journey*, op. cit., p.20.

34. Ibid., p. 20.

35. Ibid., p. 51.

36. Ibid., p. 20.

37. Reginald A. Ray, "Understanding Buddhism: Religion Without God" (*Shambhala Sun Magazine*, July 2001, http://web.archive.org/web/20050308212701/http://www.shambhalasun.com/Archives/Columnists/Ray/july_01.htm), p. 25.

38. David Jeremiah, *Life Wide Open* (Brentwood, TN: Integrity Publishers, 2003), Introduction, p. xii.

39. Ibid.

40. Ibid.

41. Ibid., xiii.

42. Ibid.

43. Ibid., pp. 164, 165.

44. Calvin Miller, *Into the Depths of God* (Bloomington, MN: Bethany House Publishers, 2000), p. 107.

45. Ibid., p. 96.

46. Peter Senge cited in "Inviting the World to Transform" (A Research Report by the Center for Contemplative Mind in Society, http://web.archive.org/web/20120625183310/http://www.contemplativemind.org/programs/cnet/inviting.pdf).

47. Sue Monk Kidd, *The Dance of the Dissident Daughter* (New York, NY: HarperCollins, 1996, First HarperCollins Paperback Edition, 2002), p. 161.

48. Ibid., p. 163.

49. Ibid.

50. David Jeremiah, *Life Wide Open*, op. cit., p. 87, citing Sue Monk Kidd, *When the Heart Waits* (New York, NY: HarperCollins, 1990), p. 71.

51. David Jeremiah and Carole C. Carlson, *Invasions of Other Gods* (Dallas, TX: Word Publishing, 1995), p. 22.

52. Ibid., p. 23.

53. Ibid., p. 29, 39.

54. Charles Swindoll, *So You Want To Be Like Christ?* (Nashville, TN:W Publishing Group, a div. of Thomas Nelson, 2005), p. 12.

55. Ibid., p. 14.

56. Ibid., p. 21.

57. Ibid., p. 55.

58. Ibid.

59. Ibid., p. 61.

60. Ibid., p. 62.

61. Ibid.

62. Ibid., p. 63.

63. Ibid., p. 65.

64. Richard Foster, *Be Still DVD* (Fox Home Entertainment, April 2006), "Contemplative Prayer" segment.

65. Ibid.

66. Beth Moore statement after release of *Be Still* DVD can be found

at: http://web.archive.org/web/20061103170812/http://www.sliceoflaodicea.com/archives/2006/04/official_statem_1.php.

67. 2nd statement issued by Beth Moore after release of *Be Still* DVD can be found at http://www. lighthousetrailsresearch.com/bethmoorethumbsup.htm.

68. Beth Moore, *When Godly People Do Ungodly Things* (Nashville, TN: Broadman & Holman Publishers, 2002), pp. 72-73.

69. Ibid., p. 290.

70. Ibid., 109.

71. Beth Moore, *Be Still DVD*, op. cit.

72. Henri Nouwen, cited in Saddleback training book, *Soul Construction: Solitude Tool* (Lake Forest, CA: Saddleback Church, 2003), p. 12.

73. Michael O' Laughlin, *God's Beloved* (Maryknoll, NY: Orbis Books, 2004), p. 178.

74. Henri J. M. Nouwen, *Thomas Merton: Contemplative Critic* (San Francisco, CA: Harper & Row Publishers, 1991, Triumph Books Edition), p. 3.

75. Ibid., pp. 19-20.

76. Ibid., p. 20.

77. Ibid.

78. Ibid., p. 71.

79. Ibid., pp. 46, 71.

80. Ibid., p. 71.

81 . Ibid., p. 29.

Index

A

Note: Certain words like contemplative, meditation, and New Age appear so frequently in the book that they are not included in this Index.

B

C

P

Q

Quaker Meditation Center 121
Quantum Spirituality 158, 159
Quartus Foundation 99

R

Rabbi Lawrence Kushner 123
Radiance Technique, the 94
Ragamuffin Gospel 82, 83
Rahner, Karl 160
Rajneesh 114
Reckless Faith 51
Redfield, James 21
Reiki 13, 94-98, 104, 106, 107, 108, 116, 122, 183, 205
Reimagining Christianity 175
relaxation skills 98
Religion and Ethics Weekly 126
Religious Science church 136
Renovare 73
Renovation of the Heart 156
repetition of sacred words 133
Rhodes, Tricia 152, 153, 154
Richardson, Cheryl 103
Road Less Traveled, The 10, 55
Robert H. Schuller Institute for Successful Church 154
Robbins, Duffy 161
Robbins, Maggie 161
Rogers, Adrian 142, 143
Romney, Dr. Rodney R. 87
Ruthless Trust 84, 140

S

Sabbatical Journey 63
Sacred Way, The 161, 174
Sacred Pathways 151, 152, 156
sacred space 9, 205
sacred word prayer 44
sacred word repetition 181

DVD Lecture Series—Featuring Ray Yungen
The New Face of Mystical Spirituality

Buy all 3 and Save—$39.95 for set

The Invisible Denomination: the New Age

The New Age movement can be likened to "an old melody played by a new band." What makes this new band significant for our times is that over forty million people, in the US alone, are now dancing to its melody. In this talk, Ray Yungen examines the source and nature of this modern spiritual movement and gives credible evidence to its widespread influence in our culture. This lecture will be of great importance because once obscure practices are now poised to touch every family in the Western world. Yungen refers to this spirituality as the invisible denomination because it is found in business, health and fitness, education, and religion but yet is not readily identifiable by the average person as an actual denomination or spiritual body. $14.95, 45 minutes—DVD

Contemplative Prayer

In his clear and understandable style, Ray Yungen explains the dynamics of contemplative prayer. Unlike biblical prayer, this "new" form of prayer halts the normal flow of thought processes and takes the participant into a mystical state. Yungen not only explains how this is done, but he takes us to the ancient roots of this prayer practice derived from eastern mysticism. Although promising much in the realm of intimacy with God, you will learn how this practice delivers a package of seducing spirits and a pantheistic view that is characteristic of the New Age. $14.95, 50 minutes—DVD

The Emerging Church & Interspirituality

In this talk, Ray Yungen unmasks the spirituality behind the emerging church movement—its roots and its teachings. He explains the role that various popular figures have played in bringing about a spirituality that has direct ties to the New Age movement.

It is essential that every believer know what the emerging church is all about and how this "new spirituality" is replacing the biblical Gospel of Jesus Christ with a mystical universalistic gospel that undermines the Cross and the foundations of true Christianity. $14.95, 35 minutes—DVD

TOPICAL BOOKLETS FROM LIGHTHOUSE TRAILS — OVER 100 TO CHOOSE FROM

The Lighthouse Trails topical Booklets are designed to share with others important truths from a biblical perspective.

What is so wonderful about these Booklets is two-fold: one, we are selling them at very low prices so just about anyone can afford to buy them (with quantity orders of 6 or more of the same title, the discount is as much as 50% off retail); and two, we are told when they are being handed out to people by our readers, people are reading them. That's the best news of all!

Each Booklet is between 10-18 pages and is written by one of the 35 Lighthouse Trails authors. We add new Booklet titles frequently. These can be purchased individually or in bulk at very affordable prices and given out. Visit www.lighthousetrails.com or request a free catalog.

EACH BOOKLET IS $1.95 RETAIL WITH THE FOLLOWING DISCOUNTS:

6-25: $1.66; 26-50: $1.46; 51-100: $1.27;

101-150: $1.07; and over 150: 98 cents each.

THESE DISCOUNTS APPLY FOR QUANTITIES *OF THE SAME TITLE.*

FULL COLOR GLOSS COVERS

5 1/2" X 8 1/2" | 10-18 PAGES

HIGH QUALITY WHITE HEAVY GLOSS PAPER

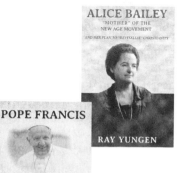

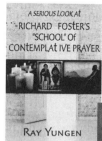

See our list of topical Booklets on the following pages.

LIGHTHOUSE TRAILS TOPICAL BOOKLETS

THROUGH IT ALL SERIES BY WARREN B. SMITH

WS-TRUTH—*Truth or Consequences*

REJOICE—*Rejoicing Through it All*

WS-PRZ—*Praising God Through it All*

WS-TF—*Being Thankful Through it All*

WS-STF—*Standing Fast Through it All*

WS-BLESS—*Blessings Through it All*

WS-HOPE—*Remaining Hopeful Through it All*

WS-FTH—*Remaining Faithful Through it All*

WS-TR—*Trusting God Through it All*

HOMOSEXUALITY

JL-MB—*The Message "Bible"—A Breach of Truth* by John Lanagan

MC-6Q—*6 Questions Every Gay Person Should Ask* by Michael Carter

HYPER-CHARISMATIC/NAR/ FALSE SIGNS & WONDERS

VIS—*"I Just Had a Vision!"* by Kevin Reeves

JL-BTH—*The New Age Propensities of Bethel Church's Bill John* by John Lanagan

WS-HL—*False Revival Coming? Part 1: Holy Laughter or Strong Delusion?* by Warren B. Smith

WCG—*10 Questions for those who claim The "Supreme Beings" of the Nations Are the True God* by Sandy Simpson

MD-KCP—*The Perfect Storm of Apostasy: The Kansas City Prophets and Other Latter-Day Prognastigators* by Mary Danielsen

KR-SL—*Slain in the Spirit: Is it a Biblical Practice?* by Kevin Reeves

DF-WF—*Ten Word of Faith Doctrines Weighed Against Scripture* by Danny Frigulti

BR-BB—*Beware of Bethel* by Bill Randles

DD-SW—*Signs and Wonders: Five Things You Should Consider* by David Dombrowski

JESUS CALLING

WS-NA-JC—*The New Age Implications of Jesus Calling* by Warren B. Smith

WS-JC—*Changing Jesus Calling* by Warren B. Smith

WS-10-RS—*10 Scriptural Reasons Why Jesus Calling is a Dangerous Book* by Warren B. Smith

ISRAEL & THE JEWS

ISRL—*Israel—Replacing What God Has Not* by Mike Oppenheimer

HH—*When Hitler Was in Power* by Anita Dittman

TP-KJ—*Who Really Killed Jesus?* by Tony Pearce

CHSLM—*Chrislam: The Blending Together of Islam & Christianity* by Mike Oppenheimer

EM—*Christians in Holland in 1941: "Should We Help Save the Jews?" (Obeying God or Man)* by Diet Eman

NEW AGE/NEW SPIRITUALITY & ITS PRACTICES

NA—*Understanding the New Age, Meditation, and the Higher Self* by Ray Yungen

RKI—*The Truth About Energy Healing* by Ray Yungen

AA—*The "Spiritual" Truth About Alcoholics Anonymous* by John Lanagan

GR-RD—*Confused by an Angel: The Dilemma of Roma Downey's New Age Beliefs* by Gregory Reid

WS-OPR—*Oprah Winfrey's New Age Christianity* by Warren B. Smith

WS-OPW—*Oprah Winfrey's New Age "Christianity" Part 2: Neale Donald Walsch, "God," & Hitler* by Warren B. Smith

SHACK—*The Shack & Its New Age Leaven* by Warren B. Smith

INDIA—*A Trip to India—to Learn the Truth About Hinduism and Yoga* by Caryl Matrisciana

RY-MR—*The Mystical Revolution* by Ray Yungen

RY-YGA—*Yoga: Exercise or Religion— Does it Matter?* by Ray Yungen

CL-YAC—*Yoga & Christianity: Are They Compatible?* by Chris Lawson

RY-MEDI—*Meditation! Pathway to God or Doorway to the Occult* by Ray Yungen

RY-BAILEY—*Alice Bailey, "Mother" of the New Age Movement* by Ray Yungen

MK-JL—*Goddess Worship in America* by Maria Kneas and John Lanagan

LP-COLOR—*Mandala Color Books: Relaxing Fun or A Tools for New Age Meditation?* by Lois Putnam

CT-FM—*Freemasonry: A Revealing Look at the Spiritual Side* by Carl Teichrib

PROTECTING CHILDREN

PTC—*5 Things You Can Do to Protect Your Kids From Sexual Predators* by Patrick Crough

GR-8—*8 Things You Should Know About Sexually Abused Boys* by Gregory Reid

BK-OC—*Popular Books That Introduce Children to the Occult* by Berit Kjos

BK-CC—*A "Common Core" for a Global Community* by Berit Kjos

LN-MA—*The Dangers & Deception of the Martial Arts* by Linda Nathan

LP-POK—*A Christian Parent's Guide to Pokemon* by Lois Putnam

HLWN—*Halloween: A Warning to Christian Parents* by Johanna Michaelsen

PURPOSE DRIVEN/SEEKER FRIENDLY

RW-DP—*Rick Warren's Daniel Plan* by Warren B. Smith

PCE—*The Peace of God versus the P.E.A.C.E. of Man* by David Dombrowski

RO-RW—*Rick Warren's Dangerous Ecumenical Path to Rome* by Roger Oakland

ROAD TO ROME (CATHOLICISM)

JC—*My Journey Out of Catholicism* by David Dombrowski

JA—*The Jesuit Agenda* by Roger Oakland

NW-EZ—*The New Evangelization of the Catholic Church & Finding the True Christ* by Roger Oakland

RY-PF—Pope Francis and the Thomas Merton Connection by Ray Yungen

RO-CM—*The Catholic Mary & Her Eucharistic Christ* by Roger Oakland

AM-FN—*A Former Nun Speaks Candidly About Pope Francis, Deception, and Mind Control in the Catholic Church* by Ann Marie
KR-CATH—*C is for Catholicism* by Kevin Reeves

SALVATION, THE GOSPEL & THE WORD OF GOD
IR-RDM—*Redemption* by Harry A. Ironside
IR-RGN—*Regeneration: "Ye Must Be Born Again."* by Harry A. Ironside
IR-GOSPEL—*What is the Gospel?* by Harry A. Ironside
WHO—*For God So Loved the World That... Whosoever!* by Harry Ironside
ST-GP—*Setting Aside the Power of the Gospel for a Powerless Substitute* by David Dombrowski
IR-JST—*What Does it Mean to Be Justified by God?* by Harry A. Ironside
MO-DC—*Did Jesus Identify Himself as God?* by Mike Oppenheimer
WS-WG—*The Awesome Wonder of God's Word*
IR-SUBT—*Substitution: He Took Our Place!* by Harry Ironside

FAITH & THE CHURCH
MK-TR—*Overcoming Obstacles to Trusting the Lord* by Maria Kneas
LT—*The Story Behind Lighthouse Trails* (LT Editors)
DD-PRT—*Preparing for Perilous Times and Finding God's Peace in the Midst of Them* by David Dombrowski

CF-AW—*The Unacknowledged War and the Wearing Down of the Saints* by Cedric Fisher
DD-CLR—*Dear Pastor and Christian Leader: Have You Grown Careless About the Gospel* by David Dombrowski
BK-AMR—*The Unseen Force Behind Rising Evil and Putting on the Armor of God* by Berit Kjos
RO-ENV—*A Christian Perspective on the Environment: How the Catholic Pope and Other Leaders Are Uniting the World's Religions Through Environmentalism* by Roger Oakland
CL-SA—*How to Know if You Are Being Spiritually Abused or Deceived—A Spiritual Abuse Questionnaire* by Chris Lawson
EX-ER—*Three Vital Questions on Navigating Discernment: 1) Should Christians Expose Error? 2) What Does Matthew 18 Mean? 3) How Should the Christian Contender of the Faith Speak and Behave?* by Harry Ironside, Paul Proctor, and LT Editors
IR-EXP—*The Expectation of HIS RETURN* by Harry Ironside
RY-TRIBUTE—*Ray Yungen: A Life Set Apart for God* (this is a free booklet)
SM-PC—*Remembering the Persecuted Church (And Why We Need to Pray)* by Susan Moore
CF-FAITH—*Faith Under Fire: Are You Growing in It or Fleeing From it?* by Cedric Fisher
IR-BRK—*Broken Vessels for Christ* by Harry Ironside

Notes

To Order Additional copies of:

A Time of Departing

send $14.95 plus $4.20 for shipping to:
Lighthouse Trails Publishing
P.O. Box 908
Eureka, Montana 59917

Call or go online for information about quantity discounts.

You may order online at
www.lighthousetrails.com
or
Call our toll free number:
866/876-3910
[ORDER LINE-USA & CANADA]

For international orders and all other calls: 406/889-3610.
You may also mail or fax your order. Our fax line is 406/889-3633. You
can print an order form from our website if you prefer.

A Time of Departing, as well as all books by Lighthouse Trails Publishing, can
be ordered directly from Lighthouse Trails or through all major outlet stores,
bookstores, online bookstores and Christian bookstores.

Bookstores may order through Ingram, Spring Arbor, Anchor, or directly
from Lighthouse Trails. Libraries may order through Baker and Taylor or
Lighthouse Trails. Quantity discounts available for most of our books.
Also check out our website for special international ordering through
one of our international distributors.

For more information:
Lighthouse Trails Research Project
www.lighthousetrailsresearch.com or www.lighthousetrails.com

You may visit the author's website at: www.atimeofdeparting.com.

LIGHTHOUSE TRAILS BOOKS

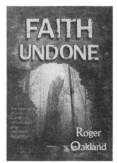

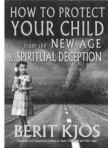

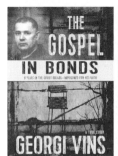

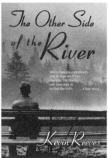

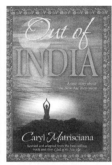

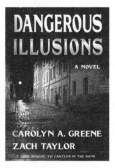

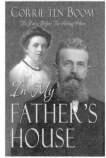

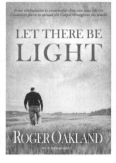

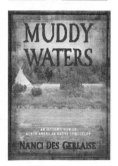

An Urgent Message to the Last-Days Church

THE
GOOD
SHEPHERD
CALLS

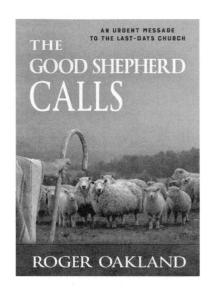

By Roger Oakland

SINCE THE TURN of the millennium, in particular since September 11, 2001 when America was attacked by terrorists triggering a global-wide spiritual paradigm shift, Christianity as we have known it has experienced a major meltdown. While many are saying Christianity is on the brink of a great revival and even a "new reformation," in reality, we are witnessing the greatest apostasy in modern-day history.

This latter-day deception has impacted every evangelical and Protestant denomination to one degree or another, and it is worldwide. The sheep have been led astray by shepherds who have neglected what they have been called to do—protect the sheep.

The Good Shepherd Calls brings clarity to what this delusion looks like, why it is happening, where it is headed, and what can still be done to warn believers and unbelievers alike.

Released 2017 by Lighthouse Trails | $14.95 | 288 pages